Making Them Like Us

Making Them Like Us

PEACE CORPS

VOLUNTEERS

in the 1960s

Fritz Fischer

SMITHSONIAN INSTITUTION PRESS

WASHINGTON AND LONDON

COPY EDITOR: Tom Ireland
PRODUCTION EDITOR: Robert A. Poarch
DESIGNER: Kathleen Sims

Library of Congress Cataloging-in-Publication Data
Fischer, Fritz.
    Making them like us : Peace Corps volunteers in the 1960s / Fritz
Fischer.
       p.   cm.
    Includes bibliographical references and index.
    ISBN 1-56098-889-4 (alk. paper)
    1. Peace Corps (U.S.).   I. Title.
HC60.5.F57   1998
361.6—dc21   98-16158

British Library Cataloguing-in-Publication Data available

Manufactured in the United States of America
05 04 03 02 01 00 99 98 5 4 3 2 1

☉ The paper used in this publication meets the minimum requirements of the American
National Standard for Information Sciences—Permanence of Paper for Printed Library
Materials ANSI Z39.48-1984.

Contents

Acknowledgments

Anyone who studies the Peace Corps must begin by acknowledging the dedication and hard work of all the men and women who served in the Peace Corps. The title of this book, *Making Them Like Us,* might appear to some as an indictment of the Peace Corps and its volunteers. Quite the contrary—as the reader will find out, the experiences of volunteers promoted a new spirit of dialogue and understanding between Americans and the rest of the world. This book does not argue that the volunteers tried at all times to make them like us. Rather, the volunteers continually struggled with the dilemmas of how much to make them like us. It is these struggles that provide the central focus for this book.

As I have worked on this book, many people have asked me if I served in the Peace Corps. Although, as the following pages will attest, the work appears to have been in many ways rewarding and exciting, the answer is no. The idea for this book did not come from a desire to examine my background. The impetuous behind this book came from a desire to connect the history of American foreign relations with a broader audience and a broader source base.

Although any errors or faulty conclusions are due only to me, I have many people to thank for challenging me to develop these broader connections. I owe my greatest intellectual debt to Robert Wiebe, who consistently prodded me into pushing the envelopes within my mind and who provided me with the ideal model of the teacher-scholar. Michael Sherry introduced me to the possibilities of stretching the bonds of traditional diplomatic history, and I still remember the moment in his office where the idea for this project was born. I would also like to thank Jim Campbell, Frank Safford, Ken Debevoise, Naoko Shibusawa, David Ruth, Ricki Shine, and Amanda Seligman for kindly suggestions and intellectual pointers along the way toward the completion of this manuscript. Thank you to William Walker and Elizabeth Cobbs Hoffman for their encouragement of my work on the Peace Corps and to the reviewers of my original manuscript, Dennis Merrill and William O. Walker III, who provided a wealth of sage advice.

The research for this project took place at a number of different locations, and I would like to thank the staffs of all the various archives I have worked in. I am especially indebted to the staffs of the Smithsonian Anthropology Archives, the National Archives, the Bentley Library at the University of Michigan, and the library at the Peace Corps headquarters in Washington, D.C. The Northwestern University Graduate School provided funding that helped in the early stages of writing this manuscript. I would also like to thank the faculty of the University of Northern Colorado Department of History for providing a caring and intellectually vigorous atmosphere to work in as I completed the book.

I am grateful to Mark Hirsch at the Smithsonian Institution Press for believing in this project and for encouraging me to work with him on this book. The entire staff at the Smithsonian have been helpful to me as this book has approached completion. The production editor, Robert A. Poarch, has been very understanding, and I want to extend a special thank you to my copy editor, Tom Ireland, for his tireless pursuit of my silly mistakes.

Finally, I would like to thank my family for their patience and perseverance in the years I have been working on this project. This gratitude extends to my parents and brothers who helped to mold my ideas as I was growing up. Thanks to Kevin, Eric, Kylie, and Shannon for their patience as Daddy spent many days and nights staring at the computer screen. Most of all, I am truly indebted to my wife, Lynn, who not only has done the lions share of raising these four children as I have written this book, but has provided the intellectual and emotional support (not to mention a keen editor's eye) that make anything I have done possible.

Introduction

My point is that an American can never really get to know a Latin. . . . The cultural prison in which we all live will never permit us to have total understanding of each other.

— JOHN FREIVALDS, PEACE CORPS VOLUNTEER

By the 1960s, Americans had built for themselves a very complicated "cultural prison." Americans clung to both a mythical vision of the past and a liberal vision of the future. On the international stage, this cultural background helped create a commitment to "develop" the rest of the world. The Peace Corps, more than any other policy or program, symbolized the desire of the United States to apply liberal ideas and American experience to mold the world's future. In looking at the Peace Corps experience, we can gain valuable insights into American culture and its interaction with the world in the late twentieth century.

The American people have always sensed the importance of the Peace Corps in American culture. The agency reached the apex of its popularity and importance in its first decade, the 1960s. The Harris Poll found that Americans ranked the Peace Corps as the "third most popular act of the Kennedy administration."[1] A quarter of a million Americans applied to be Peace Corps volunteers during the 1960s, and over 70,000 served as volunteers during that decade.[2] Hundreds of newspaper articles and dozens of books about the fledgling agency appeared in the decade, constantly bringing it to the American consciousness.

Until very recently, historians have not given the Peace Corps such a central role, and they have never examined the relationship between the agency and larger ideas within American liberal culture.[3] Since the 1960s stands as the central decade of the Cold War, most historians of American international relations have placed the Peace Corps firmly within the Cold War framework. When they have discussed the Peace Corps at all, they have usually stuffed it into traditional Cold War explanations of post–World War II foreign policy. In the textbook version, the Peace Corps served as "an instrument in the Cold War."[4] Diplomatic historians admit that the Peace Corps seemed more "constructive" than mere Cold War propaganda agencies such as the United States Information Agency (USIA), but "even though the Peace Corps was the program carrying the least Cold Warriorist character, the Peace Corps became part of the game."[5]

These historians focus on the Peace Corps only as an institution, rather than examining how the agency implemented policy. They examine Kennedy's ideas and rarely look beyond Kennedy toward the early administrators of the Peace Corps such as Sargent Shriver. But, as many scholars of American international affairs have begun to realize, "Relations are far broader, more complex, and above all, far more interesting than simply matters of government policy."[6] Merely looking at policy statements by governmental leaders misses too much that is interesting and important.

In the case of the Peace Corps, we cannot understand the relations between Americans and the peoples in the rest of the world without exploring the *implementation* of policy. To study the Peace Corps only as it exists in Washington is to miss the entire point of the agency. As one former Peace Corps staffer put it recently, "The real work of the Peace Corps is centered in the field. Most of what goes on in Washington matters little to the volunteers' daily existence."[7] This book is the first history devoted entirely to the study of the volunteers, those who actually instituted policy. Taking advantage of a huge wealth of previously unexamined primary sources found at the Smithsonian Museum of Natural History, the University of Michigan library, and the National Archives, this book seeks to understand the volunteers as ambassadors of American culture in the 1960s.[8] The Peace Corps volunteers were tasked with putting the policy into practice—they were forced to confront the relationship between American ideas about the world and the reality of the world itself.

During the years of the Kennedy and Johnson administrations, American liberalism reached the height of its power and influence. The specific tenet of liberalism concerned with America's relations with the world, liberal developmentalism, "entered its golden age in the early 1960s under John F. Kennedy's patronage."[9] This book focuses on the early and late 1960s to examine the birth of that golden age. We look to the beginnings to understand an entire era, an era that for many continues to this day. Looking at the Peace Corps in the 1960s helps us understand the fate and progress of American liberalism in the whole period of the late twentieth century.

This book argues that, in the end, the volunteers rejected the ideas of liberal international development so central to American culture and policy of the early 1960s. Volunteers' experiences overseas forced them to break down the bars of the cultural prison. Their relationship with the Peace Corps leadership, their living conditions, their work, and their relationship with the people they were working with all convinced them to reevaluate many previously held cultural assumptions. This reevaluation created a new understanding of the third world and helped point American culture in a new direction in its understanding of other cultures.

Such cultural interactions have recently become a central concern for many historians of American foreign relations. *Culture* is a protean term, with many different meanings. Drawing from the work of anthropologist Clifford Geertz, these historians have defined culture as an "integrated and coherent system of symbols, values and beliefs."[10] American culture provided one such system of beliefs, a system that provided the framework within which volunteers worked. As this book will show, the Peace Corps drew heavily from certain aspects of this American cultural system, and the volunteers struggled to understand how this cultural understanding matched the realities of the real world.[11]

These Peace Corps volunteers began their work as diplomats imbued with a set of American cultural ideas about the nations of Asia, Africa, and Latin America. Americans in the early 1960s knew very little about what was universally referred to then as the "third world," "underdeveloped world," or "developing world." As one historian has so aptly concluded, the real definition of "third world" in the 1960s was "lands unfamiliar to Americans, even those making up the foreign policy elite."[12] Americans knew it was a place of battle with the Soviet Union and had absorbed a variety of images of it from magazines such as *National Geographic*. In these images, the people of developing countries were portrayed as living in a world that was "unchanging and . . . more primitive than civilized." In the photographs in these magazines, "at many points there appear to be only two worlds—the traditional and the modern."[13] For Americans, the underdeveloped world remained a mystery, a blank slate ready to be acted upon by American policymakers.

Further, the volunteers believed in the ideology of progress they saw depicted in the pages of *National Geographic,* which trumpeted the inexorable march of "progress from tradition to modernity" in the third world since World War II.[14] Their job as volunteers, then, was to help promote this process of development. As discussed in chapter 1, American intellectuals and policymakers shared the view that development was a straightforward process, a task of moving people in the third world from 2 to 7 or 8 on a development scale of 1 to 10.

Kennedy's policymakers included this notion of straightforward development within the broader concept of "nation building," believing that the Peace Corps would be a principal participant in the process. Invented by the young minds in the Kennedy administration, this concept called for the United States to help third world nations "through the stormy times of economic infancy to economic and hence political maturity."[15]

But neither Kennedy nor his closest advisers had a strong influence on the direction of the agency. Kennedy conceived of it as a new weapon to be used in the Cold War. But as he began work as president, he became preoccupied with other matters and lost interest in building the Peace Corps. The new agency used John F. Kennedy's image and charisma as a starting point, but Kennedy had little to do with setting its direction, a job that he and his top advisers allowed the first director of the agency, Kennedy's brother-in-law, Sargent Shriver, to take on.

Shriver, and the men he chose as his top lieutenants, designed the Peace Corps to be something completely new. They began with the general concept of "nation building" and invented a specific plan for accomplishing the task, in part by making Peace Corps volunteers into a 1960s version of the mythical American pioneer, helping the inhabitants of the third world conquer their own frontiers.

We meet our first volunteers in the second chapter. The Peace Corps leadership designed a training program that, although short, was designed to mold raw American youth into this new brand of American pioneer. From its heavy emphasis on Outward Bound to its reliance on the newest methods in social science, volunteers entered a training program that attempted to forge a tight-knit cadre of tough, like-minded recruits. A few volunteers lived up to this image, becoming "hero volunteers" or "super-volunteers." Scrutinizing their work delineates the ideal pioneer image and clarifies the intent the Peace Corps leadership had for the agency.

In the third chapter we see how cracks opened up between the volunteers and the Peace Corps leadership during training. From the beginning, many volunteers felt alienated from the leadership due to the training regimen and an overzealous program in psychological testing and selection. As chapter 4 points out, conflicts continued in the field as volunteers disagreed with the ideas of the Peace Corps leadership. That leadership never understood its own volunteers or the work they tried to accomplish. Often, they treated the volunteers as immature youths, creating a generation gap that mirrored American society during the 1960s. From political to religious issues, the Peace Corps leaders and the volunteers disagreed. The agency had special difficulties dealing with "unique" volunteers, be they women or volunteers from minority groups. Most volunteers ended up feeling alienated from the agency in some way or another. The result was an independent cadre of volunteers, open to crafting their own set of ideas about the third world and the people living there.

Upon arriving in the third world, most volunteers immediately learned the inappropriateness of American cultural preconceptions. The Peace Corps leadership, often referred to by volunteers as Peace Corps Washington, expected them to live a spartan existence, in isolated mud huts in the jungle, if necessary. Actually, many lived in comfortable houses, often employing servants and occasionally living in luxury. Some volunteers felt pangs of guilt because they failed to live up to their preconceived image of the life of a Peace Corps volunteer. Rather than finding their country and its people mired at 2 on the development scale, most volunteers placed their countries on a completely different scale, hovering somewhere near point Q. The living situation of volunteers forced them to abandon the notion of straightforward development.

As they worked, volunteers began to recraft a philosophy of how Americans should relate to the third world. Chapter 6 begins by exploring the unexpected working environment they encountered at their projects. Peace Corps leaders demanded constant toil from volunteers, who would earn friends for the United States and develop the third world by the sweat of their brow. The work of most volunteers failed to fit this description. More than half of the volunteers in the 1960s served as teachers, a job strikingly different from any work performed by mythic American pioneers. Even jobs seemingly better suited to the image, such as community development, failed to live up to that image. While on the job, nearly every volunteer dealt with tensions between a faith in universalist values and a desire to teach the locals something useful. After rejecting the image, the volunteers found two ways to justify their work. First, they decided their specific jobs were important for their own sakes—completing a specific task helped volunteers fill a role in their new society. Second, volunteers realized that through their work, they could get a better understanding of their hosts and begin to redefine American understandings of the third world.

Chapter 7 examines the relationship between the volunteers and their hosts. Many faced tension over how far they should push the locals to change. Peace Corps Washington believed volunteers would make friends easily, but many found any sort of positive interaction with their hosts next to impossible. Some never overcame the problems they had dealing with their local counterparts, and they could not resist the temptation to group their hosts into a negative stereotype.

In the end, the volunteers failed to resemble either Kennedy's vision or that of the founding leadership of the agency. Rather, they struggled to create a new way for Americans to interact with the third world. They never crafted a universal ideology for themselves—they were too independent for that. Yet, in the end, new ideas emerged from the experiences of many volunteers. Democratic, egalitarian, individual, these ideas formed a different kind of understanding of how cultures interact. Volunteers developed a new way for Americans to understand the rest of the world. Their "ideology," purposefully ill defined, viewed the rest of the world in almost surrealistic terms. This new understanding had a slight impact on formal American foreign policy making, especially during the Carter administration. More importantly, it represented a profound shift in American cultural views of international and intercultural relations. With this new understanding, some Americans began to break down the walls of the "cultural prison" described by volunteer John Freivalds.

Many Americans feel the Peace Corps is a valuable program, yet they have difficulty explaining why. The idea strikes a positive chord in most, yet few know exactly what the agency does. Even the name contradicts itself, trumpeting peace in military terms: a warlike *corps* of soldiers. Analyzing these "soldiers" helps us to understand American cultural ideas about the rest of the world and international relations in the 1960s.

Kennedy, the Peace Corps, and Liberal International Development

The great battleground for the defense and expansion of freedom is the whole southern half of the globe.

I believe that this nation should commit itself to achieving the goal, before this decade is out, of landing a man on the moon and returning him safely to earth.

—JOHN F. KENNEDY, MAY 25, 1961

JOHN F. KENNEDY'S NEW FRONTIER

Perhaps the two initiatives most responsible for the brilliant luster on the administration of John F. Kennedy are the space program and the Peace Corps. Whether exploring space or "developing" the world, Kennedy had confidence that the United States, epitome of progressive modernity in the 1960s, could successfully accomplish the task. For Kennedy and American culture, the moon and the third world represented figurative frontiers to be explored and mysteries to be solved. As a matter of fact, the third world was for many Americans more of a frontier, more mysterious, than the moon.

For Kennedy, the race to the moon was important for its own sake, but more important as a symbolic test in the Cold War competition with the Soviet Union. The new relationship of the United States with the third world in the 1960s, symbolized by the Peace Corps, would serve the same purpose. Kennedy first enunciated this idea in a late-night speech in front of thousands of shivering fans on the campaign trail in Ann Arbor, Michigan:

Technicians or engineers, how many of you are willing to work in the foreign service and spend your lives traveling around the world? On your willingness . . . to contribute part of your life to this country . . . will depend the answer to whether we as a free society can compete.[1]

Kennedy, locked in the political struggle of his life, had arrived in Ann Arbor at 2 A.M. after an exhausting day of campaigning. Surprised that over ten thousand University of Michigan students turned up to see their favorite candidate in the presidential race, he felt he owed them some excitement. So he launched into a vague, ill-conceived discussion of an idea that came to be known as the Peace Corps. At a later time, Sargent Shriver wrote, "No one is sure why Kennedy raised the question in the middle of the night at the University of Michigan."[2]

Despite this lack of certainty and definition, Kennedy's idea became an immediate hit. He realized he had found another weapon with which he could attack the Republicans in general and his opponent, Richard Nixon, in particular. As a senator, Kennedy's main disagreement with Nixon's political mentor, Dwight Eisenhower, had been over foreign policy. Kennedy did not disagree with the former general over the substance of American policy, but over tactics. Kennedy prided himself on being as tough a Cold Warrior as anyone in the administration. He shared the view of Eisenhower's secretary of state, John Foster Dulles, that "the great danger is the communist system itself and its relentless determination to destroy us. . . . We and the Communists are locked in a deadly embrace all around the world."[3]

Kennedy's tough Cold War stance is, in part, what made him attractive to Democrats who had tired of the leadership of Adlai Stevenson in the 1950s. The Republicans had successfully tarred Stevenson with the brush of being "soft" on Communism. Many Americans saw Stevenson as the prototypical example of the liberal Democrat who committed such sins as "losing China" to the Communist menace. Although Stevenson was actually more at the center of the Democratic party than the left, he "was a reluctant convert to the pretenses of the Cold War." Kennedy purposefully positioned himself as a candidate who could attract votes from both Stevenson's liberal wing of the Democratic party and the more conservative, mostly southern wing. Kennedy attracted conservative Democrats by grounding many of his ideas, from the space program to the Peace Corps, in Cold War ideology.

Yet the Peace Corps had strong connections to ideas of the liberal Democrats as well. The idea for the Peace Corps was first broached by liberal members of the "Stevenson wing" of the party. Congressman Henry Reuss of Wisconsin and Senator Hubert Humphrey of Minnesota had offered up the idea of a "Point Four Youth Corps" in Congress in February of 1960, an election year. Humphrey had presidential aspirations of his own, and many saw the fiery ex-mayor of Minneapolis as the heir to Stevenson. Reuss and Humphrey wanted to incorporate an extra dimension into American foreign aid by adding a provision for nontechnical advisers to join the technical advisers first sent overseas under Harry Truman's Point Four program of the early 1950s.

The ideas of Kennedy, Humphrey, and Reuss all flowed from ideas being espoused by an influential group of intellectuals. This group, led by Max Millikan and especially Walt Rostow, explicitly connected the crusade against the Soviet Union with humanitarian ideas of foreign aid and development. Rostow's famous study, entitled *The Stages of Economic Growth*, was even subtitled *A Non-Communist Manifesto*.

Rostow postulated a general theory of economic development whereby all nations needed to undergo a similar four-stage process of growth. This process, though not without potential pitfalls, was essentially straightforward and could be duplicated by any economy. All nations began as "traditional societies," defined by Rostow as cultures mired in "pre-Newtonian" thought patterns. In other words, modern scientific ideas and technological processes had yet to penetrate these cultures. As Rostow summarized it later, "We placed economic growth and foreign aid systematically within the framework of the process of the modernization of societies as a whole."[4] Rostow's ideas accurately reflected the ideology of America's political and intellectual elite since the early 1950s. The Educational Policy Commission, formed by Harry Truman and counting among its members Dwight Eisenhower and James Conant, concluded in 1950 that "greater production is the key to prosperity and peace. And the key to greater production is a wider and more vigorous application of modern scientific and technical knowledge."[5]

Historian Robert Packenham has provided the most complete study of the theories of Rostow and his contemporaries, dubbing them "liberal international development."[6] The most important aspect of this theory was its faith in the possibilities of modern science to conquer seemingly timeless problems in a straightforward fashion. Third world problems provided another equation for modern western science to solve. The right application of the right factors at the right time would produce what Rostow called "economic take-off." Kennedy obviously bought into this metaphor, as evidenced by a speech he made in February 1959: "This year could be the year of their [India's] economic downfall—or the year of their economic take-off."[7] The image of takeoff, with its connections to the ultimate flowering of modern science, the rocket, probably appealed to Kennedy's need for excitement.

As Rostow put it, "In the end the lesson of all this is that the tricks of growth are not all that difficult."[8] Another champion of liberal development ideas (and later a strong Peace Corps supporter), Chester Bowles, summed it up this way in a memo in 1952: "How I would love to see Sears and Roebuck come out here and really tackle the problem of inexpensive distribution of consumer goods, keyed to the Indian market. Such an undertaking could open immense possibilities for village industries, which in turn could produce the goods which would give the cultivators incentives."[9] Development, then, was a clear process of pushing countries along a straight path until they took off into the twentieth century.

As we have seen, Dwight Eisenhower was sympathetic to these ideas of liberal development. However, no one in his administration felt they were important enough to emphasize. Eisenhower and Dulles followed the lead of America's first Cold War secretary of state, Dean Acheson, and centered American foreign policy on the worldwide competition with the Soviets. The world outside of Europe was insignificant except as a battleground in the Cold War. Acheson believed that "major states should dominate in international affairs" and was "wary of peoples and leaders of the emerging third world."[10] Dulles helped construct an American policy in Southeast Asia that supported French colonial rule and ignored the nationalist aspirations of the local population, because he believed this policy would best thwart Soviet interests in the area.

One of Kennedy's few initiatives as a senator had been to disagree with this attitude toward the third world. In analyzing American interaction with the third world, Kennedy disputed Dulles's bipolar view. A grand tour through Asia in 1951 convinced him that nationalism and anticolonialism were the area's crucial forces. Kennedy's most important speech as senator denounced the French occupation of Algeria. He resisted attempts to stop Point Four aid and was involved in the Friends of Vietnam movement. It was not a principled belief in helping the less fortunate that led Kennedy to these ideas. Rather, he believed the United States needed to change tactics to win the Cold War. He criticized imperialism not out of concern for the downtrodden masses, but because the nation would be "critically judged by the uncommitted millions in Asia and Africa."[11] And if the United States was judged to be a failure in this area, Kennedy believed it was doomed to lose the Cold War.

In 1958, a book appeared that seemed to confirm Kennedy's view of American foreign policy. *The Ugly American,* by Eugene Burdick and William Lederer, was a Book-of-the-Month Club selection that went through twenty printings in its first year alone. It describes an American foreign service dominated by ill-prepared and overnourished diplomats, pampered secretaries, and clownish, overpaid bureaucrats. Burdick and Lederer insisted that their work, though fictional, held closely to the truth and described a real world in which the Americans were daily losing out to the better prepared, more dedicated, and more professional Soviets.

Burdick and Lederer attacked a foreign aid establishment that had only been in existence for a decade. Many Americans had distrusted the distant and supposedly effete diplomatic corps for a long time, but the attack on foreign aid was something new. Organized, government-sponsored foreign aid began after World War II with the Marshall Plan, designed to rebuild war-torn Europe—part humanitarian gesture and part anti-Communist policy.

President Truman's 1948 inaugural address surprised many of his advisers by expanding the ideas of the Marshall Plan to the third world. His Point Four—the fourth major subject in that speech—argued that the third world needed technical assistance and monetary aid to grow and prosper. Only when prosperous could these developing nations effectively stave off the assault of the scheming, opportunistic Soviets. The apparatus created in response to Truman's Point Four was what Burdick and Lederer found especially wanting. They felt this infrastructure ignored problems specific to the third world, and they called for a drastic change in the American system of aid. Only a "small force of well-trained, well chosen, hard working and dedicated professionals" could be successful in the highly competitive Cold War world.[12] Kennedy thought so much of this book, the book jacket proclaims, that he sent a copy to every one of his fellow senators.

Kennedy and his foreign policy advisers called for a more complex response to third world problems. They promoted a three-pronged attack on the underdeveloped world. They continued to view this vast area as a Cold War battleground. But rather than ignoring the specific needs of third world nations, they thought the United States should focus on injecting military, economic, and political aid into these new nations. Policy should be designed "to enable the underdeveloped countries to 'take-off' into self sustaining economic growth." This goal, "salient and widespread among . . . the American aid establishment during the Kennedy years," formed the basis for the attraction of the Kennedy camp to the Peace Corps.[13] Though more complicated than previous attitudes, their view of the third world was still one dimensional. Every country had the chance for takeoff, regardless of its particular history, culture, or resources. The United States needed to show how it was done.

The American public was ready for Kennedy's proposals at Ann Arbor, but at 2 A.M., the newspapers were not, and few people outside Ann Arbor heard about them. The Kennedy team decided that he should formalize his ideas in a well-covered speech. They decided to put the concepts into

Kennedy's final major address on foreign policy, scheduled for November 2 at the Cow Palace in San Francisco. This would be close enough to the election to perhaps push a few doubting voters into the Kennedy camp.

Kennedy's speech that night serves as the perfect example of his belief that this new agency could serve as a humanitarian gesture and, more importantly, a new weapon in the Cold War. The main theme of the speech was Eisenhower's lackluster prosecution of the Cold War. Kennedy insisted, "We must do it better." He declared that he was the man to do it. His youthful, vigorous, exciting style would contrast markedly from the plodding manner of the golfing president. And then he declared that the substance of his policy would be different as well. Chief among these differences would be "a Peace Corps . . . well qualified through rigorous standards, well trained in the language, skills and customs they will need to know. . . . Our young men and women, dedicated to freedom, are fully capable of overcoming the efforts of Mr. Khrushchev's missionaries who are dedicated to undermining that freedom."[14]

Cold War competition gave Kennedy's Peace Corps a new twist and differentiated it from Humphrey's lofty Point Four Youth Corps and the commendable precedents from the past. From the moment Kennedy first considered the idea, the aspect that attracted him most was the opportunity to use it as a weapon in the Cold War. The proper prosecution of the Cold War became Kennedy's only substantive foreign policy issue against Nixon in the 1960 election. And the Peace Corps gave him what Theodore Sorenson later called his "only important new proposal of the campaign," a fresh and exciting way to show that his policy was going to be different from Eisenhower and Nixon's.[15]

After Kennedy won the election, the idea languished. Busy constructing his administration, he "had not the time or the opportunity to weigh the various options."[16] The American people, on the other hand, initiated a wave of enthusiasm for Kennedy's proposal. College students met in November at Princeton to discuss the idea, the AFL-CIO created an "executive council on the Peace Corps" to make sure American workers were part of the new agency, and letters flooded the Democratic National Headquarters and the White House inquiring about the subject. Kennedy realized the political potential of this idea, and on January 9, 1961, two weeks before his inauguration, he issued a press release that was a verbatim rendering of a memo that he had asked leading liberal development theorist Max Millikan to write. The memo was vague and tentative, but it reminded Americans that Kennedy was still considering the idea of a Peace Corps.

The day after his inauguration, Kennedy asked Sargent Shriver to head a task force to give him recommendations for the structure of the Peace

Corps. Then Kennedy moved on to other, more pressing matters, such as what to do about Cuba. He had attacked Eisenhower's policy for being too reactive, so he needed to prove to the country that his more proactive Cold War policy was effective. Kennedy intended to do this in Cuba.

Kennedy also had a predilection for fast answers to big problems. Cumbersome bureaucracy irritated him, and he preferred getting solutions sooner rather than later, even if they weren't completely thought out. According to Harris Wofford, one of Shriver's subordinates on the Peace Corps task force, "The President was open to any view, any analysis, any person, no matter how iconoclastic, with one limitation: Kennedy did not want to be bored. . . . The secret use of power was not boring. Foreign aid and perhaps even the Peace Corps were boring. The CIA was not." Once the initial excitement of the Peace Corps idea wore out, Kennedy was more than willing to let someone else hammer out the details while he turned to more exciting things. And, as fate would have it, the CIA presented Kennedy with an exciting possibility on the subject of Cuba just as Shriver and his committee sat down to work on the outlines of the Peace Corps. Kennedy turned his focus toward this CIA plan and away from the Peace Corps.[17]

Fidel Castro had recently taken power in Cuba, and because of his virulent nationalism and socialistic economic ideas, American leaders viewed him as a threat to American interests. Eisenhower and Kennedy believed Castro to be the prototypical example of a third world nationalist who, if not in the direct employ of the USSR, was at least easily duped by the conniving Kremlinites. Ironically, it was the supposedly plodding Eisenhower administration that decided that the best way to deal with Castro was through a bold plan that attacked him directly. After Kennedy's election, the CIA presented the fruits of this plan to the new president. Fitting in perfectly with Kennedy's desire to go on the offensive in the Cold War, it called for an American-backed invasion of Cuban exiles at the Bay of Pigs in southern Cuba. After a successful landing, the invaders would march on Havana, picking up support as they went, and topple Castro in a popular coup.

Unfortunately for Kennedy and the invasion force, the plan was a miserable failure. The exile army was much too small to make a dent against Castro's well-trained and devoted military followers. Kennedy refused to allow the U.S. Air Force or Navy to intervene directly to support the invasion. Although he believed in a more aggressive policy, he cut that aggression off before it got to the point of an actual war. Kennedy wanted to use new, unique methods of foreign involvement that fell short of war. In this case, the method failed.

The Bay of Pigs invasion proved to be a mixed blessing for another one of Kennedy's new weapons, the Peace Corps. The invasion, and the discussion and defense of it afterwards, kept Kennedy and his top advisers preoccupied when Shriver and his task force were meeting to formulate plans for the Peace Corps. This meant that the task force did not receive input from Kennedy and his advisers when they were forming the agency. Kennedy's idea that the Peace Corps would be a weapon in the Cold War could be ignored, if that was what Shriver and his colleagues chose to do. Obviously, Shriver had the interests of his powerful relative at the front of his mind. But Kennedy had very little to do with building the agency, deciding on its philosophy, and formulating its plans.

Soon a jurisdictional battle flared, which, in the end, gave the Peace Corps even more autonomy. Kennedy gave Shriver the official go-ahead to organize the agency on March 1. By April (the month of the Bay of Pigs invasion), the administration needed to decide where to put this fledgling agency on its organizational charts. Consistent with Kennedy's philosophy that it should be yet another instrument of Cold War policy, his top White House advisers suggested that the Peace Corps be made part of the existing foreign aid establishment. Exactly where was not clear—perhaps part of the old International Cooperation Administration or the new Agency for International Development (AID). Kennedy's top aides, such as Richard Goodwin and Theodore Sorenson, argued that it was only logical to put everything together, each agency serving, as Kennedy put it, as one of the "flexible tools" to deal with the Communist menace.[18] It appeared that by the end of April they had persuaded Kennedy to this logic, and that the Peace Corps would be one part of a vast foreign aid bureaucracy.

Sargent Shriver had other plans. In his three months of work on the Peace Corps, he became convinced that it could only work as an independent agency. From the beginning, members of Shriver's task force argued for independence. William Josephson, one member of the group, resisted including the Peace Corps in the traditional foreign aid establishment because it would taint the new agency with any evils associated up to this point with the "ugly American" image of American foreign aid. In short, Shriver and his aides believed they could not create the agency they had dreamed of without independence.[19]

This clash over independence instigated a bureaucratic battle that raged within the administration during April and May. The forces on the side of integration seemed to overpower even the substantial powers of the quasi-Kennedy, Sargent Shriver. But at the last moment, Shriver enlisted the aid of a seemingly unlikely source, Vice President Lyndon Johnson. Johnson believed in Shriver's cause because of his distrust of "the striped pants boys" in the State Department. Throughout his tenure as majority leader of the Senate and in his short stint as vice president, Johnson felt snubbed by the educated, eastern-elite men who had traditionally made American foreign policy. In his eyes they were arrogant and condescended toward the average American like himself. He argued that these diplomats would ruin the Peace Corps because of their "guidebooks and rulebooks and do's and don'ts." Also, there was no love between Johnson and the Kennedy aides opposing the agency's independence. According to one of the leaders in the Peace Corps task force, Warren Wiggins, Johnson "liked the way we, as underdogs, were kind of trying to kick the shit out of them."[20] So he spoke directly with Kennedy about giving the Peace Corps its independence. With Johnson's arguments in one ear and Shriver's in the other, Kennedy relented.

The victory had costs. Kennedy's advisers, miffed at their defeat, cut any direct connections between the administration and the agency. They frowned on the Peace Corps task force as "obstinate loners" and "empire builders" and decided that the Peace Corps "was on its own in the struggle for congressional support."[21] After this point, any connection between the overall goals of Kennedy's foreign policy machine and the Peace Corps would be coincidental.

Kennedy also distanced himself from this, one of his most popular programs. His advisers convinced him to let the Peace Corps sink or swim by itself as an independent agency. The next year, when Shriver went to Congress to get funding, he found out exactly how independent he was. He asked his wife, Eunice (Kennedy's sister), to act as an intermediary during a family weekend in Hyannisport by asking her brother for advice on the upcoming hearings. The president replied, "Shriver and the Peace Corps had wanted to be on their own and now they were completely on their own." From that moment, Shriver vowed that he would not ask the president for anything, even so much as "a light for a cigarette."[22] The Peace Corps was now Shriver's agency, not Kennedy's.

In Ann Arbor, the politician John Kennedy had suggested the ideas for what became one of the most popular ideas of his presidency. He saw this concept of a "Peace Corps" as another piece of the puzzle that would lead to an American victory in the Cold War. Kennedy took the precedents for such an agency and added his pragmatic, anti-Communist touch. The combination earned instant popularity and forever connected the agency to his name. Historians have argued since that because Kennedy conceived of the Peace Corps as a weapon in the Cold War, it became such a weapon. But the basic philosophy behind the agency was Sargent Shriver's, not Kennedy's.

SARGENT SHRIVER AND THE NEW FRONTIER

Although the Peace Corps was seen as John Kennedy's favorite child, the president and the best and the brightest around him allowed Shriver to control the agency's destiny. Shriver and the men he chose to form the new agency accepted the idea that development in the third world was a straight-forward, albeit difficult, process. They differed from the president and his advisers on the details of implementation but accepted the central ideals of liberal international development.

The president's advisers considered the Peace Corps leadership to be brazen "hot shots" who deserved to be ignored because of their incessant campaigning for independence.[23] Shriver used this administrative license to craft his own ideology for the Peace Corps, making it an example of a new way of dealing with the third world. Shriver, in contrast to Kennedy, tried to avoid focusing on the Cold War and did not look for Cold Warriors to serve in the Peace Corps. He consciously attempted to fashion new methods for dealing with the third world by making his organization anti-bureaucratic, representing a break from colonialist methods of the past. The agency would follow the most modern liberal development ideas by pro-moting universal humanistic values while at the same time respecting par-ticular cultural attributes. Finally, the Peace Corps would use the energizing theme of the Kennedy administration, the New Frontier, as a guiding phi-losophy. Shriver's agency would search for new pioneers to help the people of the third world conquer their own frontiers, just as the Americans of the mythic West had done in the nineteenth century.

It was a philosophy that chose selectively from Kennedy's agenda. Shriver did not share his brother-in-law's hawkish Cold War attitudes. He believed that the Peace Corps should not be a weapon in the Cold War, but a "genuine experiment in international partnership."[24] Most in Kennedy's inner circle considered Shriver too liberal to be trusted. According to The-odore Sorenson, they joked that Shriver was "the house communist."[25]

To this point in his career, Shriver's only political commitment, other than loyalty to his new family, was to the burgeoning civil rights movement. In the early 1950s, Shriver helped found the National Catholic Interracial Movement and headed its Chicago office. His main public service before the Peace Corps was as president of Chicago's school board, where he searched for ways to "break the vicious circle of race and poverty in our school system." He sent a memo to civil rights attorney Harris Wofford "saying that because of de facto segregation in housing, the school system was in racial trouble."[26] Shriver worked through the traditional liberal Democratic party to improve the lot of the underprivileged in Chicago. His background placed him in the camp of the Stevenson Democrats rather than the Kennedy-style, hard-headed realists. It also gave him a sophisticated understanding of the relationship between different cultures within the United States.

Nor did Shriver bring substantial experience in international development. He "was not a development specialist," having only brief experience as a youth in the 1930s with the Experiment for International Living.[27] The focus in this agency was to "break down the feelings of insularity, of national superiority, of chauvinism, prejudice and stereotype which had [been] erected throughout the world."[28] In other words, it was one attempt to ignore contrasts in the cultural values of different countries and create a more unified world. Shriver lived in Germany in the summer of 1936 and learned firsthand about the potential tensions within such a universal philosophy. Confronted with "flags and pictures of Hitler everywhere," he rejected those German values, choosing instead to accept "the healthy world of green forests, German songs and Goethe."[29] Shriver's Peace Corps never resolved the tension between a belief in universal morality and a defense of particular cultural values.

Although Shriver did not bring experience in government-sponsored international development or a firm Cold War ideology to the Peace Corps, he did bring with him the Kennedy mystique. "He was bright, handsome and, in the terminology of the New Frontier, 'vigorous,'" critical characteristics in this fledgling agency.[30] In many ways, Shriver was the archetype American liberal of the mid–twentieth century—hard working, earnest, and convinced that any task could be accomplished if attacked with enough energy and intelligence.

Although Kennedy distanced himself from the Peace Corps, the Peace Corps did not distance itself from Kennedy. The men entrusted with forming it set to work with Kennedy's image imprinted in their minds. This image, rather than Kennedy's policies, shaped Peace Corps ideology. Whether accurate or not, Kennedy's image motivated men and women who patterned themselves after this image. If Shriver did nothing else, he served as the perfect Kennedy surrogate.

First, and not least important, Shriver looked the part. Many who met him were immediately entranced, if for no other reason than he was "too perfectly unbelievably handsome."[31] Knowing that the dashing Peace Corps leader was kin to the handsome prince of Camelot lent a special mystique to the agency. It radiated the freshness, youth, and excitement of the New Frontier, qualities that would break any barriers to the tasks of straightforward development facing the Peace Corps.

Shriver acted the part, as well. Peace Corps office workers later referred to him as "His Bubbliness," while journalist Mark Harris called him "the Prince of Vitality and the King of Hope."[32] His colleagues relished opportunities to describe his superhuman capabilities and spunk. While abroad on Peace Corps business, "Sarge behaved like a Great White Hunter on safari with a bunch of dudes who were not quite up to it, which we often weren't."[33] Kennedy did not choose "Sarge" because he was a Cold Warrior or because he knew the intricacies of international development. He chose Shriver because he fit the image of an energetic, youthful leader who would create a dynamic agency that would and could accomplish the tasks set before it.

Shriver strived to make such dynamism a crucial part of this new enterprise. He "labored hard to enhance the popularity of the Peace Corps" by becoming "a regular keynote speaker at business meetings, commencement ceremonies, churches and philanthropic groups' meetings." He insisted that the new office radiate the same vigor he was famous for, "mercilessly draining" his staff and creating an office atmosphere comparable to that of "a campaign headquarters on the eve of a national election."[34]

Energy was central in Shriver's conception of the Peace Corps. So was newness. In the earliest days of the agency, Shriver wrote to Secretary of State Dean Rusk, "The Peace Corps is a bold, new idea requiring a bold, new effort."[35] He worked to prevent the Peace Corps from becoming an entrenched bureaucracy, something he equated with an outmoded style. Many American policymakers believed that in the third world, bureaucratic structures equaled colonial structures. Entrenched bureaucracy meant keeping the status quo, remaining conservative—Shriver wanted a genuinely liberal agency to promote progressive change in the third world. He also wanted to create a new style, one with no connection to colonialist ways of the past. He developed the policy of "in, up, and out" to help prevent such fossilization. Later codified into the Peace Corps Act, this policy allowed no one, not even Shriver or his top lieutenants, to serve for more than five years.

Shriver created and controlled this agency from the beginning. He made decisions as large as the overall structure of the organization and as small as whether any staff members could have a chauffeur (naturally, they could not).[36] His subordinates viewed him as their spiritual as well as their official leader. "The staff found unity in Shriver's electric leadership," reveling in being at the heart of the New Frontier.[37]

Shriver had little to go on when inventing a rationale for the new agency. He understood that the Peace Corps was part of Kennedy's overall strategy for the third world, and that it was tasked with promoting the economic takeoff of underdeveloped nations, which would lead to the goal of nation building. But there was a surprising "lack of clarity and rigor among officials of the Kennedy administration about the relationship between economic and political development."[38] Kennedy's "action intellectuals" had devised a theory but added few details.

With few guidelines, then, Shriver and his followers decided to take the rhetoric of the New Frontier and use it to craft the ideology of the Peace Corps. During the first year, Shriver gave a speech outlining the philosophy behind his new agency:

> If we are successful in finding the rugged Americans needed for this pioneer job, they will work clearing the jungle of the eastern Andean slopes, building farm houses, improving crops, starting education, and surveying for access roads from the jungles to the larger centers.[39]

To Shriver, his job was not international development per se or fighting the Cold War. Part of his task was sending out a group of young Americans in the Kennedy family image: young, spirited, liberal new pioneers, working to conquer the new frontiers of the third world and so promote the straightforward progress of development.

Shriver, like any American in 1960, had been exposed to a very expansive image of the mythic American pioneer, which he used as one basis for his Peace Corps philosophy. In 1960, Americans were practically obsessed with the western pioneer in many guises—cowboys, mountain men, sodbusters, and fur trappers. Pioneer characteristics included "democracy, individualism, freedom, coarseness, strength, acuteness, ingeniousness, materialism, exuberance and optimism."[40] Whether nineteenth-century American pioneers fit this description did not matter. The myth remained strong in America in the early 1960s. And, as Australian author Thomas Keneally put it, "The thing about a myth is not whether it is true or not, nor whether it should be true, but that it is somehow truer than truth itself."[41]

Life devoted a series of seven issues in 1959 to examining this myth and its centrality to American life at the time. Perhaps the most enduring symbol of the western pioneer was the cowboy. Historian David B. Davis argued that Americans in the 1950s saw the cowboy as "an enunciation of the goodness of man and the glory which he can achieve by himself. . . . We behold a dazzling superman."[42] A sweeping image to be sure, and one that Shriver wanted to harness in his vision of Americans at work in the developing world. American pioneers had succeeded in developing their wilderness. The task was not easy, but it was straightforward.

Perhaps the most important frontier characteristic was toughness.

Colorado poet Hal Borland captured the importance of this quality in one of his poems:

The High Plains are tough, tough as rawhide,
   uncompromising
And they choose their people.[43]

Shriver's generation had proven their toughness and grit on the battlefields of World War II. Beginning in the early 1950s, many of his contemporaries had expressed doubts that the current generation of young Americans possessed the characteristics of toughness supposedly developed on the frontier almost a century before. In 1952, Louis B. Seltzer, editor of the *Cleveland Press,* syndicated an editorial entitled "What Is Wrong with Us?" in which he declared, "We have everything. We abound with all the things that make us comfortable. Yet something is not there that should be."[44] By the end of the decade, the worries had reached a crescendo. During a visit by Nikita Khrushchev in 1959, George Kennan doubted that "a country in the state this country is in today, with no highly developed sense of national purpose, with the overwhelming accent of life on personal comfort and amusement," could hope to prevail against the "disciplined" USSR.[45]

The Peace Corps leadership as well as the intellectual leadership in the United States believed that such a cadre of new pioneers would help cure a malaise among the American youth of the 1960s. Robert Shaffer, dean of students at Indiana University, hoped that serving in the Peace Corps would create "a period of personal challenge" by "shattering the actual and mentally imposed limitations of provincialism, tradition and custom" and would also "combat conformity and anonymity."[46] Shaffer wanted the volunteers to live the challenging life of their forbears and in so doing regain a sense of rugged American individuality.

Nothing better illustrated Shriver's hopes for the Peace Corps than a speech he gave in Worthington, Minnesota, in October 1961 at the National Corn Picking contest—seemingly a strange place for a top-level diplomatic official to be making a major address, but a fitting spot for Shriver to outline his version of international development. Shriver declared that the people of the Minnesota prairie "understand the basis of the Peace Corps better than anyone else. Rural life in this country has always been dependent on the spirit of helping your neighbor." Not only did they appreciate the motives of the Peace Corps, but, because of their pioneer stock, they would serve as the ideal volunteers. Just like the Minnesota farmers, said Shriver, "these volunteers are not starry-eyed, impractical do-gooders. They're good, solid, down-to-earth Americans who want to use their skills to help the underdeveloped nations of the world."[47] The volunteers, due to "their volunteer spirit and radical pragmatism—their ability to improvise tactics on the ground and to overcome hidebound regimes of red tape and bureaucratic restraint," would conquer the new frontiers of the third world just as their ancestors had conquered the frontier of America.[48] Shriver conjured up the pioneer characteristics of toughness, ingenuity, and individualism in outlining his vision for the Peace Corps.

For Shriver, the Peace Corps became an ideal vehicle to prove that this generation had the same mettle as the previous ones: "The Peace Corps has made it possible for these young Americans to speak—to act. The years following the Korean war were gray years for American youth. Cries of soft were in the air. 'Did not one third of the Americans in North Korean prisons collaborate with the enemy? Did not another third die?' The sign of the new generation became a question mark."[49]

By applying the precepts found in William James's "The Moral Equivalent of War," Shriver expected to change this question mark into an exclamation point. James had argued, "We must make new energies and hardihoods continue the manliness to which the military mind so faithfully clings." Shriver wanted the Peace Corps to be a vehicle through which "the military ideals of hardihood and discipline would be wrought" into the generation of American youth.[50] He accepted the argument made by historian Arnold Toynbee in the *New York Times Magazine* in 1960 that the United States needed to "be represented abroad today by the generation of men and women who won the American West." Toynbee, who, according to Peace Corps staffer Brent Ashabrannar, "was talking our language in every word he wrote," asked, "Can the pioneer generation of Americans be brought back to life?"[51] Shriver's answer was the Peace Corps volunteer. The volunteer would first regain his or her pioneer bearings and then use them to show people in the third world the straight path to development.

Shriver designed the Peace Corps as a break from past methods of dealing with the underdeveloped world. The United States would not act as colonialist oppressor but would respect local peoples while showing them, by example, the best qualities Americans had to offer. He began by recruiting men of a similar mind-set to help him build this agency. The first kindred spirit he turned to was Harris Wofford. The day after Kennedy's inauguration, on the same day that Kennedy tasked Shriver with inventing the Peace Corps, Shriver called up Wofford, whom he had become friends with during the Kennedy campaign, and together they started a "task force" to form the new program.

As with Shriver, Wofford's major political involvement up to this point had been in the civil rights movement. A Notre Dame law professor, Wofford had become interested early in his career in the teachings of Gandhi. As early as 1952, he concluded in a law school paper that the civil rights movement needed "a Negro with some of Gandhi in him."[52] In the mid-1950s, he was immediately attracted to Martin Luther King Jr. and his philosophy of nonviolent direct action and counted himself as one of King's staunchest supporters. This commitment to the civil rights movement put Wofford even further left than Shriver, the Kennedys' "house communist." So radical did Wofford later appear that at least one volunteer joined the Peace Corps because he thought Wofford was "trying to make Peace Corps into a more tolerant, better financed version of the angry, charismatic organizations to its left like SNCC [Student Non-Violent Coordinating Committee] and the FSM [Free Speech Movement]."[53]

Wofford was not a Cold Warrior. Besides his liberal civil rights credentials, he brought with him a lifelong commitment to the World Federalist Movement. Wofford learned about Gandhi's philosophy on a trip to India sponsored by the World Federalists. As Wofford put it, the World Federalists desired to "journey from the age of sovereign nation-states to the beginning of a united world community."[54]

As with Shriver's involvement in the Experiment for International Living, Wofford's involvement with world federalism signaled his desire for a new kind of American role in world affairs. He did not argue, as some of his colleagues in the World Federalist Movement had, that communism could be compatible with world federalism. Instead, he wished to offer up world federalism as a competing ideology for both nationalism and communism, thereby creating a true New World Order. Wofford thought that American leaders missed the boat in their preoccupation with communism in the changing world of the late 1950s: "Our country and its leaders are out of touch with the changes and revolutionary pressures in the developing nations and the Communist world."[55] The Cold War contest was "of little interest to the third world."[56] Wofford, like Shriver, viewed the Peace Corps as far more than another agency on the Cold War battleground.

As a youth, Wofford believed in world federalism because he believed in universal values. He argued against the necessity of borders, because "people on one side of the line are conditioned to the erroneous fact that they are different from those on the other side."[57] The Peace Corps could become the type of program that could erase the borders, because volunteers and hosts alike would learn through interaction that they shared universal beliefs and values. Wofford's world federalism also presaged the tension within universalism that would vex many volunteers. At the same time that Wofford called for a blurring of boundaries and differences, he insisted on the value of a democracy that "puts the individual at the center."[58] Allowing individuals the right to decide for themselves potentially contradicted a call for universal beliefs.

Wofford also cut a dashing image: "He cast a spell that only the most cynical could reject. Tall, lean, handsome and eloquent, he seemed the very personification of the New Frontier. Friends and critics alike called him the 'Philosopher King' of the Peace Corps."[59] Wofford exuded energy and fresh ideas that typified the image that Kennedy's administration wanted to portray.

Wofford shared Shriver's desire to rejuvenate the American spirit in the new generation of American youth. He felt that the experience of the frontier was central to the American character: "We are a pioneering people, with the frontier still in our blood."[60] "America never wanted to turn from Thoreau and pioneering," Wofford lamented as early as 1946, "but it could not grasp at once the revolutionary way in which it might apply its dream to the whole world."[61] He believed that the essence of international development lay in recreating this frontier spirit in the developing world. Wofford defended Truman's Point Four program by arguing that "world development is a concept of American history, echoing of covered wagons on the westward trek."[62] Like Shriver, he envisioned the Peace Corps as a host of new pioneers, spread throughout the world rather than America's West. As a World Federalist, Wofford did not believe that these new pioneers should conquer the world for America, only that they should show the world's peoples how Americans had conquered their frontier, and the locals would naturally choose to follow the example. He "always talked about this common vision which kept swirling around us and moving us forward . . . the New Frontier . . . in the Third World. . . . We are sending people to bring the message of democracy and individual initiative."[63]

In January 1961, Shriver and Wofford set about creating the Peace Corps in the image of the New Frontier. Neither of them had any experience creating an agency for third world development, and both of them had a strong disdain for the international aid establishment. Both had read *The Ugly American,* which portrayed American overseas diplomats as out of touch with the tough problems of the third world. Its authors, Burdick and Lederer, believed that U.S. diplomats had "forsaken their heroic ancestors' journey into a frontier."[64] Shriver and Wofford thought they could change this image, and they were not about to bring any of the old-fashioned aid bureaucrats into their new agency.

But, facing the specifics of organization, they floundered on the rocks of inexperience. Fortunately for them, a solution came in the form of Warren Wiggins and William Josephson. Both worked in the Far Eastern Division of the ICA, the International Cooperation Association, and so seemed to personify the type of foreign aid bureaucrat loathed by Shriver and Wofford. Yet they were rebels, agreeing with the arguments of *The Ugly American* by fighting within the establishment to eliminate American extravagances over-seas.[65] The Peace Corps idea intrigued them. On their own initiative and in their own time they constructed a blueprint for the Peace Corps called "The Towering Task."

This document, rather than the credentials of Wiggins and Josephson, caught Shriver's eye in February 1961. It attracted him from the very begin-ning, because it took its title from an excerpt of a Kennedy speech calling for a "towering and unprecedented response" to the problems of the devel-oping world. It created a strategy for the type of agency that Shriver and Wofford had been trying to create during the previous month. Wiggins and Josephson argued that only a substantial and bold Peace Corps could be effective. They suggested that a small, cautious program might get lost in the bureaucratic wasteland of Washington, while an organization of up to fifty thousand volunteers would constitute a bold new step in international development. This suited Shriver and Wofford, who were looking for vitality and sparkle. In typical style, Shriver called up Wiggins late at night after reading the memo and insisted on a meeting at 7 A.M. the next morning. From that point on, "The Towering Task" provided Shriver with a detailed plan for sending his new pioneers out into the world.

After Wiggins and Josephson were brought on board, the Peace Corps shaped up quickly. Josephson, a lawyer, hammered out most of the legal details. Wiggins began to structure the organizational chart. Wofford, by now special adviser to Kennedy for civil rights, kept in touch with the White House. Most importantly, Shriver began to assemble the rest of the team that would constitute the heart of the Peace Corps leadership for the next five years.

Shriver continued to look for men like Wofford who could lead in this fresh approach to the third world. Frank Mankiewicz exemplifies the type of man Shriver chose to run his new agency. Mankiewicz, "a man after the Kennedy clan's own heart," came from an elite Hollywood family. He understood all about the importance of image: his father had written the screenplay for *Citizen Kane*. He also understood that the media would find it "irresistible" that a member of a famous film family was leading a group of "blond, beautiful and brilliant Kennedy clones through the world's mountains and jungles." He accepted Shriver's offer to head up the Peace Corps operation in Peru, not even sure of its location.[66]

Although he knew nothing about Peru and had no experience in development, Mankiewicz fit exquisitely into Shriver's vision of the Peace Corps. Like Wofford, he came with the appropriate liberal credentials, having been an active member of the ADA (Americans for Democratic Action) in the late 1940s. The issues of the Cold War did not interest Mankiewicz. Instead, he became nearly "obsessed" with an idea called community development: "[It] offends a bureaucrat's sense of order because it is basically revolutionary. I mean, the purpose of community development is to overthrow the existing order—social, political, economic." The idea fit Shriver's outline for the agency—it was new and antibureaucratic. Mankiewicz envisioned volunteers teaching the Peruvians how to help themselves and so change the world in which they lived.[67] This idea dovetailed nicely into the ideas of the rest of the Peace Corps leadership. After all, the characteristics of individuality and self-inspired work had propelled the pioneers on the American frontier. So could they propel the new pioneers, and Mankiewicz's idea of community development was the perfect vehicle to translate these ideas to the local population.

Shriver pulled off a major coup in attracting another one of the administration's top talents, Bill Moyers. Referred to as "young Bill Moyers," he became deputy director of the Peace Corps at the age of twenty-eight, at the time making him the youngest presidential appointee in history.[68]

Before joining the Peace Corps, Moyers served as the star of Lyndon Johnson's staff, and Johnson was loathe to lose him. Shriver pushed hard to get him, though, because he fit the mold. He had no experience in development. His experience had been as a Baptist minister and a political aide for Lyndon Johnson. In the best Kennedy tradition, his attributes included toughness as well as intelligence and charm. According to fellow Johnson adviser Jack Valenti, "Behind that ministerial facade and the smell of fire-and-brimstone sermons was a brass-knuckled street fighter who knew every side alley and fire exit."[69] Valenti's description conjures up a picture of the rough-and-tumble mythic American.

By reputation, Moyers was brilliant and dedicated. In 1965, veteran *New York Times* correspondent Tom Wicker wrote a glowing description of Moyers in a nine-page article in *Harper's* magazine. According to Wicker, Moyers had a "quick eye and a sharp brain," and he had become "the most able and influential Presidential assistant I have ever seen or read about."

Sargent Shriver (left foreground), active as always, hikes through the forests of Nepal in 1964 with volunteers involved in agricultural development. Photo by Paul Conklin, courtesy National Archives.

Despite his youth, people listened to him because "his scope had no limit."[70] This was the type of person Shriver wanted at his agency, and he used Moyers as a legislative liaison, helping to push Peace Corps legislation through Congress.

All of Shriver's staff recruits fit the same image. The vast majority were white men with elite backgrounds and impressive educational pedigrees. They did not represent the realistic, calculating, Cold War side of Kennedy. In fact, many were reluctant supporters of Kennedy in the 1960 election, accepting his leadership only after it was apparent that their favorite, Adlai Stevenson, would not carry the standard again. Mankiewicz stated, "My heart was with Adlai, but I knew Nixon would eat Stevenson alive." The head of the Department of Evaluation, Dave Gelman, was "staunchly for Stevenson," and it took a long time for him to be persuaded to "work for the enemy"(i.e., Kennedy). Donovan McClure, Peace Corps representative in Sierra Leone, declared that he had been "an active Stevenson supporter." The Peace Corps staff represented the left wing of the Democratic party much more than Kennedy's more realistic, centrist wing.[71]

McClure pointed out why these liberals joined one of Kennedy's most high-profile agencies: "I could instantly see what it was all about," he said. "It was all about Sarge."[72] "The Peace Corps was 100% Shriver—kind of an eagle scout on the make style," affirmed staffer Coates Redmon.[73] Shriver communicated excitement and involvement, the most hopeful aspects of the New Frontier. His recruits did not sign on to fight the Cold War. Wofford later argued that it is "wrong to look at John F. Kennedy and Robert F. Kennedy simply as Cold Warriors."[74] They did not sign on because of a lifelong commitment to international development. They signed on because the agency seemed like an inspiring approach to foreign affairs; in other words, because they thought the Peace Corps represented the most hopeful aspects of the New Frontier. Kennedy might not have thought much about the rhetoric of the New Frontier, but these men did. They were excited by the "heroics, the new Frontier 'vigah'" in the new agency, and they looked forward to molding volunteers into a personification of this idea.[75]

This guiding ideology remained relatively constant throughout the 1960s. Ironically, one of its most salient characteristics was a constant need for self-evaluation and self-criticism to prevent any petrifaction. The Peace Corps became famous for constantly questioning its own practices, programs, rules, and policies. But the basic philosophy changed little during the Kennedy and Johnson administrations. The Peace Corps remained committed to the basic ideas of liberal international development and to Shriver's pioneering version of these ideals.

Shriver remained in charge of the agency until 1966, even after Johnson appointed him the head of the War on Poverty in 1964. He always projected an image of action. The *Peace Corps Volunteer Magazine* (usually called the *Volunteer*), published by the agency, constantly pictured him circling the globe, diving into the rough-and-tumble third world frontier. One issue describes him "walking seven miles to see volunteers, then riding back in an open jeep" in Nepal. Another portrays him "skirting a puddle, walking through rain to his disabled land rover."[76] Countless anecdotes told of Shriver's superhuman abilities to sleep on airplanes, eat local food, and face the toughest challenges the third world could offer.

Shriver's deeds as director remained consistent with his philosophy. For example, Shriver wrote a letter on August 8, 1963, to the Peace Corps representatives, outlining social expectations for volunteers. Among other things, they were supposed to "eat host country food, stay healthy, speak the language, know the culture."[77] Shriver wanted the volunteers to fit into his image of the new pioneer in a strange land. Arnold Zeitlin, a volunteer in Ghana, described the emphasis on image and how it confused the volunteers as to their roles: "There was—and remains—some confusion in the Peace Corps over what was expected of the volunteer. The executives saw the Peace Corps as an opportunity to toss sheltered young Americans into ways of life supposedly more challenging than their American existences. . . . Hardship and what was called 'Shriver's hairshirt stuff' even obscured the work volunteers were invited to host countries to perform."[78]

"Shriver's hairshirt stuff," cliché though it became, accurately encapsulated the director's hopes for the agency. He proclaimed, "Because of the Peace Corps Volunteers, the world is learning that Americans have not gone soft."[79] Shriver never wavered in his hope that the volunteers could help the developing world conquer its frontiers as the United States had done a century and more before.

Harris Wofford's ideals were equally consistent. He remained in different positions within the Peace Corps through the mid-1960s, including a stint in "the bush" as director for the large program in Ethiopia. His focus remained on youth. In 1966, he made clear his vision of the Peace Corps in a letter to the volunteers, declaring, "The classroom or school in which you are teaching should be a model of the kind of society we and the Ethiopians want to achieve."[80] Wofford, like Shriver, did not picture the Americans forcing change on the Ethiopians in an imperialistic way. Instead, the American volunteers, along with their Ethiopian counterparts, would show the rest of Ethiopia how to change their world.

In 1966, just as in 1962, Wofford continued to see the Peace Corps as a rejuvenating tool for the youth of the United States. Wofford's ideal Peace Corps would serve as a "university in dispersion," a way in which young Americans could learn about the world in a setting far removed from the college campus. The volunteers would learn in "a kind of Socratic seminar writ large."[81] The Peace Corps, then, was not to be a typical development agency. It was to serve as a place for the youth of the United States to learn and have their limits tested and stretched, a challenge similar to that described by Shriver.

By 1966, the Peace Corps was no longer Sargent Shriver's agency. Everyone at the Peace Corps assumed that the mantle would fall on "young Bill Moyers." His image fit the Peace Corps perfectly, and he had an even closer relationship with President Johnson than Shriver had had with Kennedy. But that was the problem. Johnson, in the midst of his fights over the Great Society and Vietnam, could not afford to lose his most respected subordinate. Even farther from the Peace Corps than Kennedy, Johnson was not about to let a man with the ability of Moyers defect to an agency seen as Kennedy's most vibrant child.

Instead, the directorship of the agency went to Jack Hood Vaughn, who at first glance appeared to bring a different philosophy to the Peace Corps. Andrew Kopkind, in an article in the *New Republic,* applauded Vaughn's entrance because he would move away from "Shriver's hairshirt stuff."[82] After being installed as director in March 1966, Vaughn claimed that the Peace Corps must "skip quickly over its adolescence and become a responsible adult in a world it helped to sophisticate."[83] He was not as interested as Shriver in image. His goal was to "make the Peace Corps as good as Sarge said it was."[84]

Perhaps unintentionally, however, Vaughn's personal image connected well with the image that Shriver had created before him. Vaughn, after all, signed on with the Peace Corps in its earliest days, becoming the first chief of the Latin American section. He was born and raised in the farm country of Montana and liked to say of his upbringing that he "was the son of a cowboy."[85]

Vaughn's first claim to fame had been as a boxer under the pseudonym Johnny Hood. This athletic, no-nonsense, cowboy image played perfectly in Shriver's Peace Corps. Vaughn's "physical stamina, disarming sangfroid and marked inclination towards gallows humor" immediately attracted Shriver and many of the other leaders, including Bill Moyers.[86] Moyers's influence helped convince Johnson to appoint Vaughn as ambassador to Panama, and while there Vaughn established himself as a poker-playing friend of the Panamanian president. More importantly, his hearty style and his "exhausting weeks in farmer's fields" earned him the title, the Peasant Ambassador.[87] In other words, he seemed another version of Shriver's hard-working, hard-driving man of the people.

Vaughn accepted the role for the Peace Corps that Shriver had crafted. "In 1961," Vaughn wrote, "the Peace Corps took the drab concept of public service and gave it dash. It was high adventure with a purpose, a blow against the chauvinism of the 50s, a disarming, fresh approach to international relations." [88] Naturally, Vaughn's emphasis would be slightly different, but in core philosophy, he essentially agreed with the ideas of Shriver, Wofford, and Wiggins. For example, he "totally supported" Shriver's antibureaucratic five-year flush rule: "We couldn't become staid or career oriented. This was going to have to be a burst of glory."[89] Even though he had worked for years in the ICA, he agreed with Shriver that freshness, energy, and initiative were more important than development experience.

Vaughn did bring a new emphasis in community development to the Peace Corps. Mankiewicz, who had been elevated to chief of the Latin American Division when Vaughn became ambassador to Panama, served as one of Vaughn's most important lieutenants. Although, for one, Kopkind saw the rhetoric of community development as a break from Shriver's Peace Corps, as we have seen, Mankiewicz's community development ideas fit perfectly with Shriver's conception of the volunteer as a new pioneer.[90] American youth would take their inbred know-how and individual initiative and teach people in developing nations how to find and use these characteristics in themselves. As Vaughn put it the year before he was appointed director of the Peace Corps, "I doubt that we can stress self help too much."[91] Vaughn's techniques may have been new, but they were still based on the original conceptions articulated by Shriver, Wofford, and Wiggins.

After Vaughn's directorship, the Peace Corps leadership underwent a fundamental change, due for the most part to the election of Richard Nixon in 1968. Never sold on the idea of the Peace Corps to begin with, Nixon had the added incentive of doing everything in his power to mitigate the legacy of his arch rival, John F. Kennedy. As soon as possible, Nixon ordered the end of Peace Corps independence by folding it into VISTA (Volunteers in Service to America), creating a single entity for all volunteer agencies. This effectively ended the golden era of the Peace Corps, introducing new complications and new questions that move beyond the scope of this book.

We must keep in mind, however, that although the philosophy at the top of the bureaucracy changed after the 1960s, the cultural legacy lived on in the volunteers and in American culture at large. We will return to this issue in the conclusion, but should remember that the ideas of the early

1960s carved an indelible imprint into the agency and into American culture. Understanding these ideas and their fate helps us understand more than just the 1960s—it helps us understand the progress of American liberalism in general from the 1960s up until the present day.

In sum, the overarching philosophy behind the Peace Corps changed little during the 1960s. The Peace Corps leadership believed that they could send young Americans out to change the developing world for the better. Their new, antibureaucratic agency would represent a fresh approach to the third world. Using the values supposedly bred into all Americans, this cadre of young Americans would help the rest of the world become as successful as the United States. Kennedy's New Frontier would allow young Americans to stretch to their full potential as young pioneers, changing both the world and the United States in the process.

The New Pioneers

FINDING AND PREPARING THE NEW PIONEERS

Shriver and his agency wasted no time in beginning the search for volunteers to participate in this new adventure into the third world. Shriver was told early on, in newspaper articles and by important government officials such as Lyndon Johnson, "that if the wrong type of person were selected to go overseas, the Peace Corps would face embarrassment at home and abroad."[1] Shriver needed to forge an elite corps of new frontiersmen to fulfill his dream. This search for excellence created the impression that the Peace Corps "was elitist, even though that wasn't the intent, but that's how it turned out."[2] It seemed to many that the recruits were even physically perfect: "They all had wonderbread faces and daffodil smiles and china blue eyes and soft white arms and pumping vital hair, smooth, limber and American."[3] After passing muster as prototypical Americans, these perfect volunteers would take their American qualities into the darkest recesses of the globe.

To ensure that they considered only the elite, the Peace Corps asked applicants to undergo a battery of tests before they applied. First, they had to complete a lengthy application and obtain six personal references. Next came a six-hour exam and a thorough medical check.[4] Only after successfully completing these tasks would a recruit be invited to training.

Most recruits were not only perfect, they were young. Many factors contributed to the leadership's decision to focus on youth. First, everyone acknowledged that young people had less of a stake in careers and families and so could more easily serve in a foreign country for two years. An important dimension of the Peace Corps, as Wofford so often stated, was to educate America's youth. Not only did people in the third world need to see how America's pioneers worked, American youth had to be reminded of their own pioneering roots. Shriver, in discussing the War on Poverty, claimed, "Like the Peace Corps, the focus is on young people and their education."[5]

Most importantly, the image that Shriver created for the Peace Corps demanded youthful energy. He radiated a youthful exuberance and insisted his subordinates do so as well. Shriver wanted his volunteers to bring to the third world an American brand of youthful enthusiasm. Like many Americans, he equated age with frailty and European-style decadence. Youthful Americans would provide a clean slate on which Shriver could write his prescription for the new pioneer.

As Alan Weiss put it, "They were young! Unspeakably, unthinkably young."[6] Even evaluators, constantly sent to the field to rate the performance of volunteers, often commented on their conspicuous youth. Paul Bell, evaluating a group in Guatemala, commented, "The striking thing about this group was its age—the average age of these fourteen Peace Corps Volunteers on their date of entrance to training was 20."[7] Many early critics of the Corps, including Richard Nixon, belittled it as a "kiddie crusade." Defenders of the Peace Corps answered, "World War I and World War II were also children's crusades, yet they [the soldiers who fought these wars] had no opportunity to shape the world in which they lived," while the Peace Corps volunteers would.[8]

Shriver did not search for only the supremely talented of the young generation. Eugene Burdick and William Lederer, hired by Shriver to do a Peace Corps evaluation, declared, "Any extreme deviation from the average is likely to be more troublesome than it is worth."[9] The Peace Corps wanted intelligent volunteers, but they did not want overzealous idealists or obnoxious extroverts who could not be trained in techniques appropriate to the new pioneer.

They found this intelligent but normal and well-rounded individual in what became known as the B.A. generalist. These were recent graduates from prestigious colleges and universities who had degrees in a nontechnical discipline, usually in the humanities and social sciences. Part of the attraction to the B.A. was practical. Graduates with degrees in science were more likely to shy away from the Peace Corps because opportunities in the work force were more lucrative and abundant. Also, a larger percentage of science graduates had firm career plans. B.A. graduates were more likely to be unsure of their career path and more likely to be attracted to the two-year sabbatical offered by the Peace Corps. As an article in the *Peace Corps Reader* put it, "Who else but the educated young generalist from the established middle class can take two years off, learn a new trade, work like hell, maybe live in a dump and not get paid much?"[10]

But there was a philosophical attraction to the B.A. generalist as well. They fit into the category of intelligent but malleable volunteers described by Burdick and Lederer. B.A. generalists suited Shriver's image of the lonely frontiersman, forced to rely on nothing but his own guile to survive. They resembled a "renaissance man, a jack of all trades—the BA generalist who is still able to adapt to most anything."[11] According to George Carter, director of the Peace Corps' West African division, "BA generalists are more flexible . . . and they are more receptive to Peace Corps training."[12] For Shriver and his agency, this was most important, because training was the arena in which they envisioned molding these raw recruits into new pioneers.

Shriver and his top aides provided few specific guidelines for the training program. Because most recruits would be recent college graduates, and because the Peace Corps viewed itself as an educational institution, it seemed natural to rely on American universities to do the training. Wofford was especially keen on this idea, as we have seen earlier, in his desire that the Peace Corps be a "university in dispersion." Practical concerns also dictated using universities to run the training programs. George M. Guthrie, who helped run early training programs for volunteers going to the Philippines, described the early days as "marked by an almost indescribable haste and confusion." No one knew what they were doing at Peace Corps Washington, but they needed to get the job done quickly, so "they had no choice but to give wide scope to the universities and hope for the best."[13]

But "nobody knew exactly what they were training the volunteers for."[14] The trainers knew they were preparing the volunteers to enter the third world, but they generally shared American cultural ignorance about these countries. As an answer to this problem, the trainers presented the fledgling volunteer with a mixture of philosophies. They latched on to Shriver's new pioneer ideal, mixed it with ideas from the Cold War and with assumptions about the relationship between volunteers and host nationals. An early document discussing the purposes of the Peace Corps presented the vague idea that "the volunteers will get special orientation and training on factors which have made it possible for the United States to rise to a position of world leadership and great wealth."[15]

Photos such as this one, depicting a trainee hard at work in language training, dominated Peace Corps literature in the 1960s. Many volunteers criticized their language preparation: this volunteer is in the midst of learning eight different Micronesian languages during a twelve-week training period in 1966. Courtesy National Archives.

The Peace Corps leadership had to develop a training program from scratch, inventing everything from a coherent training philosophy to a daily schedule. Shriver decided that the most practical length of a training program was eight to twelve weeks, enough time to introduce trainees to basic Peace Corps ideas but not too much time to dampen the enthusiasm of the mostly young volunteers. The leadership left the details up to the specific training institutions. The staff of most training centers, realizing they only had the trainees for a short time, decided to keep them busy as much as possible. The typical training schedule asked the trainee to work from 7 A.M. to 10 P.M., six days per week, with one-hour breaks for lunch and dinner.[16]

The Peace Corps Act provided some specific guidelines for the trainers to follow. The act encompassed three goals: to provide developing countries with trained manpower, to help promote a better understanding of Americans by the peoples served, and to increase American knowledge of other peoples and cultures. This last part of the act seemed easiest for the trainers to attack in a university-based training program, and so the trainers designed courses in world affairs, communism, and local culture.

To fulfill the second part of the act, the trainees had to understand what it meant to be American. Hence, the trainers designed extensive courses in American history and government. More importantly, training "emphasized self-reliance, decision making and confidence building," all characteristics inherent in the American pioneer.[17]

The most complicated aspect of training was "providing trained manpower." This became tricky, because different countries were asking the volunteers to do different jobs. Training programs needed to teach all the languages and all the skills necessary within only a few months.

Perhaps the clearest mandate given those who were to train the volunteers regarded language instruction. Speaking the language of the locals seemed to stand at the center of the Peace Corps philosophy. Everyone remembered Burdick and Lederer's searing images of mute, arrogant American diplomats not bothering to learn a nation's language. Only if a volunteer knew the local language could he truly understand and respect local values. The most prevalent early newsreel images of Peace Corps trainees showed them hard at work in the language labs, listening to tapes of exotic foreign languages.

But learning languages did not become the heart of Peace Corps training. Although using tapes for learning language was innovative, it was not successful. James Cross, later a volunteer in Senegal, complained about the "drills done without knowing meaning or any visual association. This is OK for children, but not for adults."[18] The academic language training provided little connection to the real-world situations the volunteers were being thrown into. Training for Cameroon included only courses in African languages, which meant that they could not converse at all with the many Cameroonians who spoke French.[19] In Peru, few volunteers "arrived with a bilingual level of fluency in Spanish," and, even more problematic, none understood Quechua or Aymara, the Indian languages of the majority of the people they worked with.[20] The trainers made little use of native speakers to help teach the classes, instead relying on tapes to do the job. Almost every evaluation in the 1960s stressed that the volunteers had received too little language instruction at their training sites.

Why, if speaking the native language was so important to the philosophy, did the trainers put so little emphasis on it? Part of the answer comes in the Peace Corps' *counterpart* concept. Shriver and the other Peace Corps leaders envisioned the volunteer showing the host-country nationals the keys to development. They would do this by picking out a small number of host nationals to work with. These people would serve as counterparts, and the counterparts would impart their received wisdom to the rest of the local population. These counterparts, just like those depicted by Burdick and Lederer in *The Ugly American,* would be "exceptional in their possession of a latent gift for American-style progress." The mythic American frontier that Peace Corps Washington used as a model overflowed with pairings of pioneers and Indian counterparts. The Peace Corps' idea, like Burdick and Lederer's, "conformed to the pairings of frontier counterparts in mythic tradition," a Tonto for every Lone Ranger.[21] The volunteer only had to know enough to communicate his ideas to the counterpart, obviating the need for extensive language training. The Peace Corps leaders envisioned volunteers, with their American values, dealing with the different values of the third world through an intermediary. This implied a creation of distance between the American volunteer and the people of the host country.

The trainers had other ideas on how the trainees should use their time. Volunteers spent much time listening to lectures on world affairs, American studies, area studies, and communism. Julius Amin relates that in preparation for work in Cameroon, trainees spent over half their training in these lectures. The trainers realized that the volunteers lived in a different world from that of their mythic ancestors a century and a half before. Being a pioneer would not be enough. Volunteers would have to deal with the Cold War and clashing value systems.

Regardless of the feelings of the leadership, many trainers felt the most important part of the training in world affairs involved teaching about communism. "Trainees preparing for the first overseas teaching project, in

Ghana, spent less time learning Twi than they did the theory and practice of Marxism."[22] In part, the trainers were reacting to fears of organizations such as the Daughters of the American Revolution that these naive American youths would be easy pickings for sinister communist spies. The trainees needed to become acquainted beforehand "with the tactics which the professional communist organizer will use." There was a "real and immediate danger here that a professional Marxist or communist organizer, without revealing his identity, will 'take over' the Peace Corps Volunteer."[23]

The trainers devised elaborate means to teach their pupils about the evils of communism. Every trainee received a pamphlet entitled *What You Must Know about Communism.* One trainer, Paul Jacobs, relates how he accomplished the task for a group being trained to go to the Philippines: "We put on a demonstration of how a Communist would answer the questions of a group of PCVs [Peace Corps volunteers]. . . . The discussion between the trainees and the acted-out Communist party official seemed to have an electrifying effect on the trainees. . . . Perhaps it would be possible to build such a discussion into all programs with the cautionary note that it takes a skilled person to enact the role of the communist party official."[24]

Although the Cold War was de-emphasized by Shriver and other Peace Corps leaders, the volunteers were given a heavy dose of Cold War propaganda during their training, especially in the early years. The classes in communism also exemplify the incompleteness of the belief in universalist ideals. Volunteers were taught to accept all values, yet communism was unacceptable. Just as Shriver rejected fascism but respected Germans, volunteers were taught to reject communism but accept those who might believe in it.

The volunteers, especially the B.A. generalists, needed technical training for the job they were going overseas to perform. Peace Corps training recognized this need. For example, the group bound for Cameroon, whom Amin examined, spent 110 hours of their training in "technical studies, to include knowledge and skills required to perform the assigned job overseas."[25] The program introduced Peace Corps teachers to basic educational philosophies and techniques. Those bound for community development were given an introduction to basic development techniques, and so on down the line of all the jobs the Peace Corps worked on.

But job training received little emphasis. The trainers felt it was more important to give the trainees an overall philosophy on how to deal with this unknown, undeveloped world than to give them specific job training. The 110 hours spent by the trainees for Cameroon represented less than 25 percent of their training. Much of the training might have been specific, but

Not all frontiers required skills such as horseback riding. At a Peace Corps training site on Key West in 1966, volunteers learned pioneering skills more typical of the tropics, such as basket weaving. Photo by Carl Purcell, courtesy National Archives.

it had little connection to the jobs the trainees were supposedly training for. According to volunteer Paul Cowan, most of the technical courses he took were "insubstantial."[26] Many trainers defended the lack of job training because they believed it to be superfluous. Instead, they "argued for 'role centered' vs. job centered training; a more open, ambiguous, less structured training."[27] The Peace Corps believed that other things, such as the role they fit into as an American in the third world, were more important to the volunteer than the job they did.

This lack of technical and language training prevented the volunteer from understanding the specific country or situation he or she was going to. One training evaluator said about a training program in New England: "I do not think that Shawnee [the name of the training center], with all its good intentions and all its genuinely valuable training, can give the volunteers anything approaching the true experience of living in an Indian village."[28] The training center did not focus on training recruits to succeed in their projects. Part of this stemmed from the leaders' aversion to bureaucracy. They wanted to create a new type of fluid aid system that gave the volunteers maximum control, rather than a well-oiled machine that accomplished tasks while alienating local feelings.

Rather than giving the trainees practical job suggestions, the educators tried to develop ingenuity in their students. One course training science teachers was "a barehanded approach to science: the scientific method and five senses are all that is needed to achieve an understanding and appreciation of nature . . . using materials they are reasonably certain will be available in the field (bottles, cans, bamboo, string, etc.)."[29] This faith in using one's senses fit Shriver's image of how a new pioneer was supposed to act.

Theoretically, Americans had an innate sense of how to act on a frontier. In a book written in 1966 that canvassed volunteers all over the globe, Edna McGuire described some of the "basic life skills" given to volunteers. During training, "girls labored over a kettle," while a "group of men were lashing rough boards together with heavy twine in the hope of producing a table." Other chores included learning to make soap and even "how to pick a good horse."[30] Regardless of where they were going, volunteers were trained to fit the image of nineteenth-century American pioneers rather than of skilled development workers in the twentieth century. American myths about what "undeveloped" life would be like dictated the direction of training.

Occasionally, trainers modified the training so that it took into account local conditions. Training for Micronesia included "boat building, spear fishing, coconut husking, weaving palm fronds and climbing coconut trees,"[31] even though these volunteers were being trained for teaching jobs. The trainers believed they needed the primitive survival skills of Robinson Crusoe, rather than the wilderness skills of Daniel Boone. But the necessary characteristics were the same for Crusoe and the pioneers—ingenuity, toughness, and individuality.

According to trainer John Snyder, "Our object is to teach every trainee to be a jack-of-all-trades and a master of one." Trainees became this self-sufficient type mostly through living the spartan existence of a pioneer. The trainers believed they could create this personality type by putting their elite charges into the right sort of environment. In the Vermont training program, where Snyder taught, trainees "lived in a crude wooden huts with tarpaper roofs and sand floors. Each hut shares walls with neighboring huts, which limits privacy. . . . Outdoor latrines are an uphill walk away, a pace especially difficult to negotiate by flashlight. Cold showers are located halfway down the mountainside."[32] This submersion in the pioneer lifestyle sometimes had little connection to conditions in the new home where the volunteers would serve. According to Paul Cowan, an ex-marine taught the group how to use a compass, then quit, realizing his lesson was useless since Guayaquil was on the other side of the Equator."[33] The details did not matter. The important thing was to create the complete volunteer, one who could help teach natives how to deal with their frontier in the same way Americans had supposedly dealt with their own. After training, volunteers would be able to serve as exemplary new pioneers. One volunteer on his way to Africa described the end product this way: "a composite of a competent, if amateur, Africanist, well briefed if slightly practiced teacher, articulate spokesman for the American way, and healthy mind in sound and flab free body."[34]

The pioneer image, and hence the volunteer image, demanded this ideal "flab free body." Physical education became central in the training regimen for every potential volunteer. According to anthropologist Robert Textor, there was "an underlying assumption that physical energy and athletic prowess were somehow going to make a vital difference."[35] The trainers believed that the third world, with its jungles, deserts, and mountains, required that the volunteers be made into tough, physically fit individuals. The volunteers needed to live up to the image of a sinewy frontiersman. "We will use physical training as a vehicle to measure a man's stamina, courage and resourcefulness," said William Sloane Coffin, the director of the Peace Corps' first training camp.[36] One volunteer described the morning regimen this way: "Can you imagine doing for physical education 140 jumping jacks, 120 situps, 120 touching toes, 30 pushups, and 100 jumps in place; then in the pool five laps of crawl, three laps of breast stroke and two of side stroke?"[37]

Another favorite exercise demanded of the trainees was "drown-proofing." This technique was a complicated method for preventing oneself from drowning even if one fell in the water completely clothed. One volunteer gave the details: "We pick up the ring from the bottom of the pool and swim one width of the pool under water with our hands tied and then with our feet tied. . . . This was done mostly so that if you were ever caught in an accident or had a cramp and one member of your body was incapacitated you could stay alive, travel and even save someone else."[38] If volunteers got unexpectedly caught in the middle of a wilderness lake or raging jungle river, they would be prepared. Just as Huck Finn had to be prepared to swim the Mississippi or John Kennedy had to be prepared to swim in the Coral Sea, volunteers had to be prepared to swim in the jungle waters of the third world frontier, even if they had difficulty speaking the language once they dried off.

Part of the rigorous physical training included a technique called "drownproofing." These women, training in New Mexico in 1964, made water wings out of blue jeans to train themselves in water-survival techniques. Photo by Paul Conklin, courtesy National Archives.

The Peace Corps expected volunteers to keep themselves in top physical condition and health while at their posts. Peace Corps health officers worried about a misunderstanding of health conditions in the host countries. Even before the founding of the Peace Corps, health officials fretted that "the relatively antiseptic conditions common to the United States do not prevail in most regions in which the Peace Corps will be operating."[39] Health trainers warned trainees to stay away from anything that might make them ill, from the water to fresh vegetables to local beer. They were admonished to take "extra precautions, such as vitamins and dietary additions."[40] This made some volunteers so paranoid that they thought "it would be more dangerous to be a Peace Corps Volunteer in Ecuador than a soldier in Vietnam."[41]

The Peace Corps trainers were caught in a bind. They insisted on creating self-reliant volunteers in the world of twentieth-century science. They hated offending third world cultural standards of sanitation and health but could not accept that conditions in the third world and the United States really were the same. Often, trainers erred on the side of too much caution because they believed the volunteers were innocent youths, needing protection. One volunteer complained that "training gave us too many preconceived ideas. One of them was this boiling water and this medicine kit. We are given an overprotective attitude."[42] This attitude exemplifies a problem that would surface again and again in Peace Corps Washington's relations with its volunteers. The agency demanded that the volunteers live the self-reliant life, accepting "stomach aches and parasites as some of the unpleasant facts of life."[43] But at the same time, the agency viewed the volunteers as immature youths who needed an overdose of health training to be protected from their own mistakes.

The most important part of the trainees' physical conditioning took place in a program called Outward Bound. This program, originally developed in England to help train the British army and find out "why some people survived in life threatening situations and others didn't," became the key element for teaching young Americans how to be new pioneers. The program combined physical exercise, such as hiking and jogging, with learning wilderness survival skills, such as compass reading. It also created psychological stress by asking participants to survive such adventures as a solo hike.

Bill Haddad, one of the leaders of the Peace Corps Training Division, called Outward Bound "more heroics, more of that New Frontier 'vigah.'"[44] Gerald Caplan, the chief psychiatrist in the Peace Corps Medical Division, summed up the purposes behind this sort of training: "Trainees were required to learn survival techniques and develop high physical condition. Here the emphasis was on a highly conditioned elite group (e.g., U.S. Marines, Special Forces, Green Berets, etc.)."[45] Caplan's comparison to the Green Berets provides an interesting image of the Peace Corps volunteers. Shriver and his aides envisioned their corps as equally elite, equally tough, and equally trained as the most elite American fighting forces. Both the Green Berets and the Peace Corps volunteers were "quintessential symbols of renewal . . . and the youthful desire for change that Kennedy gave mainstream political meaning."[46] Both were asked to serve in the third world, fighting the Cold War and recapturing the essence of the raw frontier.

The Outward Bound program demanded physical fitness and determination. Trainee Esther Warber described some of the training in her diary: "We received instructions in map reading, first aid, mountain climbing, rock climbing, survival, jungle living, latrine making and cleaning, vegetable preparation, jungle direction finding, rock cracking, mudjugging [push-ups in mud] and drown proofing."[47] The trainers intended this litany of survival skills to create the ultimate self-made person. Volunteers would survive anywhere, under the harshest conditions.

Rock climbing and rappelling classes, central to the Peace Corps Outward Bound experience, exemplified the search for tough and hardy pioneering volunteers. Photo by Paul Conklin, courtesy National Archives.

Training in 1964 for jobs in Brazil, these volunteers prepare to brave the New Mexican wilderness on a four-day Outward Bound experience. Photo by Paul Conklin, courtesy National Archives.

The training program did not make volunteers fluent in the languages of the third world. It did not give them a thorough preparation for the jobs they were sent to do. They were not given complete specific technical instruction on how to teach or develop a community. They were not even given a thorough immersion in the culture of the host country. They were given lectures about that country and had some knowledge of local history, customs, and beliefs. But nearly all volunteers felt that training fell short of giving them an adequate understanding of the culture of their country.

However, training was not designed to do any of these things. Instead, it was designed to mold these young, unsophisticated Americans into a cohesive platoon of pioneers. The training program focused on making the trainees "remember" what it was like to face an untrammeled frontier. The trainers prepared the minds and bodies of these youths so they could face the rigors of the third world, and they instituted procedures to guarantee that only the hardiest survived.

THE FRONTIER ADVENTURE

The founders of the Peace Corps believed that they were sending American youth out into the new frontier of the third world. Rather than merely a rhetorical device, this idea had concrete connections to the imagined frontier of the United States in the late nineteenth century. The training program was designed to create a cadre of old-stock pioneers from the American youth of the 1960s. The agency's leadership expected volunteers to be "a sort of combination of Paul Bunyan, Astor and Schweitzer."[48] The volunteers were trained to expect conditions in their host countries similar to those of the mythic American West, complete with excitement, romance, and hard living. For some, the reality came close to these expectations.

A few entered the Peace Corps in search of adventure, excited by the prospect of leaving their mundane lives for the uncharted jungles of the third world. Mary Williams, a volunteer in Colombia, pointed out the importance of excitement: "With a definite mission in mind (and spirit) we came to the Peace Corps seeking adventure. We are finding it. . . . We're having a damned good time."[49] They wanted to taste the cultures of the world and entered the experiment with eyes open, ready to accept what came to them.

Some of the youth joining the Peace Corps sensed a connection between its task and the mission of their pioneer ancestors. They wanted to be the Marlboro Man, riding their horse not on the plains of America's old

Marlboro Man or Peace Corps Volunteer? Volunteer Tom Qualia, the model new frontiersman, strides through the Bolivian village of Jalsuri on a break from teaching classes in sheepshearing and rabbit and chicken farming. Courtesy National Archives.

West but on the plains of Bolivia, Tanzania, or Afghanistan. "The Peace Corps mystique," wrote Richard Lazarus from Colombia in 1967, "of the exotic, rugged, individualistic volunteer who hacks his way through jungles with a machete in one hand and a Marlboro in the other . . . that's a pretty picture and one that many of us, who found ourselves wandering around a college campus trying to figure out what we were going to do with ourselves after graduation, found appealing."[50] Some chose to work on the most difficult projects just for the challenge. "I signed up for community development work," one volunteer wrote, "because it seems to me to be the most exciting, revolutionary and challenging work the Peace Corps offers. That last sentence sounds like something out of a recruiting brochure, but I really believe it."[51]

A recruiting brochure stressed that "the volunteer must be prepared to live a pioneer life" and warned that there would be no recreational facilities, travel would be by foot, food might be strange, and tropical diseases might be prevalent.[52] Potential volunteers were told to expect the harshest, most challenging conditions, and many prepared themselves to face these hardships in the forthright manner of the pioneers of the old West.

Many of the evaluators sent by the Peace Corps to examine the effectiveness of programs sensed this feeling among volunteers. One evaluator said, "While still in the U.S., the Peace Corps Volunteers see their role as pioneers in working out a new kind of life for 'emerging peoples.'"[53] These volunteers could not separate their visions of the third world from their preconceptions about the emerging America of the nineteenth century.

So Kennedy, Shriver, Wofford, and the rest of the Peace Corps leadership sent the volunteers off into this new frontier. The first group of youthful volunteers left prepared for a new and exciting chapter in their lives: "The girls were bright in their summer dresses, the men were turned out in their Sunday best. . . . Inside, the President and his brother in law, Sargent Shriver, looked for all the world like fathers of the bride as they greeted each of the young guests."[54] It didn't take long for the young volunteers to change into clothing they felt more appropriate for their surroundings. According to one group of foreign nationals, this included "a skin tight pair of blue jeans, cowboy boots and broad brimmed hat, in perfect taste at a rodeo in Montana or Texas."[55]

Some volunteers stepped immediately into pioneer roles. Anne Wilson waxed historical: "We arrived in the Philippines on October 12, 1961—remembering that October 12 had been an auspicious day for Columbus in discovering his new frontier and hoping it would hold great significance for us and our new frontier."[56] Even after their arrival, the most intriguing aspect of volunteers to most Peace Corps outsiders was their pioneer-like qualities. After visiting her daughter, one mother wrote to the *Volunteer* about her experience roughing it and her opinion on why American youth were so well suited to that type of life: "I slept well on their rope bed. . . . Since then I've been happy knowing that these unselfish young persons, raised with the comforts and softness of our way of life, can face reality and the basic problems of daily living in another culture with courage, concern and convictions. No doubt most Volunteers are from pioneer stock, who know a little rough going is more exciting than smooth sailing."[57] Not only did observers note this volunteer ruggedness, they thought it was the critical idea behind the Peace Corps and its success. Magazines and journals bemoaned the fact that "American pioneering spirit might seem, except for the orbiting astronaut, to have gone out with the days of social and political vitality." But they rejoiced that such spirit and vitality could "happen" in the Peace Corps and declared that "young people made it work."[58]

These observers noted specific character traits that they felt described both the mythic American pioneer and the Peace Corps volunteer. Lawrence Fuchs, a Peace Corps representative in the Philippines as well as an American studies professor whose research specialty was the American character, felt especially qualified to comment on the "peculiarly American" traits of the volunteers, which included "personal independence, achievement, and mission."[59] Furthermore, the volunteers were "planful, organized, hurried, restless consumers of time who were driven incessantly to accomplish task upon task." Just as for Americans in the wild West, these characteristics could lead the volunteers astray. One evaluator describes a group of volunteers in the Dominican Republic with a mixture of admiration and dismay as "the guys in the cowboy movies who come in from the range to shoot up the town."[60] Another compared volunteers to soldiers in World War II, because they were a "tough, self-confident, independent bunch of veterans. The war and headquarters seem awfully remote. Their concern is with the immediate day-to-day task of living." This evaluation went on to describe how one volunteer had a knack for "hard drinking," another a "striking talent for Community Development and for women," while another was so wild, he was "worthy of a separate chapter."[61] Reading this evaluation, one can picture the wild inhabitants of a dusty prairie town in a Hollywood movie.

Volunteers felt anxiety about living up to the image of the "American" pioneer. This image included everything from intense work to an ability to live the rough life with common people. Volunteer Fred McCluskey wrote to a friend, "There seemed to be a tremendous pressure to do something spectacular, to inject the community with a tremendous dose of energy and remake it overnight."[62] Another volunteer felt pushed not only to act the part of the pioneer American, but to look it as well. "I don't think I want to stay with the professors even if the opportunity presents itself," he wrote. "I want to get down there with the real folks in the grubbiness—mix in as I become one of the great unwashed."[63] The mythic westerner was not an academic, but a hard-working man of the people. Volunteers had been trained for that life, and many intended to live it. "Many said they thought of themselves as pioneers," one evaluator wrote, "and felt they had demonstrated the kind of determination to stick with the job under trying circumstances that a pioneer is supposed to possess."[64]

Many prided themselves on possessing one of the wide array of pioneer characteristics, such as a thirst for adventure. Volunteer Michael Parrish said, "I painted myself as gutsy adventurer." In letters home to his parents, he began: "Well, I got it—malaria!" or, "Killed a little cobra last night!"[65] Chad Bardone described his grit and courage: "Heading upstream in a 25 ft. dugout canoe. . . . The river is muddy, fast, and dangerous. . . . I must admit I felt a little like 'a great white hunter' as I sat in the raised bow of the dugout canoe and appraised the hostile jungle shores."[66]

Some volunteers believed that their host country even looked like the mythic American frontier. According to Raymond Stock, "Climbing some of the hills, reminded me of the desert chase scenes in old Hopalong Cassidy pictures."[67] Another volunteer jumped into the role of Huck Finn, rafting on boats made from banana trees down wild rivers through the island of Mindanao, which he described as "the new frontier of the Philippines, like our wild west. There it is Indians; here it is head hunters."[68] William Buss described his experience as "not unlike an evening on *Bonanza*, because in many ways Mato Grosso is reminiscent of the early American west. . . . Here are the boom towns, the agricultural settlements, cattle drives, gold digs, and gun fights. Just substitute palm trees for pines."[69]

Thinking of their host countries as the American frontier helped volunteers see a path for development. One in the Philippines put it this way: "It is still quite primitive, but it is also a pioneer country in the process of change. . . . He [the volunteer] is there to see it grow and develop and perhaps to aid in a small way."[70] For some volunteers, living on the frontier epitomized the Peace Corps experience. Jerald Posman, in Tunisia, summed up the feelings of many in his generation: "To many people, the Peace Corps is possibly the last frontier. The frontier in America was tamed more than a half-century ago, and to recapture the spirit of adventure and challenge that disappeared with this frontier, many see two recourses. The first is war; the second is the Peace Corps."[71]

Some early Peace Corps projects tried to capitalize directly on this pioneering spirit. Sargent Shriver hoped that schemes for colonization in some of the host countries would mirror the mythic effort of colonizing the American West. One evaluator described a project in Ivory Coast designed to "open up the 'trackless' southwest region with roads. . . . [The government] would induce the subsistence-level farmers on the perimeter to move in and start rubber and palm oil plantations."[72] Chad Bardone describes a similar project in Bolivia that planned to move locals to a deserted area and show them how to live on the untamed frontier.[73]

As much as the Peace Corps leadership liked this kind of project, they were few in number. Most host nations did not have the land or the desire to back such pioneering schemes. But just because there were few explicitly pioneering projects does not mean that few volunteers acted like pioneers. If the images of the *Volunteer* provided the only evidence, it might seem as if all volunteers lived a life harkening back to the mythic West. Part of the purpose of the magazine was to show volunteers doing exciting things, which in turn would serve as a recruiting vehicle for the Corps as a whole.

This aspect of the magazine is clear in the earliest issues. The second issue shows a set of pictures of "the rough and furry life near the top of the world" in Nepal. The article talks about twenty-mile treks to work and the lucky volunteer whose station the magazine dubs "the most remote in the world."[74] These images reinforced the idea that Peace Corps volunteers had to adopt a new lifestyle in the remote frontiers of the world.

A picture essay that appeared in 1963 epitomizes the experience of pioneer volunteers. It describes the life and work of Jo and Dud Weeks, volunteers in the remote regions of Sabah, a small principality in Malaysia. Both have matinee-idol looks, and one picture centers on Dud's bulging muscles as he trudges up a muddy trail with their daily water rations. Both are pictured in different images leading prim and neatly tailored scout troops of local children. Here they are following the American method of teaching how to deal with the frontier through the vehicle of scouting. Their project was actually to teach English to the children, a mundane enough activity, but the job fades into the jungle background as the reader's focus remains fixed on the surroundings. Ingenuity stands out as one of the most important virtues of the pioneers. One image does show Jo teaching, but only so we can glimpse the children racing to the blackboard in an ingenious game devised by the Weekses. The photo essay concludes with a picture of "Dud writing a letter by hurricane lamp," conjuring up visions of Robinson Crusoe or even Abraham Lincoln reading by candlelight.[75]

The story and images of Dud and Jo are not isolated in the collections

"Supervolunteers" Dennis and Louise Wheeler on the three-hour canoe ride from their tiny jungle village to the nearest town. The picture's original caption praised them as "jacks of all trades," living "off the land" in the obligatory thatched hut. Photo by Pickerall, May 1968, courtesy National Archives.

of the *Volunteer*. In January 1966, the magazine unambiguously connected the Peace Corps to Hollywood cowboy imagery by printing a picture of a returned volunteer posing with Steve McQueen during the filming of a movie about China.[76] The June 1963 issue put the image front and center on the first page, with a photo of "mountain man" William Unsoeld, with full beard, covered by ropes.[77] Other issues show volunteers teaching banjo playing in the Ivory Coast, gathering twigs in Peru, and "elbows deep in Curds and Whey" in Cyprus.[78] The June 1964 issue pictures Harriet Osborne teaching the local women how to bake apple pies. Not only are the pies themselves the ultimate expression of frontier Americana, but Osborne herself bears an uncanny resemblance to Aunt Em in the Wizard of Oz, the stereotypical pioneer woman.[79] These images fit precisely the image Americans had of their own mythic past. Pioneers gathered wood, played banjos, and occasionally found themselves up to their elbows in preparing food, especially apple pies.

Sometimes the magazine mixed images reminding Americans of their own frontier with exotic images of far-off jungles and romantic locales. An October 1966 photo essay shows a Senegalese, dressed only in loincloth, working as a blacksmith.[80] In Afghanistan, the volunteers had to boil their water, like any self-respecting adventurer, but they had to do it in a samovar.[81] In Borneo, volunteers sat down to a feast of roast deer, much as Daniel Boone might have done, but with dense jungle in the background rather than piney forest.[82]

Many pictures depicted volunteers in labors that were not pioneer pursuits but were nonetheless distinctly American cultural activities. In Nigeria, we see volunteers sponsoring a soap-box derby, an event common among Cub Scouts in the United States and designed to teach handicraft skills common to American frontiersmen and their descendants alike.[83] We view female volunteers teaching dressmaking to their students in Venezuela, just as female pioneers made their own dresses, and just as many American women were expected to do.[84]

The *Volunteer* was not the only publication to push this mythic volunteer image. Ingenuity, of course, stands out as one of the most important virtues of the pioneers. *National Geographic* devoted much of its September 1964 issue to describing Peace Corps work around the world. One story illustrates the connection between Peace Corps volunteers and the image. Earle and Rhoda Brooks left a legacy of "cleaner streets, a stronger community spirit, new friends for the United States and lively children who might have died without help." Beyond that, the article and the pictures make clear that their pioneer character created this success. For example, Earle Brooks

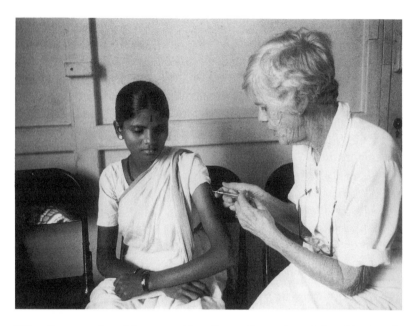

Lillian Carter, mother of future president Jimmy Carter, showed that older Americans could fit the Peace Corps' specifications for caring volunteers quite adequately. Photo by Vern Richey, 1968, courtesy National Archives.

displayed frontier ingenuity by fashioning a makeshift guitar out of scraps in five minutes: "It became a young boy's most cherished possession." And, naturally, the first song the sensible Brooks taught the youngsters to play on the guitar was "At our house, we boil the water."

The Brookses also exemplified the tension all volunteers experienced over their belief in universalism. They decided to adopt two of the local children.[85] In doing so, they accepted that two children born out of a different culture could be loved, literally, as their own. Yet the adoption also implied that they could raise these children better themselves than "the natives," because they were American and had both financial and cultural advantages to impart to these children.

The mystique included the necessity of hard work. In order to break the sod or drive the cattle on America's old West frontier, the pioneers relied on back-breaking toil. In the Peace Corps, as we have seen, they had a phrase for this toil: "Shriver's hair shirt stuff." Many accepted this idea as an important part of their Peace Corps identity. One group, whose project was to dig wells, "liked the hair shirt side of our project, especially compared with the jobs of the volunteer English teachers."[86] Some thought it important that they were challenged just getting to their job. Roy Furomizo, assigned to the mundane task of inoculating children against malaria, recounted his not-so-mundane trip to work. First, he and his partner had to endure "a rugged, four hour jeep ride to our point of departure," and then, after the locals gave them a lunch of roast wild pig, they hopped on a raft in which they "floated through magnificent teak forests, raintrees and rolling hills," with the "monkeys chattering" all the while.[87]

For many volunteers, grueling work became central to their happiness in their job. Each of a group of geologists in Ghana "worked at the head of a crew of 30 or 40 men who cut trails through the jungle, dig pits where the lateritic soils are deep and outcrops scarce, and sample stream beds and gravels."[88] This group blazed a trail through virgin jungle in search of mineral wealth, not unlike the mythic gold digger in the Yukon, out to scratch his fortune from the dirt and rock of Alaska. Pioneer volunteers felt they needed ceaseless work. In Brazil, Frances Cunha wrote in her diary, "This is really for me, life among these people is really different. When we are at the nursery in the A.M. we are busy every minute."[89] Lillian Carter, mother of a Georgia politician destined to be president, exulted after one day, "I'm so tired and *refreshed*. I just *love* busy days."[90]

If the volunteer's usual job was not challenging enough, the ethic dictated that they fill up the day with a wide variety of extra work. Lawrence Fuchs described the overabundance of projects completed by volunteers in just one village in the Philippines: "They built libraries, toilets, began model gardens, started poultry and 'piggery' projects, ran nutrition seminars, and organized summer camps in the mountains." Not only that, Fuchs argues, but the "Volunteers were never satisfied," driving themselves to the limits of their endurance as the mythical cowboys might have done.[91]

Volunteers were expected to use pioneer common sense to solve any problems they might encounter. Ingenuity was perhaps the most esteemed quality in a volunteer, and those who displayed it were trumpeted as ideal. The study commissioned in 1960 to examine the possibility of a Peace Corps argued that this was a major reason for creating the agency. According to the study, "do-it-yourself represents a deep and lasting current in American life," but it was "a quality which may often be lacking from peoples emerging from other culture patterns."[92] All volunteers agreed that ingenuity was expected of them. One group from Peru "claimed that every Volunteer must have one or more technical skills. However, during the discussion they strongly defined 'technical' as meaning handy-man type proficiency."[93] One

Peace Corps representative even went so far as denying the volunteers in his country a moving allowance, forcing them to use their ingenuity to find or make their own furniture.[94] Peace Corps leaders claimed that the reason B.A. generalists were so attractive was that they were more enterprising than trained technicians. Technical specialists could be "resourceful only under specific conditions. He cannot make those conditions himself. He expects them to be given."[95]

The prize for the most ingenious volunteer might have gone to Robert Drew, a community developer in Costa Rica. Drew organized a "Snake Rodeo" patterned after one he had seen in Sweetwater, Texas. The purpose of the rodeo was to collect snakes so that venom could be extracted and sold to researchers in the United States. Drew's unique event netted $350 for the local community center. One of the more popular activities during the rodeo was the crowning of a local "snake queen."[96] Drew used his know-how and his knowledge of what worked in a frontier town to rid the town of snakes and help build the community.

Some combined their desire to work hard with ingenuity to create an entirely new project for themselves. In Cameroon, Carl Awsumb, an architect by trade, found he wasn't working hard enough. So he decided to start an architecture school. To do this, "He had to find his own students . . . design desks, had them built locally. He substituted chip boards for about 1/5 the price of ordinary drawing boards."[97] By saving money, working with his hands, and using his mind, he became the quintessential pioneering volunteer.

In some cases, the Peace Corps seemed to be looking for an explicitly frontier type of ingenuity. Teachers in Nepal were lauded in the *Volunteer* not for their teaching, but because they made "a soils survey in the area; produced a new type of ox yoke and a new type of bridle."[98] In Iran, Jim Grant invented a makeshift hand-operated washing machine that cost only $15.[99]

No matter what job volunteers worked at, they were expected to use their ingenuity in fashioning local materials to serve their needs. Nurse Cynthia Erskine "made a pipette cleaner by fitting a distilling apparatus to the water tap. . . . A small electric hair dryer allows us to dry our slides quickly—a boon during the rainy season."[100] In Peru, volunteers invented a process to extract lanolin from the water left over after washing wool.[101]

Teachers were not supposed to be immune to inventive ideas. In Nyasaland, Dave Koehler used "bricks, soccer balls and anything else relevant in teaching geometry. Pieces of wood, metal, and cardboard of assorted shapes and sizes are turned into optical benches, spring balances and other pieces of scientific equipment." Carol Schnebel, in Jamaica, encouraged kids to "use natural materials where possible," and they "concocted mosaics out of sea shells, postage stamps, and paper and magazine pictures. . . . The children had never done crafts work before, and these exercises taught them to use their ingenuity and imagination."[102]

Peace Corps teachers were supposed to have their eyes on the future, helping their host countries progress out of their frontier past toward a more civilized future. A vignette from a book by volunteer Leonard Levitt illustrates this hope. In this scene, Peace Corps teachers marvel that they have taught their students a complex scientific concept about time completely foreign to the students' parents—that while it is day in Tanganyika, it is night in the United States. Levitt could "just picture these old men all over Africa nodding their heads, smiling in fascination night after night, just like listening to a great fairy tale."[103]

The teacher's job was to live on the frontier and educate its young inhabitants about the worlds of science and civilization beyond the frontier. In so doing, many volunteers became popular among the younger generation, and some became icons. One school in Ghana had two pictures hanging on the wall at the school entrance: one of the president and founder of Ghana, Kwame Nkrumah, the other of the local Peace Corps volunteer.[104] Many volunteers became the town luminary. On arrival in the Philippines, John Halloran wrote, "To say we have been received hospitably is a vast understatement. We are celebrities, exotic Americans, and the curiosity of the whole town."[105] After the unfortunate death of volunteer Stanley Kowalczyk, the town wrote a communal letter to the Peace Corps expressing their admiration for Kowalczyk's "unreserved liberality, simplicity, exemplary patience, keen enthusiasm" and complimenting him for "scarcely resting in building the bridge."[106]

Volunteers often developed closer ties to their students than to any other host nationals. Eric Broudy, a teacher in Liberia, said, "The most meaningful relationships I established were with my sixth grade students. The children, I found, were more responsive to true friendship and understanding than were their parents."[107] Polly Kirkpatrick wrote, "Most of my friends are under six years old. . . . I love them all."[108] Many children appreciated the efforts put forth by their American teachers. One student wrote in a volunteer guest book, "Thank you for your good behavior and sympathy toward your students."[109] Teachers attended student-run banquets in their honor, and it became commonplace for volunteer teachers to receive cookies and flowers at the airport prior to departure.

Friendship became an important goal of volunteer teachers toward their students. Some volunteers received all the inspiration they needed from the children and these friendships, such as the teacher in the Philippines who found, "The children elevated your spirits until you believed you were at least the equal of Captain Marvel."[110] Volunteers felt more comfortable working with youth, because they did not have to contend with fully developed cultural values. They could assume, without offending their egalitarian conscience, a superior role in relationships with children that they could not assume with the students' parents.

Even better than friendship with the host nationals was becoming part of their family. In Costa Rica, Anna Zentella became a godmother for all the children of a local family.[111] Roger McManus, in the Philippines, saw the locals go one step further in accepting him as one of their family. When McManus's parents visited from the United States, they received a hero's welcome: "We could never have imagined the reception we were to receive at this little makeshift airport. . . . We were showered by flowers and leis by a smiling, happy throng."[112] It became part of the Peace Corps volunteer ethos to "form a brotherly type of love for these people. . . . They mean something to me which I have never really felt before."[113]

Volunteers expected to form an almost mystical bond with the host nationals. This hoped-for bond led some volunteers to "a romantic attachment to the villages, a kind of return-to-nature attitude about the villagers. Its [sic] the simple existence."[114] The volunteers realized that there was no such thing as the perfect noble savage and that their hosts were more complicated than others might imagine them to be. Paul Cowan argued that the poor were not unsophisticated and that many were more organized than his project assumed them to be.[115] But many volunteers clung to their expectations about the host nationals living close to a state of nature, out on the frontier. And because of this, what they needed to improve their hosts' lives was a dose of the qualities that Americans used to conquer their frontier. This belief added to the strain volunteers felt about their universalist philosophy. If volunteers assumed, as some did, that mythical American frontier values would help improve the lives of their hosts, that implied that these values were better than the values already adhered to by the locals. Some volunteers had no trouble accepting this value judgment. One wrote home and asked his family to send him a copy of *The Diary of an Early American Boy.* "That fits just what the Ecuadorian campesinos need," he wrote.[116]

The volunteers felt pride in what they were doing because they were focusing their attention on the ignored host-country nationals. Charlene Duline, working on a nutrition program in Peru, put it this way: "For the first time in their lives, most of the poor people of Peru are learning that someone cares about them. For the first time they are seeing Americans who live and work as they do—Americans different from the tourists who breeze through leaving a wake of money."[117] And the volunteers respected their hosts, even while believing them to be anachronisms in the world of the 1960s. Angene Wilson described a scene that she believed epitomized the Peace Corps. "The woman with the wrinkled groundnut-brown face," she wrote, "and faded head tie and sagging breasts which have fed 14 children, all dead. She grins toothlessly when you say 'ma-ke' or 'good day.'"[118]

Many Peace Corps projects had at least one volunteer who seemed to epitomize all of the qualities of the perfect volunteer. These "hero volunteers" or "supervolunteers" represented the ultimate standards in Peace Corps conduct. Sargent Shriver was fond of describing such hero volunteers whenever he could. He told of one, a basketball coach in Tunisia, who "saw high winds blow down his baskets. Undismayed, he proceeded to teach dribbling and passing. As a result, he has a team of excellent court players who have never had a chance to shoot."[119] The hero volunteer showed uncommon ingenuity, courage, and hard work—in short, an overabundance of the values associated with the image of the pioneer volunteer.

It is no accident that Shriver chose a sporting example to illustrate his idea of the hero volunteer. It was a commonly held view that if volunteers could successfully bring the American idea of sports and physical fitness into a country, they were serving the Peace Corps ideal in the best way possible. Many of the values Americans associate with sports are also associated with the frontier myth. When volunteer Carlos Naranjo saw that Saint Lucia had "little recreation of any kind," he "went into action." He became an instant "hero" on the island because he introduced basketball. According to the Peace Corps representative, "Many would say the introduction of basketball to St. Lucia is the most significant thing the Peace Corps has done for the island."[120]

The more common hero volunteer did everything and was seen everywhere. Rex, in Guatemala, fit this mold. A "handy jack of all trades who loves to build and tinker," he was "very quiet but energetic and resourceful" and "had numerous Community Development projects going on on the side."[121] In other words, Rex worked especially hard and displayed his ingenious talents but did so in a humble manner.

Evaluator Richard Richter described another hero volunteer he encountered in Ghana in disbelieving detail: "He's raising chickens and turkeys, coaching the track team, building a solar cooker with his physics students, running the science club. He's started a chess club. He's taught a little Twi to two Russian teachers and he plucks a guitar and sings a little bit with his students because they get a bang out of it."[122] Like any good cowboy, this volunteer plucked a guitar—and still found time to break down Cold War barriers by teaching the local language to his country's arch enemies! Richard McManus, in the Philippines, qualified as a "super-volunteer" as well. He worked himself mercilessly, putting on plays as well as teaching, earning money to build a building at school. He showed his love for the locals, took them hiking, played volleyball with local boys, and even started a scout troop![123]

Some American volunteers displayed uncommon courage in defending the rights of the downtrodden in their host countries. One saved an entire school from corporal punishment with an ingenious stratagem. Every time the monks who administered his school beat the students with broomsticks, he took a broomstick from them and returned the favor: "The broomsticks disappeared in 24 hours."[124] Here is the volunteer as small-town marshall, meting out justice in an unjust world. This volunteer also took a firm stand on the merits of a local custom, rejecting it out of hand.

The hero volunteer often fit in well in his locality, whether out in the bush or in the barrio. But they related to the host nationals in a way befitting the mythic western pioneer. Cowboys, remember, were rough around the edges and had a tendency to run wild. Hank Dawson could "outdrink, outcurse and outfuck the men in his barrio, which made him seem heroic to his friends."[125] Hard drinking seemed characteristic of many hero volunteers. In fact, the Peace Corps created a case study for use in training describing a volunteer named Owen whose "rough and ready way of doing things won him considerable respect from all of the younger Peace Corps volunteers."[126]

The *Volunteer,* always the leader in creating the volunteer image, led also in creating the image of the hero volunteer. The assistant Peace Corps representative in Ecuador wrote about a volunteer with the unbelievable name of Peter Gladhart, who traveled throughout Ecuador, organizing 4-F (like 4-H) clubs for children. These clubs taught the kids proper agricultural techniques. Peter was always greeted with a "'Hola, pedro . . . Hola, pedrito.' He became so bound up in the community that they probably would not let him leave if he wanted to. His friends say 'Pete is so acclimated here he takes a bath as infrequently as we do.'"[127] The author could not resist mentioning, "When he isn't working, Pete thinks most about mountain climbing."

Many other volunteers might have snickered at the image that Gladhart displayed, due to its purity and perfection. But he was a real person. He exemplified how a volunteer could accept the customs and lifestyle of the host country while at the same time trying to teach the locals new customs and lifestyles. Because he fostered hard work, ingenuity, and democratic ideals, and was a rough-hewn adventurer, he also served as one of the ultimate examples of how volunteers could be pioneers on the frontier of the late twentieth century.

3
The Other Side of Training

Upon joining, many volunteers immediately made clear what they thought the Peace Corps was not. The new volunteers did not join to promote the United States and its values to the rest of the world. One volunteer put it this way: "I was not coming here [Malaya] to sell American culture. . . . I was coming here to help these people solve any particular problems they might have."[1] The volunteers did not want to be imperialists or colonizers in the traditional sense of the terms.

Many volunteers came into this experiment with what they considered a positive view of the people of the third world. Their view of third world peoples might have been "exotic . . . idealized . . . and naturalized," but "the exotic other" was "by definition attractive."[2] Imperialism or colonialism might stifle this attractiveness and the inexorable march of "progress from tradition to modernity" they saw occurring in the third world since World War II.[3] They did not want to slow this march with outdated conservative ideas.

Many joined because they felt energized by Kennedy's election as president. They answered his call to "ask not" by joining the young leader's newest, most electric agency. Many volunteers accepted Kennedy's liberal ideals of international development. John Rex, soon to become a teacher in Ethiopia, was attracted "by the enthusiastic . . . young man who had just become leader of our country. He was not the balding or grey-haired oracle who spoke in platitudes of complacency. . . . Not only did he seem to be telling the truth, but he seemed to be talking to me, and I wanted to answer."[4] Michael Tudor, who served in one of the first groups in Nigeria, gushed about Kennedy: "I was in love with him. He was my hero. Eisenhower never made me feel like a citizen, but Kennedy made me feel that way."[5] Virtually every Peace Corps volunteer echoed this sentiment. Many young Americans became Kennedy supporters in the election because of the Peace Corps. For example, A. W. Lewis claimed, "My first interest in the Peace Corps arose during Kennedy's campaign, and I am sure that his dedication and vigor were prime motivational factors in my joining a movement to demonstrate to developing nations the concern . . . on the part of young Americans."[6] Many volunteers joined because the Peace Corps, like Kennedy, seemed like an energetic, youthful method of dealing with the third world.

Although this image did motivate many volunteers, not all volunteers imagined themselves as the Marlboro Man. Some prospective volunteers viewed the Peace Corps in ways slightly different from Shriver's new pioneer image. For example, they noted the similarities between Peace Corps volunteers and missionaries. According to an article in the *Catholic World,* many joined because of "a realization that man is lovable and redeemable, and a conviction that each man is his brother's keeper."[7] Many volunteers wanted to help improve the lives of people in the third world. This implied that the volunteers knew how to live a better life, an attitude that caused problems for some of them. They wanted to help, yet they also wanted to respect the culture of the people they were helping, and it was not often possible to do both.

Although such idealistic notions convinced many to join the Corps, other volunteers immediately sensed the possible dangers in such idealism. Volunteers and Peace Corps administrators later denigrated idealism as a reason to join the Corps, but they recognized its importance nonetheless: "The Peace Corps attracts a lot of members of our generation who have sort of a mindless idealism. They're idealistic about things they don't know anything about. . . . When you get involved . . . the idealism tapers off. Too many idealistic people I've known don't know enough about the situation."[8]

Peace served as the primary ideal for some. Most volunteers did not know that the name Peace Corps was almost discarded because it sounded too much like a cynical, Soviet-style propaganda effort. Americans, especially some volunteers, took the name seriously and believed that the agency and its volunteers were contributing to peace in the world. Many volunteers came from a generation that had grown up during the Cold War, and they saw the Peace Corps as a way out of it. Here, at least, seemed to be one universal value that did not trample on anyone's culture. They were anything but Cold Warriors, for they put a interest in peace ahead of a desire for American "victory." One said she was making a "conscientious effort in behalf of the peace race."[9] Another mused, "Most of all, I would like to be a peacemaker." She spent her free time as a volunteer in Nigeria touring the battlefields of Biafra and helping those devastated by the civil war there.[10]

The most general comment that can be made about volunteer motivations in joining the Corps is that they were varied. Some joined to become new pioneers; some joined to become missionaries; some joined to make peace in the world. Most joined for a variety of reasons, with none paramount. Eminent sociologist David Riesman, who served on the Peace Corps' National Advisory Council, reflected this attitude by saying, "I think it should be recognized that most people's motives are mixed and that it is right not to be wholly clear about one's motives."[11] Journalists and others who examined the Peace Corps inevitably asked trainees and volunteers why they had joined. The answers always varied, and the questioner would come up with a long general list like this:

> Most are motivated by the same things that motivate the student movement in this country. They want to do something worthwhile with their lives; they are willing to take some risks and put up with inconveniences; they have a fairly broadminded view of the problems of the developing area. And most important, the way they go about implementing their ideas is outside of the normal, established channels of action.[12]

In other words, those who looked at motivations did not know what to make of them. Volunteers bristled at any attempts to categorize them or their motivations, which points to one way in which they and their motivations can be categorized. They wished, above all else, to be recognized as individuals. Lawrence Fuchs emphasized this point: "The single strongest unifying motivation of volunteers appears to have been the desire to improve the world as *individuals on their own*"(Fuchs's italics).[13] Ironically, this desire to be individuals often fit in nicely with Shriver's image of the new pioneer but would also cause friction between the volunteers and their leaders in Washington.

Even before arriving at training, volunteers felt uneasy with some Peace Corps requirements. First, there was the background check, and these checks were thorough: "Everyone from your Little League manager to the FBI is questioned."[14] As one woman put it, "The civil service commission was around investigating me. How about that. . . . He talked to the housemother and then asked her for the two kids who lived near me. . . . They really go into it pretty thoroughly. It gives you kind of an odd feeling."[15] This odd feeling of being watched and having one's life exposed grew during training.

Next, the potential volunteers had to think about the serious business of training. Immediately, they recognized that the training program was no summer lark. Lillian Carter called it "the hardest thing I've ever encountered."[16] The training program overwhelmed the volunteers in its scope and the energy level required to complete it. "Peace Corps training is like no other training in the world," volunteer Moritz Thomsen wrote, "having something in common with college life, officer's training, marine basic training and a ninety day jail sentence."[17] Trainees were shocked out of whatever complacency they might have had with the rigors, uniqueness, and intensity of the program.

The biggest jolt came to their bodies. The daily regimen of physical education produced sore bodies and complaining minds. The trainees couldn't believe what their instructors put them through: "I'm sure he thought we were superhuman. At any rate, everyone was walking a different gait, groaning at every step, and even sore."[18] Many trainees accepted the emphasis on physical training in the belief that they needed to be physically fit to survive the rigors of the third world frontier. The trainees reveled in some of the tasks that allowed them to play pioneer, such as "learning what foods we could use from the woods and how to fix them."[19]

The majority of trainees agreed that their most enjoyable training experience was participating in Outward Bound. Paul Cowan claimed it was the only part of training that made any sense at all.[20] Trainees "learned how to look at ourselves and others without luxuries and how to react under strain and pressure," and they appreciated the challenges presented by raw, primitive surroundings: "When you first look at the mountains it 'ain't' easy to make up your mind to play human fly and just go scooting up."[21] In general, however, what they liked best about Outward Bound was not the ruggedness of it but the opportunity to learn how to work as a team with the other trainees and to use that feeling to help their confidence. A group of trainees at the University of New Mexico in 1963 thought "the outward bound part of the training was regarded as favorable by most and the reason stated pertained to confidence building—doing something that was thought to be impossible."[22] They also enjoyed the chance to be outdoors. The solo hikes became an excuse "for the fun of camping out under the stars," rather than a good chance "for us to be entirely on our own, as we may be sometime in Niger."[23]

This reaction, while resembling what the trainers were looking for, was not the one they were expecting. They wanted to create new pioneers, while the trainees wanted to reach the limits of their individual expectations, which might or might not have anything to do with acting like a pioneer.

This was not the only dissonance between the expectations of the trainers and the actual reactions of the trainees.

Some trainees resisted the mold from the beginning. Not all of them were young. The leadership, of course, realized this and did not openly discourage middle-aged or even senior volunteers from signing up. As we saw previously, Jimmy Carter's aging mother volunteered. But most of the older trainees felt alienated by the harsh conditions and the emphasis put on physical fitness. One woman in her fifties, training in Berkeley, said she felt "humiliated in front of the young people. I just don't think I should have been made to run and do some of the other things they did."[24]

Some trainees enjoyed the physical fitness and survival training but made no connection between that training and their coming job in the third world. "After we'd been at camp a few weeks," one trainee wrote, "they started a weekend camping project called soloing. . . . The staff thought it would be a good experience for us to be entirely on our own, as we may be sometime in Nigeria. However, those of us who volunteered had other reasons!"[25] The trainees were willing to explore new experiences but were often unwilling to be molded into new pioneers or anything other than a group of recent college graduates out to have a good time. Frederick McCluskey described the focal point for his training period in this way: "The 60 hours a week of planned courses has not prevented most of us from seeing the sights around New England and raising plenty of hell after hours. . . . The boys here are really interesting; they like to have a good time, they drink a lot and they aspire to the Latin American ideal of 'macho,' masculine, reckless, fearless."[26]

Many observers were struck by the similarities between Peace Corps training and military boot camp. Brent Ashabrannar commented, "If the volunteer didn't feel like a new recruit at boot camp, it must have been because he was too tired to feel anything."[27] George Sullivan noted that the Peace Corps training center in Puerto Rico was "comparable in many ways to a World War II Army basic training center or navy boot camp."[28] The similarity was not accidental. Volunteers were being toughened for the rough adventure ahead. The whole experience became almost surrealistic, prompting one trainee to comment, "They do fantastic comic strip things, like swinging from vines."[29]

And while the training focused on comic strip things, many trainees realized that the training ignored other, more practical issues. The courses did not seem to be helpful. Some trainees for the Cameroon project complained about the "unnecessary emphasis" put on the communism classes and described the American studies classes as "a lot of academic garbage."[30]

At times, the disconnectedness between training and reality seemed absurd. Here, trainee LeGrande Sanders learns how to start a tractor in the freezing temperatures of Montreal while training to be a mechanic in Guatemala.

Many courses had nothing whatsoever to do with the project the volunteers were entering. Paul Cowan's training "included 24 hours of industrial arts yet this didn't fit the project." As Cowan complained, "There was no reason at all someone going to work for the Department of Taxation needed to learn how to build a latrine."[31] The leadership might answer that on the new frontier of the third world, one had to be prepared for anything.

Even the Peace Corps' own evaluators thought that the volunteers did not need to be so heavily prepared for the influence of communism, at least in the Philippines: "The communism question is certainly not one which is likely to arise . . . and this should be a consideration when the training division schedules its programs for Philippines training."[32] Training prepared trainees for the trainers' hypothetical third world, and in many cases this world had no resemblance to the real third world of the 1960s.

Volunteers quickly noted the inadequacy of their technical training. The entire contingent of one El Salvador project "all considered technical studies the most glaring failure" of their training program.[33] One group of trainees felt so deeply about the failure of their training program that they petitioned the trainers for a more effective program, and when there was no reply, they went on strike. They demanded a more practical training program, and insisted "that the Peace Corps failed to take the trainees and the training seriously."[34]

Protests about the lack of specific technical training became a training-period staple in the 1960s. For example, the Peace Corps designed many projects to help improve agriculture in specific countries. This fit well with Shriver's conception of the Peace Corps, because Americans had learned how to live off the land in their mythic past and would intuitively be able to understand and teach farming to the less fortunate farmers of the third world. Trainers assumed that the exact knowledge of American agricultural techniques and practices would work in the third world and at an agricultural extension center in Lawrence, Kansas: "Both agriculture and home economics were taught as if the Peace Corps Volunteers were to be employed as minor assistants in extension work in the state of Kansas."[35] Oftentimes, these agricultural extension volunteers were taught nothing about what they were going to cultivate in their project. One group being trained for work in Guatemala received "no training in tropical agriculture; e.g., they didn't know what yucca, cacao, mango, papaya were."[36]

Everything considered, most trainees took the obstacles of training in stride. They realized they were part of an experimental program and were willing to give the agency a chance, although some aspects of training, such as the classes in communism, seriously strained the leadership's credibility. Their youth helped, for many had little to compare the training program to, and it inspired awe just to be part of Kennedy's exciting agency. A few began to question the vague training methods. Most reserved judgment on the training until they arrived at their project and could test what they had learned. But one aspect of training rankled all volunteers from the beginning. The Orwellian practice of "deselection" alienated trainees and caused them to question the purpose of the agency they were so eager to join.

The trainees understood that they were being watched and tested by the trainers, and this made them uncomfortable. The Peace Corps' own evaluators noticed it: "Over and over again we heard Volunteers complaining that Peace Corps training sets a negative tone from the beginning."[37] As Moritz Thomsen put it, "In all three phases of our training we were studied and appraised like a bunch of fat beeves about to be entered in the state fair."[38] They felt goaded and poked, and were crushed by the battery of tests: the "Levinson F. scale, the Barron ego strength scale, the Taylor Manifest anxiety scale, the Stein self descriptive test, etc."[39] At times it became laughable for the dazed trainees: "We started taking psychological tests, and the laughter started getting a little raucous. 'Have you ever talked to God? Do you think your private parts are beautiful?' But these damned things went on for weeks, tests so long, complicated and boring that toward the end we were too punch drunk to lie."[40]

The trainees resented more than the constant testing and psychological prodding they had to endure. They began to realize that the trainers designed much of the program to test their limits and subject them to stress. Even the Outward Bound program, which many trainees enjoyed, had darker purposes. One trainee wrote, "I believe the hike was intended to serve primarily as deliberate harassment in order to test the individual's psychological stability."[41] Another believed that "sleeping on a mat and walking in the mud from one end of the island to the other were interpreted as parts of a program designed to see if the person could make the grade."[42] To trainees, every activity seemed designed to test their ability to work under strain. This first exposure to the agency gave the future volunteers an impression vastly at odds with Shriver's nonbureaucratic goal. As far as they were concerned, during training the Peace Corps assumed the role of the ultimate faceless bureaucracy.

This pressure led some trainees to the breaking point. One wrote home: "It is such a strain, like being threatened all the time. I'm *not* leaving—they might *send* me—so if I have to leave, please, please don't blame me, for God's sake. I don't see *how* I can try any harder, but I will."[43] Volunteers lost confidence, questioned their own abilities and their own personality. This is what the trainers intended, for they wanted to mold these volunteers into something completely different, and if that meant major personality adjustments, so be it. But they did not expect trainees to rebel against the entire training process because of the stress. Some realized that the stresses were false and had no relation to the projects they were being sent to perform. Volunteer Roz Parris wrote a letter to the editor of the *Volunteer* complaining about a training site that created "phony stress" that more closely resembled a "fraternity initiation" than an actual Peace Corps volunteer job.[44]

Outward Bound also had a psychological dimension. Trainers demanded that trainees complete the Outward Bound program "without flinching." The trainers realized that "in this slice-of-volunteer-life approach to training, there is a risk that the trainee will take one look and say: 'I quit; this is not for me.' Even so, the Peace Corps would rather know before the person goes overseas that he was not cut out for a Volunteer's life."[45] The program trained individuals to become hardened, elite warriors for peace and eliminated anyone not up to the demanding task. Bill Steif, a newspaper reporter assigned to write an article on Peace Corps training, described his difficulties lighting a fire in the rain and eating snails, but also his need to look untroubled because, if he looked otherwise, "What would the Peace Corps Psychologist say?"[46]

In fact, the Peace Corps Psychologist became the ultimate symbol of the alienation between the volunteer and the Peace Corps leadership. The psychologist became the main villain in the drama euphemistically referred to as "deselection" by the Peace Corps leadership. Although the agency paid lip service to the idea of individuality, it designed the training program not to foster the ideals of self-reliance but to mold immature youths into acceptable volunteers. The Peace Corps volunteer was to become the example of America and American values in whatever village they served.

Sargent Shriver relied on the newly burgeoning sciences of the mind to help him select who should serve in his elite corps. Only twenty years earlier, at the advent of World War II, psychiatrists had convinced the U.S. military of the merit of psychiatric screening of potential inductees. They convinced military leaders that psychiatric screening could save the military millions of dollars by "weeding out potential psychiatric casualties before they became military responsibilities."[47]

The leader of this movement and coeditor of the journal *Psychiatry,* Harry Stack Sullivan, decided by the end of the war that "drastic and very extensive changes in the usual patterns of human thinking and behavior would have to be made, and quickly."[48] He led a successful movement to convince his fellow psychiatrists and social scientists to use their disciplines to promote the correct type of thinking in all areas of human endeavor. By the late 1950s, many Americans had accepted a central role for social scientists in general and psychiatrists in particular in helping to guide their institutions in the appropriate direction. Christopher Lasch refers to this as "the new psychiatric imperialism of the 1940s and 1950s" and argues that by 1960, "enlightened opinion now identified itself with . . . the substitute of medical and psychiatric authority for the authority of parents, priests and lawgivers."[49]

This movement fit Shriver's preoccupation with everything modern and fresh. Writing about the Peace Corps in 1964, George Sullivan stated,

"In no other government agency does the psychiatrist play such a dominant role as he does in the Peace Corps. The credit for this goes to Sargent Shriver," who insisted that "the most advanced concepts of behavioral sciences be used in every area of volunteer service, in selection, in training, and in assessment."[50] Rather than keeping the new agency under control using a far-flung and complicated bureaucracy, the leadership would use psychological techniques to provide direction while at the same time creating a less authoritarian atmosphere. The Peace Corps depended on psychiatrists and psychologists to define the image of an elite volunteer. Gerald Caplan, the chief psychologist in the Peace Corps Medical Division and the author of a manual for Peace Corps psychologists, wrote, "It is essential that these persons be screened out, both for their own protection and for the good of the Peace Corps."[51]

As soon as the psychologists and psychiatrists got a toehold on training, their accepted expertise in matters pertaining to personality and attitude pushed them to the forefront of the training team. Some Peace Corps staffers objected to this. Thomas Scott, director of Private Organizations for the Peace Corps, complained that training and selection had become "an area rapidly giving way to the testers and psychiatric cultists."[52] In the training program for Cameroon at Ohio University, Director Roy Fairfield insisted, "The Peace Corps psychiatrist should not play so central a role," but he was rebuffed by Washington.[53] As time went on, Peace Corps Washington gave psychiatrists and psychologists an increasingly central role, and in May 1963, the leadership suggested that "all future leaders of completion of service conferences be either psychologists or psychiatrists."[54] Peace Corps Washington provided these men (they were virtually all men) carte blanche to decide which trainees fit the profile of Shriver's ideal volunteer.

These psychological professionals searched for a variety of maladies that would disqualify trainees from being Peace Corps volunteers. "The newness of the work and the lack of tradition lead to a situation where there is no generally held set of expectations," wrote Caplan.[55] Consequently, the psychologists formed categories into which to put trainees, and Caplan filled his manual with a long list of disqualifying conditions: "psychoses: psychotic, history of psychotic illness, suicide attempt, weak personality structure. neuroses: obsessive compulsive behavior, phobic reactions, history of prolonged care by a physician, etc." Serious mental illness served as a warning flag that a particular individual should not be sent overseas as a volunteer.

The Peace Corps psychiatric community took its job one important step further. Lawrence Fuchs wrote, "The most influential psychiatrists and psychologists in the U.S. have revealed an enormous preoccupation with the problem of personal independence in the assertion of self."[56] Or, put another way, "Ego, ego and more ego was the general hang up in those days."[57] Self-assertion became the dominant focus for the Peace Corps psychiatrists. Ironically, in trying to insist that all trainees assert themselves, they called not for individuality, but conformity to a particular personality type.

The psychiatrists and psychologists intended to find this corps of self-assertive personalities by testing the trainees. The psycho-testers used "the sentence completion test, the Minnesota Multiphasic Personality Inventory, the f-scale, and the autobiography, all in the conventional manner."[58] Next, they subjected the ratings from these tests "to nonstepwise discriminant analysis."[59] The uninitiated—that is, nonpsychiatrists—could not be involved in these super-professionalized testing techniques, giving the psycho-testers even more control over the deselection process. Ironically, reliance on these standardized tests worked counter to Shriver's goals for an antibureaucratic Peace Corps.

The psycho-testers depended heavily on personal interviews and ratings of the trainees. In one training program, each trainee had a one-hour psychiatric interview with one of eight psychiatrists from the Albert Einstein School of Medicine. These psychiatrists created a rating sheet that included, among other things, "psychopathology, flexibility (could have incapacitating symptoms), ego strength, ego function, character typology (could be found hysterical, compulsive), anxiety, mood alteration, etc."[60]

They barraged the trainees with questions: "Do you have thoughts too bad to say?" "Would you sneak into a theater?"[61] Through a combination of formal tests and less formal, but complete, interviewing, the psycho-testers decided whether the "ego strength" and so forth of the volunteers was up to the task of serving as one of Shriver's new pioneers. One trainee "had to go back for several interviews with the staff psychiatrists" because his "level of idealism wasn't as high as they would have liked."[62] By the time the tests were finished, one volunteer said, they were "one of the most studied groups in history."[63]

Caplan established strict rules to guarantee that the psychiatrists and the psychologists remained separate from the trainees. His manual proscribed the tester from relaxing to such an extent that he would identify completely with the trainees and become, or try to become, one of them: "If this were to happen, he would have no beneficial influence on them, and most probably they would feel that his 'palsy walsy' approach was either a symptom of a distorted desire to re-experience vicariously the joys of a lost youth, or else a guise to hide some Machiavellian mischief."[64] This edict against becoming pals with the trainees erected another wall in the training bureaucracy—walls, as we shall see, that alienated some volunteers and defined the terms in which the training program would later be evaluated.

The psycho-testers also felt the necessity to create testing situations that controlled the trainees' social behavior. They created role plays in which trainees would act the parts of volunteers in uncomfortable situations. One case study involved volunteers getting arrested for drunk driving, while in another, volunteer "girls" wore shorts that were too short for local customs.[65] Caplan warned psycho-testers not to be domineering in presenting case studies. "Often, however, there are Peace Corps policies which can be brought to bear. The discussion leader should discuss possible solutions and the relevant Peace Corps policies with the trainees, but no attempt should be made to lay down the law."[66] Caplan realized the potential tensions in forcing trainees to accept certain values, but he thought the trainers should unobtrusively do it anyway. After the role play was completed, the psycho-testers would add another piece of information to each trainee's file.

Constant testing created stress, and the psycho-testers intended it to. They developed situations "designed to be as stressful as seemed clinically feasible so that observation could be made of the trainee functioning under anxiety laden and constantly changing social conditions," and then the "field assessment officer" would "record the behavior and verbalization of each of the trainees."[67] With the leader's full blessing, the psycho-testers made training as stressful as possible to be sure the trainees could survive under the harsh frontierlike conditions that everyone believed awaited them. Too little tension, they thought, might "fail to evoke the response patterns for assessing the long term effectiveness" of volunteers.[68] The trainers thought that this would "create situations in which the trainees could actually experience a degree of acclimation to a different culture so that they would be somewhat conditioned to culture shock."[69]

Because of this testing and evaluating, the trainers created an Orwellian atmosphere. Their use of the terms *deselection* and *selected out*, rather than *termination, firing,* or even *letting go,* points to their penchant for Orwellian doublespeak. The Peace Corps leadership, wedded to their nonauthoritarian ethos, was horrified when their agency was criticized for such practices. The Department of Volunteer Services insisted nothing the Peace Corps did qualified as "brainwashing." The agency wanted to be considered a part of the government that appreciated the opinions of others. On the contrary, they argued, everything the agency did was "solely and simply to help the volunteer fortify himself."[70] But the atmosphere created by the psycho-testers was undeniably troubled and induced understandable paranoia.

The Orwellian feeling went beyond basic atmosphere. Every training program had its share of "mysterious little men from Washington in black suits whose names we never learned," who "appeared from time to time and broodingly watched us."[71] Often, those in charge of selection acted more overtly. Don Chamberlain, sent to evaluate a training center at Penn State, described a blatant example of Big Brother tactics: "One member of the staff is assigned to visit the various discussion groups, classes, etc., with a master sheet containing each trainee's picture. She makes notes about how they participate in discussion and so forth. This, of course, is done in front of the trainees and is about as subtle as a sledge hammer."[72]

The psycho-testers did not stop at their personal observations and psychological tests. They pitted the volunteers against each other, making the trainees into unwilling informants. Trainees' individual psychiatric interviews progressed from questions about their sex life to questions about the suitability of other volunteers.[73] Al Carp, director of the Division of Selection in 1965, insisted that the Peace Corps was not acting as Big Brother and that he was not turning the trainees into moles. He claimed, in defense of the practice, that "the judgments of fellow trainees are among the most reliable indicators for a trainee's potential."[74] Whether or not this point is true, the effectiveness of a practice does not mean that it is not Orwellian.

Perhaps the most unique psychological tactic was used by the training program for a group going to Ceylon, now Sri Lanka. Volunteer Katie Mayer described this program, called a "week of discipline," in her journal. The trainers structured this week believing it was "reasonably certain that anyone unable to observe a week of discipline while in training will be unable to observe two years of discipline in the field." During the week they created a series of rules designed to test the trainees' tolerance, discipline, and patience. For example:

— Arrive early to class.
— Sit, stand and walk decorously. There will be no lounging, slouching, standing with hands in pockets.
— Women trainees will not smoke at all in public.
— There will be no body contact between the sexes.
— No meal may include more than one dessert.
— Eat everything on your plate.[75]

There was merit in restraint for Americans going to the third world, and some host country nationals frowned on women smoking in public. Here we see the Peace Corps impressing upon the trainees the importance of accepting the values of other cultures. The trainers believed they needed to shock the trainees by showing them how they might have to adapt to the strange customs of their host country. But for the most part, these rules were designed not to train but to annoy. They were invented to test the trainees, to make sure they didn't crack, and to guarantee that they could fit the mold Shriver designed for them.

Some volunteers felt that the training program was designed to stifle individuality and create an army of automatons to send to the third world: "The America that the Peace Corps psychologists seemed to manufacture for export was a sterile paradise. Through mechanisms such as the peer rating and the selection process, they hoped to produce a standardized volunteer which would be germ free and physically pure."[76]

Trainees unanimously and vigorously disagreed with the philosophy behind the psycho-testing program. The possibility of deselection haunted them the most. The trainers rarely discussed how the decisions on selection were made, and this caused tremendous confusion. Paul Jacobs, in evaluating a training program for the Philippines, related the feelings of the trainees: "They were not clear as to who participated in the selection board, what the selectors said, what role the written evaluation played. . . . One girl was told she ought to do something about her hair."[77] Trainee Frederick McCluskey expressed his exasperation with a program in which "the factors determining the selection were elusive or somewhat arbitrary. The dividing line was extremely thin."[78] This lack of clarity caused a situation in which "panic was everywhere."[79] The trainers did not try to alleviate matters. "The basis of the board's decisions remained hidden behind plastic phrases," ex-trainee James McDonough wrote after suffering the ignominy of deselection.[80] Trainees came to believe job skills made no difference and only hoped they had the qualities the psycho-testers felt qualified them as volunteers. Julia Chang, while teaching in the South Pacific, insisted that "the agency deselected many people who would have made wonderful volunteer teachers but who did not have the will or were not physically able to adjust to mud huts."[81]

Trainees who survived were encouraged to forget about their former brethren so they would not feel "hate, bitterness and self protection."[82] The psycho-testers and the other trainers purposely built a wall around the process, alienating the trainees and forcing them to look askance at the training program and at the Peace Corps in general. Everywhere they went, the trainees felt watched. Even their social get-togethers were suspect. "The scuttlebutt about the party," according to Alan Weiss, "is that it is for observation of one's behavior in a psycho-social milieu."[83]

When asked about the selection process, representatives from Peace Corps Washington only worsened the situation. In one training program, the leader created a "Big Brother is watching you atmosphere by firmly stating that he and his staff were to be spies."[84] Since the Peace Corps told the trainees little about the process, and the actual participants in the process remained so aloof and mysterious, the trainees resented and feared them. Some made up diabolical personas for them. One trainee described his "de-selection officer" as a man with "beady, dark eyes set in the back of his head like two pieces of highly sophisticated radar . . . and rumor had it that he had worked for army intelligence during the war."[85] The selection process not only offended the trainees, it frightened them to such an extent that it is difficult to imagine those who became volunteers viewing their leaders positively.

Another result of this system was a perceived tendency to eliminate unusual trainees. The trainees believed that to survive, they had to toe the Peace Corps line. Anyone who failed to conform would be selected out. An outside consultant, Zygmunt Nagorski, noticed this and wrote: "Usually the training program is especially troublesome for rebels. They have to be molded into at least a semi-collective shape requiring collective loyalty. Their sharp edges have to be dulled, without affecting their natural sharpness. . . . The task is difficult and often brutal; it is a job which tends to break weaker rebels."[86] The Peace Corps tried to shape the trainees, but some refused to be molded. Forty-one from Peru sent a letter to the *Volunteer* in 1966, insisting, "Selection should be altered radically to avoid phasing out the exceptional trainee; to assure the selection criteria depend on more than the biases of the individual psychologist."[87]

Many trainees and outside observers were convinced that this system hurt the Peace Corps by creating conformity. In a bit of intended understatement, volunteer John Freivalds declared, "Diversity was not a word you would use to describe the training program."[88] The training program in general and the selection process in particular gave the Peace Corps a reputation that would have made Shriver blanch. "Peace Corps training is now about the squarest thing in the agency," the director of the Peace Corps training center in Puerto Rico wrote. "It reeks of the very values that the most creative and involved students now roundly reject."[89] The Peace Corps could not recruit these talented, unique students because its selection and training process was not designed to accept them.

The Peace Corps evaluators knew about this problem, as well. An evaluation of projects in the Philippines reproached training because it "left no room for spontaneity and individuality. The high attrition rate of training they tended to attribute to the selecting out of trainees who refused to toe the mark, were outspoken in their remarks, but who were stimulating people, thus leaving 'bland' conformistic candidates."[90]

The volunteers mocked this aspect of training once they got to their posts overseas. One composed a song that ridiculed Shriver's search for conformity:

We are marching in formation
down the middle of the road
For to turn to either left or right
is dangerous we're told
Sargent Shriver wants his teachers
always docile never bold
And the Peace Corps marches on
Glory, glory mediocrity.[91]

Most volunteers saw little sense in the Peace Corps training program. They did not want to be molded into new pioneers. They wanted to be prepared for the specific jobs they were going to perform. Most of all, they did not want to deal with the psycho-testers and the deselection process, which alienated the volunteers and placed a barrier between them and their nominal bosses in Washington.

As the volunteers boarded planes for their new posts, most did not know what to expect. Many had not been trained for their specific jobs, and after training, most had little idea what would happen to them when they stepped off the plane. Just before one group was sworn in as brand new volunteers, they were reminded one last time of the process they just completed and the disillusionment that went with it. As they disembarked a plane in Dallas after a final month's training in Peru, Peace Corps selection officers told them to step right or left at the end of the exit ramp. Those who were told to go left were deselected and received a ticket home. Those who went right were "the winners." One of them wrote: "[We were] herded into a little office where, still tired from the trip and dazed at losing more of our friends, we raised our right hands and were sworn into service."[92]

Shaky Relations

The Peace Corps Leadership
and the Volunteers

Despite the outwardly successful appearance of some volunteers, most had a shaky relationship with the Corps leadership and liberal ideals of international development. Shriver and his trainers did not have blank slates on which to write their version of the new pioneer. The Americans who joined the Peace Corps, while indeed mostly young, came from a variety of backgrounds and joined for a variety of reasons. Problems arose both in the training program and in the relationship between the leadership and the volunteers overseas. These difficulties led many volunteers to question the development philosophy of their leaders and opened their minds to new ideas about how to relate to people in the third world.

Peace Corps volunteers could never fit the image that their leaders in Washington envisioned for them. Their leaders never allowed them to be independent. Although the agency consciously worked to avoid the pitfalls of entrenched bureaucracy, it constrained the actions of the volunteers through an elaborate system of formal and informal bureaucratic devices. The relatively youthful volunteers interpreted this bureaucratic separation as part of the generation gap so central in the minds of youth during the 1960s. Such stresses and strains, picking up from the stress of training, separated volunteers from their leadership and allowed the volunteers to develop their own ideas about international development.

Even though the leadership said they expected volunteers to live a rough and independent life, volunteers were discouraged from a life of hardy self-reliance. Like a protective parent, Peace Corps Washington could never permit the volunteers to become too independent. One volunteer in India asserted, "I think the Peace Corps overprotects. It's like a big brother."[1] In an article about the staff, Lewis Butler, Peace Corps representative in Malaysia in 1963 and 1964, admitted that the whole idea of Peace Corps staff contradicted the Peace Corps image. The staff, he wrote, "will oversee and be ultimately responsible for the behavior, well-being, work performance and conduct of the Peace Corps Volunteers."[2] One Peace Corps representative believed the young volunteers "simply don't take responsibility."[3]

Peace Corps Washington and the representatives in the field tried to prevent volunteer irresponsibility by creating an elaborate set of rules—yet another surprise for many volunteers, who expected to be treated as self-reliant adults. Paul Cowan expressed shock that "Peace Corps in the field had a set of regulations every bit as strict as those that governed us in training." Volunteers in Ecuador could not carry firearms, drive cars, climb mountains without permission, leave their project sites, write newspaper articles without permission, eat in the expensive Hotel Quito, or marry Ecuadorians.[4] Most volunteers felt such rules were "childish" or, as a group of Peruvian volunteers put it, "inane, unrealistic and ridiculous."[5] But, according to one evaluator, Peace Corps Washington could not afford to accept the volunteer view "that more faith should be placed in their individual judgment."[6]

Responsibility became a watchword for Peace Corps staffers. Volunteers should be "made to recognize their responsibility." They had to realize that "a Volunteer does not have a private and public life, he is always held to the standard of a Volunteer."[7] Volunteers, naturally, resented this attitude. The problem, according to those in Guatemala, was that they were "being made to feel irresponsible until we are proven responsible. Such rules represent paternalism."[8] Volunteers disagreed with Peace Corps rules not because they thought them to be inappropriate, but because they disliked Peace Corps Washington's lack of trust.

Perhaps the one rule that they complained about most involved using automobiles. In Nigeria, the main topic of conversation at Peace Corps staff meetings was often Peace Corps vehicle policy.[9] Most Peace Corps representatives forbade the use of private transportation by volunteers in their country. One evaluator expressed surprise that "by far the hottest issue [at a completion-of-service conference] I am sorry to say was that of transport and practically all of them felt that the Peace Corps should provide them with motorcycles or cars." These volunteers, in Ghana, felt that the most important thing was doing their job well, and they believed this required reliable transportation. The evaluator, speaking with the voice of Peace Corps Washington, disagreed. Even though the rules against using cars might restrict movement and freedom of choice, they were important to make sure volunteers lived as new pioneers. Without any irony, this evaluator, William Mangin, continued by moaning that the volunteers had "little if any sympathy and understanding for the concept of a self-reliant, independent and self-motivated Peace Corps Volunteer."[10] Mangin did not focus on the fact that volunteers lost independence of movement when not allowed to use a car. Another evaluator, Dee Jacobs, agreed that even though Peace Corps volunteers looked the part, there was "a certain lack of maturity" among them exemplified by their "abuse of jeep privileges."[11]

"Looking the part" became an important rule that some representatives created for volunteers. In Jamaica, volunteers had to be clean shaven. They joked about this rule in a poem published their in-country newsletter:

To Volunteers boasting a beard
LBJ said, "Young man, you look weird."
Although you may crave 'em
The Peace Corps says shave 'em!
Look sharp! Feel sharp!
And be Sheared![12]

It must have been difficult for volunteers to picture their predecessors, the mythic nineteenth-century pioneers, as beardless. Facial hair and long hairstyles became symbolic in the 1960s of the separation between youth and the older generation. Rules about hair length, designed to enhance volunteer image, instead increased their distrust of their unfeeling bureaucratic leadership. The general Peace Corps policy on beards stated, "The Peace Corps feels that a group of Volunteers who suddenly decide to grow shaggy beards as a lark, or as evidence of 'roughing it,' may hurt the Peace Corps."[13]

Trouble sometimes found the volunteer who did not fit the preconceived image. A full-page picture in the January 1968 issue of the *Volunteer* reflects the tension about image between volunteers and leadership. It pictures a volunteer on his way to Micronesia, not dressed in the "Peace Corps uniform" discussed earlier—blue jeans, cowboy boots, cowboy hat, and Marlboros. Instead, he is wearing a bohemian plaid jacket and beard and carrying a beat-up guitar case. This picture, when printed in American newspapers, provoked "several thousand not so kindly words for official Washington mailbags and editorial writers," such as, "What a disgrace to this country to send a bum like that out to represent us."[14] Some Americans could not accept that some volunteers did not fit Shriver's image or understand how this volunteer could be a good representative of American values.

Many agency staffers believed a neat, clean-shaven appearance was critical to volunteer success. An evaluation report on Malaysia chastised volunteers for "appearing at government offices—when they appear at all—unshaven and in dirty clothes, almost as though to communicate to the officials the low esteem they hold them in."[15] It is not clear how volunteers, trained to swing from trees and survive solo hikes, were supposed to understand the critical importance of wearing a coat and tie on certain occasions. Some Peace Corps leaders thought rules on appearance were senseless. Richard Hopkins, director of the training center in Puerto Rico, argued in 1966 that the Peace Corps should eliminate all such rules. Although staffers "might be appalled by beards and beatnik appearance," in his opinion they should have allowed the volunteers to learn for themselves that such appearance was counterproductive.[16] Apparently, Hopkins's advice went unheeded.

Some Peace Corps representatives dictated not only how volunteers dressed, but how they wrote as well. Many volunteers believed that the "very active public information office plants the stories about the Peace Corps that are printed, and undoubtedly certain information is withheld."[17] Arnold Zeitlin was reprimanded by his country director because he sent a letter to *Newsweek* describing his comfortable living conditions. He was told, "The Peace Corps people in Washington are upset. They prefer controlling news stories about the Peace Corps."[18]

In most countries, volunteers issued newsletters to keep abreast of the goings-on among their fellows. Usually, these newsletters took the form of tabloids, chattily spreading volunteer gossip. Occasionally, they examined more substantial issues. And occasionally, Peace Corps representatives censored such articles. There is evidence that such censorship was a conscious policy of Peace Corps Washington. In an evaluation report of projects in the Ivory Coast, Philip Cook insisted, "These papers must be carefully screened by the Peace Corps Representative to prevent objectionable material from finding its way into print." Cook believed it was "odd that any Volunteer could be so naive as to think he could express himself, without restraint, on matters vital to public policy without danger of serious repercussions."[19]

In another censorship incident, all the editors and writers of the newsletter in the Philippines resigned because they claimed their articles were censored by Arthur Purcell, the Peace Corps representative. They asserted Purcell only wanted "yes men around him" and insisted on the discipline of a marine platoon. Purcell even managed to order one volunteer home because of a "mental illness" that turned out to be fabricated.[20] Such heavy-handedness exemplifies how many Peace Corps staffers managed to alienate and set adrift their volunteer charges.

Some Peace Corps representatives also restricted volunteer movement. A group of volunteers in Peru expressed "'general dissatisfaction' with the rule that Peace Corps volunteers could visit only three countries outside of Peru on vacation. This the group regarded as a restriction on freedom of movement."[21] Whether or not this sort of a rule made sense, the volunteers resented it because it was imposed upon them. The image of a volunteer as a self-reliant free spirit made it even more difficult for them to accept this sort of restriction.

Peace Corps Washington felt uneasy about the volunteers' relative youthfulness. The agency's leaders wanted youth, because they felt youthful Americans could best express frontier ideals. At the same time, they worried that these youths were not ready to be ambassadors for the United States. Most belonged to an older generation and never seemed able to trust the youngsters they sent out as volunteers.

Many outsiders who wrote about the Peace Corps in the 1960s noted this generational impasse and often commented on the volunteer's youth. The *Economist*, a British magazine designed for a sophisticated readership, commented, "Perhaps the most extraordinary thing about the kids is how ordinary they are. Relatively few are intellectuals. . . . They are for the most part unsophisticated and inexperienced."[22] Whether the volunteers matched the *Economist*'s level of sophistication, the fact that this respected journal referred to people in their lower and mid-twenties as "kids" says something about the generational disdain held for volunteers. "Older" Peace Corps leaders felt the same way. Brent Ashabrannar, at one point deputy director of the Peace Corps, insisted he "never called the Volunteers kids, but I did think of the early ones as Mr. Kennedy's boys and girls."[23] Lawrence Fuchs consistently referred to the volunteers as "boys and girls." At one point, he chastised them because "dozens of the Volunteers were stereotypically adolescent in their relationships with the staff."[24] Some volunteers were forced to resign while overseas because their superiors thought they lacked maturity. One named Julia was terminated because her "immaturity in judgment" was "obvious and her logic" was "starkly simple."[25] A country representative in Somalia believed the volunteers in his care to be nothing more than "a bunch of neurotic, infantile whiners."[26]

The volunteers often recognized their youth and their lack of experience. Efrem Siegal, after returning from his project in West Africa, reflected on his experience and decided he had endured a good deal of chaos. But he admitted, "Not all of the change was due to disappointment. A good deal of it was simply growing up."[27] Michael Parrish also served in western Africa, specifically in Niger. Twenty years after his service, he wrote a postmortem for *Life* magazine entitled "The Peace Corps Revisited" in which he complimented his Nigerian hosts for being "surprisingly forgiving of our youth." He admitted that "in our early 20s, we embraced both adult responsibilities and the temptations of the times."[28]

Drugs exemplify one temptation of the times succumbed to by youthful volunteers. Just as we have little idea of the percentage of the total population that used drugs in the 1960s, we also have little idea of the percentage of volunteers who used them. Without question, however, volunteers experimented with drugs. Murray Cox tells of "dropping my first acid during Peace Corps training in Hawaii. . . . I was positive I could see beneath the water and watch the currents between the islands."[29] Robert Gaudino believed marijuana was used "by a fair number of Volunteers, and most often in a convivial and social way. For many, it is a first experience."[30] Paul Cowan contended that in his group in Ecuador, twenty-eight out of fifty volunteers smoked marijuana regularly, and of those, three were sent home because of the practice.

Cowan's point sheds light on how drugs symbolize the generational split between the volunteers and Peace Corps Washington. Cowan quit smoking pot because his Ecuadorian hosts saw it as a sign of degeneracy and would not work with anyone who used it. But he defended his fellow volunteers because he felt their use of it was their business, and he objected to attempts to prevent its use. He wrote an entire section detailing the surreptitious means by which the country representative tried to smoke out the perpetrators. Cowan's generation had different ideas on drug use from those held by the generation of the country director and Peace Corps Washington, and they did not understand one another. The Peace Corps representative asserted loudly, "There is no generation gap in the Peace Corps," but the Ecuadorian volunteers merely shrugged him off as out of touch.[31] Just as at home, some volunteers used drugs, and some did not. But the important thing was that nearly all volunteers believed it should be up to the individual to decide whether or not to use drugs.

Even though many volunteers recognized their own inexperience, they resented being told about it by their elders in the Peace Corps. As progressive as the Peace Corps leadership thought themselves to be, in many cases volunteers did not view them this way. In 1965, Harris Wofford called for a "new, youthful climate more receptive to imagination and innovation."[32]

At the same time, other Peace Corps staffers viewed volunteers as "too often gruff, unpolished, inconsiderate, and all too often insulting, patronizing and downright childish."[33] Volunteers complained about these staff attitudes. In the Philippines, they demanded "mature support which was founded on respect for them as individuals—not on paternalism. . . . They felt they were patronized and not treated as informed adults."[34]

Volunteers resented nothing more than being patronized by the Peace Corps hierarchy. Many thought the Peace Corps staff was "arrogant" and naturally condescending.[35] Arnold Zeitlin contended that Peace Corps Washington "vacillated between stern papa and sugar daddy."[36] Philippine volunteers complained that "the Manila staff generally treated them as very young, immature and, at times, irresponsible people."[37] Volunteers in the Dominican Republic could not understand why "they kept telling us to 'think for yourselves' but they treated us like children."[38] Jerald Posman, in Tunisia, put his finger on the central problem in an article in the *Volunteer* in 1968. He pointed out how difficult it was "when a Volunteer is praised for self sufficiency and then given guidelines of behavior." He argued, "Every Volunteer, as a mature individual, had the right to decide personally the rules which shall govern him." In concluding, Posman called for Peace Corps Washington to give more autonomy to volunteers.[39] Richard K. Lazarus agreed, writing in a letter home about the restrictions he contended with and how, given the chance, he would change things: "I thought it was better to make a few mistakes rather than just quietly accepting the 'father knows best' attitude which has recently become so popular among U.S. presidents and Peace Corps staff members."[40]

During the 1960s, Lazarus's call went unheeded. Even in an area that most volunteers considered sacred, political rights, the Peace Corps attempted to control volunteer actions. The agency bolstered this practice with strong arguments. Volunteers could hamper their effectiveness by inserting themselves into the political turmoil of the host country. The leadership designed the agency to be apolitical, and if that image was tarnished, host governments might be less likely to invite future volunteers. Finally, the leadership had no desire for volunteers to damage the image of the United States by becoming involved on the wrong side of an internal political matter. Some accepted this policy. Chilean volunteer Lee Leardini maintained, "I am thoroughly convinced that Peace Corps Volunteers should avoid host country politics, as well as our own national and international problems," because there were "sufficient social and economic obstacles to overcome to keep a Volunteer thoroughly occupied for two years."[41]

Despite these reasons, most volunteers felt violated by the Peace Corps rule suppressing political involvement, viewing it as another example of generational arrogance and bureaucratic meddling. Peace Corps Washington, as the benevolent father, could decide what volunteers could and could not do. The volunteers, as immature children, could not be trusted to make decisions of a political nature. John Freivalds felt this keenly. Referring to a political crisis in his host country, Panama, he wrote: "Here one's Peace Corps training fails. It tells you to live, eat and work like the natives. However, when they suffer, especially politically, do not get involved. We are employees first, human beings second." Freivalds objected to being made into a "political eunuch, just because the Peace Corps leadership did not feel comfortable with a touchy political situation."[42]

Freivalds was not the only volunteer trying to cope with a period of political unrest. The Peace Corps had a definite model for how volunteers were supposed to act in such a situation. According to one of the most important leaders, Warren Wiggins, "the Peace Corps avoids involvement in short range objectives of political stability." In Nigeria at the time of the Biafran civil war, "volunteers received copies of a State Department telegram clearly warning that those making political statements could not continue their service."[43]

In other words, volunteers were supposed to stay out of political crises altogether, acting like the volunteers in the Dominican Republic during a coup in 1965, when they served as nurses and medics during the street battles, attending to both rebels and government supporters.[44] Many of them treated wounds inflicted by American soldiers sent by Lyndon Johnson to support the government. Yet they were serving as compassionate noncombatants, a role even Johnson accepted. One apocryphal story even had it that some Peace Corpsmen were stopped on the street by armed rebels and then released because, as the rebels said, "You're not Yanquis, you're Peace Corps."

Most volunteers found it impossible to act in such an apolitical fashion. Even the reality of the Dominican crisis did not fit the image the Peace Corps and U.S. government tried to portray. As they were serving as neutral noncombatants, the volunteers drafted a petition to send to Lyndon Johnson, insisting the U.S. Army pull out of the country. They argued, "Our Dominican experience convinces us that the Constitutionalist Forces have overwhelming popular sympathy." Luckily for the volunteers, Bill Moyers intercepted the petition before Johnson saw it, saving them an ignominious exit from their posts.[45]

Volunteers all over the world had difficulty remaining apolitical. Arnold Zeitlin describes a situation at the O'Reilly School in Ghana, where he taught, proving this point. When Ghana's leader, Kwame Nkrumah, imposed a curfew on the nation because of an attempted coup, Zeitlin noticed that "at school, students wrote about the curfew in their English compositions." How could he then be expected to remain apolitical? As he put it, "We couldn't avoid politics at O'Reilly."[46] Paul Cowan described a situation that caused his suspension in Ecuador. The people that lived in his village, mostly Indians, were not allowed to enter a nearby modern supermarket. He tried to organize a petition drive to prevent their exclusion but was stopped by the Peace Corps representative in Ecuador. Such a petition drive, it was decided, would be too political.[47] University teachers in Venezuela believed it was "difficult—if not impossible—to establish a neutral area where studies may be undertaken without a political taint."[48]

A volunteer in Panama argued the volunteer line in saying that volunteers should "forget about that crap. If I can help this way, I'll do something."[49] After all, wrote Alicia Teichman, "One can't help but be interested and active as it involves so much more than simply discussing. I suppose it's a feeling similar to what the pioneers of America felt when we were improving and developing."[50] The volunteers turned the Peace Corps ideology on its head, insisting that in a frontier world they had to be involved in politics. But some Peace Corps leaders could not allow volunteers complete independence, because that might be dangerous. American diplomats overseas viewed volunteers as "idealistically irresponsible."[51] Even the smallest and most vaguely political actions were prohibited. Ed Smith created a questionnaire to help him teach his students English, but it was censored because he asked such questions as, "What newspapers do you read?"[52] Actions like this stripped volunteers of any feelings of independence that the agency attempted to foster.

Nowhere did this paradox become more obvious than regarding American involvement in Vietnam. Although the leaders tried to keep the agency separate from politics and the issues of the Cold War, sometimes the issues became so important that the agency had to face them. Shriver, Wofford, and Vaughn wanted to focus on issues other than the fight against worldwide communism, but as much as they wanted to assert their independence, they were still part of a government fighting a war against communists. And by the late 1960s, the war had become so important that the leadership and the volunteers had to confront it.

Most volunteers felt confused about the war. In a letter home, Richard Lazarus complained that after "mom's barrage of speeches, articles and magazines began arriving, I don't know how I feel about the war, I'm not even sure of my position on the bombing of the north, the issue I originally disagreed with you on."[53] Some supported the war. Brian Walsh disagreed with those who said the Peace Corps and the army were incompatible, insisting, "The same sense of service to his country and humankind that led him [Walsh] to devote two years of service to the Peace Corps also caused him to step into a military transport plane." David Livingston expressed a more frightening opinion. He believed "military service is more important, more crucial. Defense of your country is primary. Given the choice of using a piece of chalk and a blackboard in the bush, or using an M-16, I'll choose the M-16. It's a better convincer."[54] For Livingston, at least, there was little tension over whether to change the values of the locals. The only tension he faced was in how to do it.

Despite such sentiments, most volunteers opposed the war. Paul Cowan expressed shock that anyone could support such a "ghoulish war."[55] According to one completion-of-service conference report, "There was fairly general agreement that U.S. policymakers don't understand revolutionary pressures and don't seem to know how to deal with them."[56] One wrote a letter home to her boyfriend, pleading with him not to join the marines: "I sure as hell hope the marines don't call you. I feel so strongly about that war, using taxes to kill instead of fighting poverty. I know the ROTC has done a lot for you, but still, would you go to kill?"[57] Many volunteers could not help comparing their daily life in the Peace Corps to the seemingly similar situation in Vietnam.

Some wrote letters and sent petitions to the president and their congressmen. In Ethiopia, volunteers staged a vigil in front of the U.S. Embassy. John F. Kennedy would have been surprised to see how far the philosophy of the volunteers had strayed from his original intent of a Peace Corps helping to fight the Cold War. Nothing came of these small protests until 1967, when a volunteer in Chile named Bruce Murray signed a petition opposing the war. Peace Corps Washington responded by ordering Murray and the other signatories not to attempt to make their petition public. Murray reacted by sending a letter to the *New York Times,* complaining that the Peace Corps limited his First Amendment rights. On the direct orders of Jack Vaughn, the Peace Corps expelled Murray.

The Murray Incident, as it has become known, is most interesting because it illuminates the relationship between volunteers and the Peace Corps leadership. The country director in Chile called Murray's letter an example of "childish petulance." Murray, on the other hand, believed that "part of the job of a Peace Corps volunteer is to give an opportunity to citizens in a foreign country to know an American citizen in all the varied aspects of his personality including his thoughts on important issues." Here, then, is another example of differing views of responsibility. Volunteers felt that Murray, as a responsible individual, should be able to speak his mind.[58] They also thought they understood the conflict in Vietnam better than their leaders. While in the Peace Corps, they gleaned "an inside appreciation of the problems of a peasant society, and those problems are analogous to many of those in Vietnam."[59] Peace Corps leaders saw Murray as one "supported by taxpayers' money, and many millions of those taxpayers did not share their [the signatories'] views on Vietnam."[60]

After his termination, Murray found that he had been mysteriously reclassified 1-A by his local draft board, making him immediately available for induction into the army. Murray sued the draft board and the Peace Corps, complaining that he was wrongfully terminated and that the agency and Selective Service Administration conspired against him. Although the court tossed out the conspiracy charge, many volunteers saw this as another example of the Peace Corps not living up to its promise of remaining independent of the federal bureaucracy. The court did uphold Murray's contention of wrongful termination and ordered the Peace Corps to expunge any record of it from Murray's files. It also ordered the draft board to reinstate his volunteer 2-A classification.[61]

As Murray's case attests, status at the local draft board remained a primary concern for many volunteers. Because of their ideological difficulties with the war, many joined to postpone their entry into the draft. Robert Marshall, who served in Libya and Tunisia, discussed his thoughts at the time: "Everyone at Harvard was very eager to find something that would get them out of the draft. . . . The Peace Corps was one of the easier options and also a noble one."[62] They weren't exactly draft dodging, and neither were they "affirming a belief," but they were "fleeing a war that had frightened and confused our generation."[63] The older generation had difficulties understanding this. Some, such as Richard Nixon, opposed the Peace Corps from the start because they didn't want it to become a haven for "draft dodgers." Others, like Shriver and Wofford, suggested making service to the country mandatory, regardless of whether it was in the military, the War on Poverty, or the Peace Corps. Many volunteers had difficulty with this idea as well. Robert Thomson asked, "What sort of society is it that . . . programs its members into suitable roles which they are demanded to assume on pain of imprisonment?"[64] Volunteers did not like to be told what to do.

The Peace Corps leadership had difficulty relating to the ideas of the younger generation, such as the radical political orientation of some volunteers. One example of the generational difference is differing views about Communism and the Soviet Union. As we have seen, the agency exposed volunteers to a campaign of anti-Communist information during training.

Some Peace Corps staffers might have been ambivalent about this propaganda campaign, and some leaders disliked the emphasis they were forced to put on this part of the training. Nevertheless, from the volunteers' perspective, the Peace Corps leadership represented an older generation with a relatively inflexible Cold War outlook. Therefore, the volunteers found themselves surprised at the actual encounters they had with Communists and Russians.

In Ghana, volunteers "worried about Peace Corps/Washington's political paranoia about the Russians and the Chinese." According to one report, "Some were told not even to trade stamps with the Russians because of their evil ways."[65] The volunteers, who considered themselves more open minded because they came from a new generation, evaluated their situations and found the Russians did not live up to their sinister image. Because the United States and the Soviet Union both saw Ghana as a critical battleground in the Cold War competition in Africa, volunteers in Ghana faced this issue more directly than other volunteers. The Soviets also sent development workers to Ghana, and naturally Peace Corps volunteers and Soviet volunteers interacted. The American volunteers emphasized the similarities and ignored the differences. As one Peace Corpsmen stated, "They regard themselves as the same as the Peace Corps; and I do, too. They serve the same function I do." This idea certainly would have been rejected by John F. Kennedy. Representatives from Peace Corps Washington could not accept it either. One evaluator, Richard Richter, commented that even though the Soviets seemed the same, they were not. They dressed the same and even looked the same, but, Richter wrote, "Clearly, Peace Corps Volunteers are better teachers, are better liked, have more Ghanaian friends and have fitted more fully into the fabric of Ghanaian life."[66] This may have been true, but the statement differed from the assessment of the volunteers. On the issue of Communism and the Soviets, the volunteers' beliefs and the views of the Peace Corps staff did not connect.

Volunteer and staff beliefs also clashed on the subject of religion. The traditional liberal ideology of the Peace Corps leadership called for a strict adherence to the doctrine of the separation of church and state. This idea became central in the Peace Corps philosophy. The Peace Corps leadership felt this to be especially important because the volunteer's job resembled the job of a missionary. Because of his Catholicism and that of his brother-in-law, Shriver felt it critical to separate religion from his Peace Corps. Even when talking to the Vatican about recruiting seminarians to work for the Peace Corps, Shriver made it clear that "they would be forbidden to proselytize on the job."[67] Peace Corps staffers had little patience for religion or what they considered to be religious zealots. One evaluator wrote about a "girl" who worked at a teachers training college in Cameroon: "[She] presents a problem. She is very religious and told me that 'God had sent her on this mission.' I believe she has a mental problem and will have to be pulled out." [68] Peace Corps Washington attempted to ignore religion because it was an issue they felt had no bearing on their job.

But, as one Peace Corps staffer admitted later, "The Peace Corps has slipped up on religion. We're negligent in not providing religious outlets for the Peace Corps volunteers. . . . The army had chaplains; every government agency did until the Peace Corps. . . . We don't even know or ask what faith they belong to." [69] One reason this presented a problem is that the host nationals did not share the ideology of religious separation held by the Peace Corps leadership. In Cameroon, one Protestant school "flatly told a Volunteer she was not wanted because she was Catholic but the mission had to take her because the Cameroonian government had insisted upon it." [70] Obviously, the Peace Corps leadership should not be criticized for its actions in this case. But it is clear that in this case and many like it, Peace Corps Washington never envisioned the problem.

Some volunteers considered religion to be central to their lives and their jobs to be similar to that of missionaries. One religious writer pointed out that, in essence, the volunteers took a "vow of poverty" during their two-year stint abroad. He continued, "We have not fully understood how closely related the Peace Corps is to the greatest traditions of Judeo-Christian faith." [71] As another article put it, volunteers believed, just as missionaries did, "that man is lovable and redeemable," and they carried "a conviction that each man is his brother's keeper." [72]

Volunteers found out time and again that they could not ignore their religious background. Myron Gildesgame faced this problem in Ecuador. Engaged in small talk with some neighbors, he suddenly found himself on the topic of religion and told them he was Jewish: "What's that, they asked. Don't believe in Jesus; not baptized. I had a hard time explaining what a Jew is and what I believe." [73] Anne Wilson wrote of her Christmas experience. While other volunteers went to a Christmas party or the local mass to see how the locals celebrated the holiday, she "offered a small, humble prayer to God that our mission would really be a success in bringing peace to earth and good will to all men" and spent the night reading the Bible. [74]

Ironically, the Peace Corps ethos demanded the utmost respect for the religious beliefs of host nationals, while ignoring the religious beliefs of its own volunteers. The story of Richard McManus illustrates this point most poignantly. McManus, a Christian Scientist, struggled with his conscience during training when required by the Peace Corps to take vaccinations. He wrote home about the experience: "I had to make a demonstration over the typhus and polio shots, which were trying to make me ill. Not being accustomed to medicine I had to declare emphatically who it is that has power over man—God or matter. Needless to say, the physical body was calmed." Once at his post in the Philippines, he began to suffer from occasional high fevers: "All I had to do was to put my trust in God, for God is our strength. Within the hour all signs of the supposed reality [the sickness] had vanished, and I was completely healed. The next day our Peace Corps leader came to rush me to the hospital, but found me perfectly well with a normal temperature." Soon after, McManus suffered the ultimate irony. He died after one of these bouts with fever. The Peace Corps doctor determined the cause of death to be a reaction to the antimalarial medication McManus had taken to "fit in" as a volunteer. The Peace Corps was not to blame for his death. But his tragic story underscores the distance between the Peace Corps staff and the volunteer on religious issues. The Philippine staff never attempted to understand McManus's ideas on religion because they were so far removed from their own.[75]

In general, the Peace Corps leadership did not understand its own volunteers. From politics to religion, the leadership treated them like children. And the volunteers believed that the agency did not "understand why the Volunteer is there, what he can and cannot do."[76] As Frederick McCluskey put it, "A few sacrificing individuals 'lowering' themselves to the level of a backward people, even if some of our knowledge rubs off on them, will not get at the basic ills of society, the injustices, the lack of opportunity."[77]

The Peace Corps prided itself on procedures designed to ascertain the feelings of its volunteers. The evaluation reports and completion-of-service conference reports that provided information for this study are just two examples of the many mechanisms designed by Peace Corps Washington to take the volunteer pulse. But the volunteers felt they often talked past the leadership. Carl Pope put it this way: "True, it [the Peace Corps] elevated the need to hear practically to the level of sacrament. But was it hearing without listening?"[78] Volunteers even believed the Peace Corps had its own language, comprehensible only to Peace Corps Washington and the overseas staff. Volunteers in El Salvador "continually poked fun at 'Peace Corps-ese.' The questionnaires were received with derisive laughter."[79] John Freivalds mimicked the process volunteers felt staffers followed when solving a problem: "Volunteers, what do they know? No, let's leave them out of it. We'll get some outside help, you know, let's be more objective."

Volunteers felt alienated by Peace Corps Washington. Those that failed to live up to the image often felt lost and confused. One volunteer described this feeling on her project in Afghanistan: "What I should be doing is a decision I have to remake frequently. Is one supposed to be a drone doing exactly what one is asked, be it typing a letter or editing a story? Or should one be a gadfly always harping on some point like the need for standard spelling? Or how about that lovely term from chemistry—the catalyst?"[80] The pioneer image and the attendant philosophy failed to give volunteers much of a guide for how to live, plunging many into confusion.

Nothing better illustrates the split between Peace Corps Washington and the volunteers than the cases of female and minority volunteers. Few of the intellectuals and politicians who dreamed of the Peace Corps in the 1950s envisioned female volunteers. The original bill in the Senate, sponsored by Hubert Humphrey, did not include women. Yet 40 percent of the volunteers in the 1960s were women. After their arrival, many women felt like appendages. In Thailand, "the four girls in the project considered themselves to be a complete afterthought. They felt that they never worked out, and they doubt that single American girls working in villages could ever work out in Thailand."[81]

Although no one believed women should be explicitly left out of the Peace Corps, no one seemed to give much thought to how they would relate to the purpose of the Corps. The new pioneer, like the mythic pioneer of the nineteenth century, was a masculine concept. The myth was built in large part on a western fiction that was "overwhelmingly macho. Men are in charge, while women are important mainly as commentators and motivators."[82] These fictional men experienced adventure, first in the American West and later, as American interest in the outside world increased, throughout the world. According to one analyst of this adventure fiction, the "Adventure experience was the sacramental ceremony of the cult of manhood."[83] Many characteristics of the image were, not coincidentally, also qualities Americans in the early 1960s connected to men.

Outsiders had difficulty talking about women and Peace Corps volunteers in the same breath, even if they were describing a female volunteer. For example, Pulitzer Prize–winning newspaper correspondent Bill Mauldin had difficulty reconciling his image of the all-American girl with the reality of such a girl at work in the Peace Corps. "She is a doll," he wrote, describing a volunteer. "Judy has one of those solid, middle-class American, peaches and cream faces that goes with school proms and gardenia corsages and here she was wading through raw sewage."[84] Some staffers not only ignored women, they had difficulty believing women could do the job. One evaluator said, "No talk of deadbeats would be complete without a discussion of girls

Volunteer women attempt to navigate the frontier in the pioneering vehicle of the 1960s, the jeep. According to the original caption, these Colombia-bound "girls" sorely tested the patience of their instructor. Photo by Paul Conklin, courtesy National Archives.

in the program. I saw few girls—married or single—who were accomplishing anything outside of their home. . . . We should only send single females to cities—the only places they can function."[85]

In part, the Peace Corps leadership and the American public tried to stuff volunteer women into the new pioneer image. In an issue devoted to the Peace Corps, *National Geographic* presented a special essay on the life of female volunteers. The article depicts the transformation that the women underwent as they were trained for the harsh environs of the third world. Like any good pioneer woman, these "soft-hearted city girls had to learn to kill chickens for their dinner." It was difficult for them: "Girls who have plucked only cellophane-wrapped fowl from supermarket racks suddenly found themselves told to slaughter their own food." As American culture viewed it, these women were about to enter a primitive world, and so had to prepare themselves for the chores of primitive women. Yet as girls of modern 1960s America, they were expected to mingle feminine charm with those primitive chores. Hence, "smiles mingle with sadness as the girls dip carcasses in scalding water to loosen pin feathers." While they went about their womanly chores, the "male members of the group are absent, learning to milk goats." The article concludes by arguing that women on the new frontiers of the third world have to be adaptable, because "to manage a

During training, women volunteers were often asked to practice stereotypically female skills such as basketweaving and sewing. This group of women was training for jobs in Morocco at a California training site in 1967. Courtesy National Archives.

home in western Venezuela, a girl should be a carpenter as well as a cook and a seamstress."[86]

The Peace Corps image of the woman pioneer resembled that of the male volunteer. Women were accepted "if they showed the time-honored signs of hard toil, dirt and sweat."[87] One advertisement, distributed to campuses nationwide, used images to recruit the acceptable type of female volunteer. This ad depicts a woman in full Victorian costume, complete with flowered bonnet and chin-high neckline. The caption reads, "Should a gentleman offer a Peace Corps assignment to a lady?" The ad was intended to rankle college women, whose image of Peace Corps life was the opposite of the image on the poster.[88] One popular image was of American women coming to the rescue in the modern version of the mythic trusty steed, the jeep. Philip Cook, in an evaluation of the Ivory Coast, pointed out that "the idea of seeing young, white women venture out into the villages by jeep to teach clearly appeals to the Ivoiriens."[89]

At the same time that female volunteers were supposed to fit the new pioneer image, they were expected to fit the image of the American woman in the 1960s. Betty Friedan outlined this image, "created by the woman's magazines, television, movies, novels, columns, etc.," in her pathbreaking work on women in the early 1960s, *The Feminine Mystique*. American women were supposed to be "young and frivolous; fluffy and feminine; passive; gaily content in a world of bedroom and kitchen, sex, babies and home."[90] Friedan dedicated her entire book to showing how completely this image permeated American society in 1963.

Most Peace Corps staffers also adhered to this view of women. Richard Hancock, the Peace Corps representative in El Salvador, described what he considered to be a model female volunteer in an article in the *Volunteer*. He described Beva Fegely, an older volunteer from North Dakota, who made her El Salvador home into a model home, "demonstrating what can be accomplished in homemaking at modest cost."[91] Richard Starkey, after saying that women had nothing to offer in Turkey, amended his statement by commenting that the "only good ones kept themselves busy by making their houses into showpieces."[92]

The Peace Corps' founders believed that "certain projects are better suited for male Volunteers and vice-versa."[93] Although "it was once believed that women would not be eligible for the Peace Corps," as Roy Hoopes wrote in *The Complete Peace Corps Guide*, the leaders quickly changed their minds on this issue. Nevertheless, they continued to confine women to traditional female roles: "Women are very much needed in the Peace Corps—as teachers, home economists and nurses."[94] In Brazil, "while men encourage building hen houses, planting new crops, etc., women are helping Brazilian girls improve their families diets by introducing balanced meals and by showing them how to preserve perishable food by drying, salting or canning."[95] In 1960s America, women had certain roles to fulfill, and female volunteers were supposed to show the women of the third world how to fill those roles.

Many female volunteers felt an inescapable conflict between these two images. In the January 1968 edition of the *Volunteer*, a woman with the pseudonym Jane wrote a letter to the editor complaining of an article in a previous issue. The letter asked exactly how women volunteers were supposed to act, since the article accused them of being "unladylike, too bold, too competing, too demanding, too everything."[96] But Peace Corps leadership terminated a female volunteer because she "lacked the strength and desire to overcome some formidable obstacles." In an exit interview, Kevin Delaney said, "She strikes me as an average to below average Volunteer who doesn't feel too strongly about anything."[97] Women volunteers could not be too bold, or they would be unfeminine. Yet they could not be too weak, or they would fail as new pioneers. In an evaluation of the El Salvador volunteers, Thorburn Reid found one he called the "most sullen Volunteer I have had the misfortune to interview." He blamed her sourness on his belief that she was "spurned by a male, and is reputedly still pining over him, whose Latin politeness she apparently interpreted as serious interest." All was not lost because, he concluded, "When she ventured a smile she seemed quite attractive."[98]

Many female volunteers worked hard to resolve their conflicting identities. The Peace Corps even distributed a pamphlet to show how volunteers could retain both identities. This document emphasized, for example, how Jeanette Killingsworth "enjoys being a girl." It pictured her doing "girl" things, such as swimming, smiling over a meal she made, and taking a nap. Most importantly, the brochure described her trip to the beauty parlor. While there, "Jeanette indulges in a hairdo, choosing an exotic style from the hairdressers' collection of old movie magazines. 'I guess I'm crazy. As soon as we start back to Julau my glamour gets sand blasted in the back of the Land Rover.'" Even though Killingsworth knew the act of feminine defiance was fruitless, she did it anyway, because she thought it was important to retain her feminine identity. Her husband accepted the eccentricity for the practical reason that "the dryer electrocutes the bugs in her hair."[99]

This pamphlet also discussed the dilemma faced by a twenty-six-year-old woman volunteer in the Philippines. "Overseas, girls lose the feminine role they had in the United States," she worried. "They do things like building, hanging doors and that sort of thing. . . . The first time you hang a door you get a kick out of it, but about the third time you begin to wonder why there isn't a male Volunteer to do it for you and maybe you're not quite the girl you used to be."[100] She was not the only one who worried about losing her feminine identity. The *Volunteer* published a letter to the editor from a volunteer who wrote, "Since joining the Peace Corps, I have often heard (and read) that female Volunteers have lost their femininity."[101] The writer insisted that they had not: it was only hidden under the Peace Corps veneer.

In their jobs, most female volunteers accepted the necessity of living up to the image. But in their personal time—while socializing, going on dates or to parties—female volunteers tried to keep their American feminine qualities. Peace Corps Washington wasn't sure this was possible. One memo from the Office of Volunteer Services queried, "Can women expect to be treated as 'one of the boys' in work situations and still expect to retain the privileges accorded them because of their sex?" According to Peace Corps Washington, the answer was yes. They found that even after a day of gritty Peace Corps work, female volunteers could still be "flirtatious and coy."[102]

Many Peace Corps staffers vigorously defended the feminine purity of the volunteer women, much to the women's chagrin. In a memo to Jack Vaughn, one staffer from the Training Division pointed out the necessity for women to "assume the same feminine role as she assumes in the States. There should be a thorough and continuous examination of what, in fact, that role is in the States."[103] Alicia Teichman, one volunteer who worried about being controlled in this manner, wrote to a friend at home:

> The male members of the staff are always watching out for us single girls as they are worried that the boys may have "sexual or girlfriend thoughts" instead of student-teacher thoughts. You know me well enough to know that I enjoy talking to people on other topics besides school—I mean trying to get to know them "as they are." This is what people seem to think one isn't allowed to do. I've been thinking of transferring to a girl's school where I might be more effective, but I'm faced with the question, am I giving up?"[104]

Teichman could not do her job effectively without the male staffers trying to impose their ideas of American womanhood upon her.

Peace Corps Washington, with its incomplete picture of the third world and of the volunteers' job there, feared this alien world might jeopardize the volunteers' American femininity. In part, this meant the leaders regulated the personal lives of female volunteers even more rigorously than they regulated male volunteers. Female volunteers were given a slew of warnings that "in some areas of the world, a girl must be careful of the circumstances in which she is seen with a man."[105] Not all of these warnings came from Peace Corps headquarters. The male leaders in the host countries also enforced their ideals of femininity on the female volunteers, and male volunteers contributed to the problem as well. Eeta B. Freeman, working in Pakistan, curtailed her social activities because "John," a fellow Peace Corps worker, told her she was "getting a reputation among Peace Corps Volunteer men for dating 'natives' so often." As a result, Freeman decided to go "into hibernation: cutting down my appearances in public places with Pakistani men. I'm scared for my job: if locals start gossiping about me, my job will be ended."[106] The male volunteers could not allow a paragon of American femininity to be soiled by a native. Women also had to be careful to hide their feminine wiles, lest they become too much a temptation to males in the area, volunteer and host national alike. A report on volunteers in Peru described one male volunteer who became so frustrated and uncomfortable that he was unfit for effective work "because he believed one of the volunteer women he worked with was too much of a tease."[107]

When it came to sex, the Peace Corps was even more protective of its female volunteers. The activities of male volunteers offended the sensibilities of some Peace Corps leaders. One Peace Corps doctor in Turkey wondered "if the Volunteers in these households have informed their parents of their living conditions (i.e. 'co-habitation')."[108] Walter K. Davis, a staffer in the Peace Corps Training Division, wrote a memo to Jack Vaughn in which he expressed mild shock at a group of male volunteers who kept mistresses. But even though he thought it inappropriate behavior, he accepted the defense: there were many men running around with women, no one would know, the volunteer said it was personal and not affecting his work, and, most importantly, "any man around who didn't have a woman was suspected of being strange."[109]

Female volunteers, on the other hand, could not be allowed to act in such a manner. One in Ghana understood that "sex in Ghana is extremely casual" but insisted she was "not suggesting any girl change her morals."[110] In 1966, the Peace Corps distributed a training manual that made its position clear. This manual presented case studies of potential problems in "social behavior." One case discussed the lives of two female volunteers. One wondered whether or not to tell the other that she was being a "fool in love."[111] She did not, and her friend became pregnant. The lesson for volunteer women: stay away from men while overseas.

This manual, distributed in 1966, appears to have been the first conscious effort made by the agency to examine the issue. Earlier, it was almost ignored. Arnold Zeitlin comments, "No one suggested volunteers avoid sexual relations with Ghanaians or, for that matter, with each other."[112] Walter Davis went to Nigeria and evaluated projects there. As a result of his observations, he wrote a memo to Vaughn on the problem. He noted that "the girls in this group felt that more detailed information should be provided [during training] on the local mores of the country. They should be informed to not hesitate to tell an unwanted male visitor to get out of their house or leave them alone."[113]

One issue that the Peace Corps leadership could not ignore was that of pregnancy and abortion. Sargent Shriver, who considered himself a faithful Catholic, made the agency's position very clear as early as 1963. His directive to all Peace Corps representatives read:

> The policy on abortion is likewise clear. In our society, abortion is almost always an illegal act, and most people consider it morally wrong. The emotional consequences, moreover, are serious and may lead to profound psychological harm. If termination of pregnancy is being considered for medical reasons, then the return of the Volunteer to the United States for medical evaluation is mandatory.[114]

On this issue, Shriver and the agency leadership did not veil their paternalism. They would decide what was in the best moral, emotional, and psychological interest of the volunteer, and regardless of any changing mood among the women of the United States, abortions would not be allowed.

Pregnant volunteers, it turned out, were almost always sent home, whether or not they needed medical evaluation. In an interview of two recently terminated volunteers, John Griffin lamented "two more victims of the send-home-the-pregnant-ones policy." Griffin thought their firing was a travesty, since "both seemed like high level volunteers."[115] Lawrence Fuchs reported that in the Philippines, ten out of twenty-three female Peace Corps volunteers sent home during his tenure as director were separated due to "problemful misbehavior connected with romance and sex." Four male volunteers were also given a ticket home—none because of similar "problemful misbehavior."[116]

Shriver and the other male leaders instituted these policies despite the lonely objections of a woman in the Peace Corps hierarchy. Betty Harris, who called herself "the token woman executive," had been a coworker with Shriver at *Newsweek* in the 1950s. Shriver appointed her deputy associate director of the Office of Peace Corps Volunteers, and, because of her journalism background, she also decided to start a volunteer newsletter, which soon became the *Volunteer.* (Harris later helped to found *Ms.*) She did not intend to be another pretty face: "I had come to do serious work, not some nicey-nicey ladies job."

Harris considered looking after women's issues part of her "serious work." Her first involvement with these issues came at an emergency Saturday morning meeting about a volunteer who had gotten pregnant. She called the subsequent conversation "ludicrous": "These grown men realized that possibly the pregnant Volunteer had got herself in the 'family way' by means of intimate contact with a *national.* Oh, god!, the guys were just falling apart." Harris angrily reported, "One fool present at this meeting actually suggested that we 'can' women Volunteers altogether. No one ever suggested that our male Volunteers might be shacking up with female 'nationals,' getting *them* pregnant, or what the implications of *that* might be in the host country."[117] Harris believes that it was this experience, and others like it, that got her involved with the women's movement. If the most progressive agency in the government could act like this, the only hope was to agitate outside of government for a change. Her experience and alienation represented that of all female volunteers.

Although female volunteers were not supposed to have sex, they were still supposed to look and act sexy, a problem central to those described by

Betty Friedan. The *Volunteer,* founded by the feminist, most pointedly illustrates this inconsistency. A volunteer named Michael T. Field, serving in Ghana, wrote a letter to the editor in January 1965 complimenting the magazine for putting a pretty woman on the December cover. Then he wrote, seemingly with tongue in cheek: "There has occurred to me another way in which you could improve the overall attractiveness of the format. This would be to have the center of the magazine a foldout photograph of a young Peace Corps lady, dressed as would be expected of tropical climates where most of us are stationed, suitable for removal and framing." The amazing part of the story is not that such a volunteer existed or even that the magazine printed the letter, but that the magazine obliged his whim and printed another picture of "Miss December" for him that was "suitable for removal and framing."[118]

Such ignorance of women's feelings and women's issues pervaded much of the Peace Corps staff. One evaluator commented despairingly about the women volunteers in the Philippines: "Impressionable, previously lonely, emotionally immature females fall prey to the male attention and are believed sometimes to mistake physical attraction for love."[119] Another example involves a female volunteer who was assaulted and raped in New York just before her training began. The training staff stated that they were "particularly concerned about her strong desire to visit New York to talk to the detective involved in the case. They see this as evidence that she has not really come to emotional terms with her problem. While I was there, she was forbidden to go to New York with a group of other trainees who were planning a trip." To Shriver's credit, after reading this memo he jotted a note in the margin: "You'd better give this several second thoughts."[120] The point is that the training staff had no ability to relate to or even understand the trauma suffered by the victimized volunteer.

When it came to sexual matters, the Peace Corps leadership displayed a lack of sensitivity toward married volunteers of both sexes. Betty Harris reports that during the same meeting in which they discussed wayward women, the leadership discussed the possibility of married volunteers having children overseas. Telling the story with her own special verve, Harris begins by asking, "What if a married Volunteer got pregnant by her own husband? Oh! Oh! What if our precious, upper middle class American flowers got pregnant in one of those dirty, backwater countries? Surely, the Peace Corps would send the couple home."[121] Her implication was that, regardless of the opinion of the couple, the Peace Corps would not allow the volunteer woman's femininity to be sullied in the grime of a third world country. This feeling was strong in the Peace Corps hierarchy. Charles

Wingenbach, in a book written in 1961 to outline the parameters for the Peace Corps, declared bluntly, "The general rule should be that the couple return to the United States."

The Peace Corps position regarding minorities differed from its position regarding women but reflected similar disconnection and caused similar alienation. Most in Peace Corps Washington had little interest in or knowledge of women's issues. The same can not be said of issues regarding minorities. The two most influential early Peace Corps leaders, Sargent Shriver and Harris Wofford, came from the early civil rights movement of the 1950s. Wofford was good friends with Martin Luther King Jr. and was John Kennedy's special assistant for civil rights. He tried to push Kennedy to move faster on civil rights and admitted afterward that despite his best efforts, Kennedy's record on civil rights was mixed.

In their deeds as well as their philosophy, Shriver and the Peace Corps leadership attempted to make the Peace Corps a model governmental agency in the struggle for minority rights in the United States. As Shriver put it, "We deliberately recruited as many Negroes and representatives of other minority groups as possible for jobs in every echelon."[122] One of the black leaders recruited by the Peace Corps was C. Payne Lucas, country director for Niger under Shriver and director for all of Africa under Jack Vaughn. In 1968, he published a pamphlet enunciating the Peace Corps philosophy: "The Peace Corps knows that a world based on the pigmentation of one's skin cannot survive. The Peace Corps is convinced that anything less than a total struggle against the twin evils of racial superiority and poverty can only represent a mission of suicide."[123]

The Peace Corps official line and fervent hope was to follow the tenets of King and create a color-blind society. Whenever possible, evaluators and staffers would stress how the agency was succeeding in this mission. Shriver was fond of relating a story about Carl Jorgenson, a Harvard-educated black volunteer in Nepal, the son of an NAACP leader, "tall, young and handsome," who befriended a local communist and proved to him that African-Americans could succeed in the United States.[124] Most volunteers also fervently supported racial equality. Eeta B. Freeman marveled that "in west Pakistan, we have a white Little Rock engineer working with a Little Rock Negro teacher—and very well."[125]

Unfortunately for these hopes, few minorities volunteered for the Peace Corps. Even in the first group of volunteers recruited, only 4 of 124 were African-Americans.[126] By 1967, only about 5 percent of the total number of volunteers who had served in the Peace Corps were African-Americans, and, the Peace Corps estimated, only 2 percent of recruits in 1967.[127]

A study commissioned by the agency but undertaken by an independent entity in 1968 stated, "Currently, of 8,000 Volunteers, only 111 are black," which put the figure closer to 1 percent.[128] These figures point to a dismal success rate for an agency specifically targeting minority groups.

What explains the failure to recruit African-Americans as volunteers? The study mentioned above, conducted by Pinkett-Brown-Black and Associates, provides some insight. Many young African-American youths during the 1960s concluded, "It's a luxury Black students can ill afford," because "it takes two years out of your life when you could be proving yourself."[129] Many black college students felt the sting of economic reality after graduating from college. They believed they had to make their investment in college worthwhile, especially because many were the first in their family to attend college. The *Volunteer* ran a story in 1968 echoing these sentiments: "To most Negro college seniors in the class of 68, the Peace Corps represented a two-year interlude which they could not afford," because "career pressures were more intense" than for white students.[130] The volunteer ethic, or "vow of poverty" as one critic called it, made no sense for a group of people striving to escape poverty.

But Lucas and the rest of the Peace Corps leadership had difficulty understanding that the reason many African-Americans did not join the Peace Corps is that they felt no connection to it. The leadership fought an uphill battle, because the volunteer they worked so hard to create, the new pioneer, seemed foreign to black Americans. Mythic pioneers were explicitly white, even consciously Aryan: "Steady-eyed, eagle-faced men with tawny mustaches . . . remind you of their spiritual kinsmen, the heroes of the Icelandic sagas."[131] The new pioneer eschewed material wealth, while graduating blacks sought wealth in a society that had historically denied it to them. The new pioneer lived individually, while black Americans were working to build a sense of group identity. The values of the new pioneer stemmed from the myths of frontier America, a myth that portrayed whites as the pioneering heroes, and blacks, when pictured as all, as bumbling slaves.

The Pinkett-Brown-Black study confirmed this belief. When asked to describe their image of a volunteer, the African-American students responded with a variety of answers, all outlining their alienation. One described the volunteer as a "middle-class white. Those who have been totally removed from life. That's why a Rockefeller had to go and get lost in Africa." Another felt the Peace Corps involved Americans where they did not belong: "It's similar to the white liberals going into the ghetto. It's the same thing . . . they think they're perfect." Another was even blunter, comparing the Corps to British imperialism: "[The Peace Corps] is an extension of what is considered throughout history to be the white man's burden—to go out into the various cultures and swamp them with what they have and exploit them in every way, form, and fashion that they can."[132] Many black Americans did not want to join an organization they believed was simply an extension of the type of patronizing world they had suffered in for many years.

Undoubtedly, the Peace Corps leadership would have responded that this is not what the Peace Corps did, and the volunteers were not all mid-dle-class white kids out to take on the white man's burden. They may have been right in thinking this, but they had created the image, and in this case, the image backfired. In most cases, African-Americans had no desire to be new pioneers. Many felt that the blacks who did join the Corps were selling out. The Pinkett-Brown-Black study quoted one African-American as say-ing, "If we did a poll on blacks who go into the Peace Corps, I venture to say they would probably be without political sensitivity about the struggle for black liberation." Another declared, "There are blacks brought up in a middle class society who don't see what's going on because they don't want to see what's going on."[133] He believed that blacks who joined the Corps ignored their own culture and background to become something they could not hope to actually become—the new pioneer. African-Americans, then, had yet another reason to feel alienated from the Peace Corps leadership and its ideas about international development.

Native Americans encountered an even bigger problem in the Peace Corps. Due to the minuscule number of Indian volunteers, the Peace Corps hierarchy, always attuned to the need to recruit all types of volunteers, instituted a program in 1969 to recruit more Native Americans. This pro-gram, dubbed Operation Peace Pipe by the public relations department, sought to work with an existing institution called Oklahomans for Indian Opportunity. Headed by the Comanche wife of a U.S. senator, this group sought to "help draw American Indians more fully into the mainstream of the nation's culture and economy while preserving and building up their pride of heritage."[134] This presented a huge problem in the Peace Corps. "Drawing them into the culture" in the Peace Corps meant making them into new pioneers. This meant teaching Native Americans to be just like the people who, in myth as well as reality, had slaughtered their ancestors.

Project Peace Pipe was a recipe for disaster. And a disaster it was. Project Peace Pipe #1 lost 90 percent of its trainees, and only five out of the thirty-four recruits for Project Peace Pipe #2 stayed the course and became volunteers. Lawrence O'Brien, previously a chief aide to Kennedy, "blistered the Peace Corps for cultural insensitivity" on this undertaking.[135] Jack An-derson wrote an article for the *Washington Post* savaging the Peace Corps

These volunteers were part of Operation Peace Pipe, a failed attempt to recruit Native Americans as volunteers. Courtesy National Archives.

for the project. He quoted an internal report blaming the failure on "racism . . . bungling . . . bureaucratic deafness . . . and sheer ignorance."

This attack must have deeply wounded the progressive Peace Corps leadership. From the agency's beginnings, it had prided itself on an open view toward minorities. But in trying to create new pioneers, the agency guaranteed it would fail with most minorities, especially Native Americans. One Native American was asked why he dropped out of the project. His response: "Peace Pipe seems like an effort to make us nice little WASPS so that we can fit in." That is exactly what the Peace Corps tried to do. It made a strong effort to recruit all types of Americans: blacks, Hispanics, women, and Native Americans. But once they were in the Corps, these recruits were expected to live up to its exacting image. As the internal report put it, "The Peace Corps has extremely limited capacity to tolerate, much less include, people of minority backgrounds—in fact, the system has been designed to reject them, one way or another."[136]

The actions of Peace Corps leaders and staffers pushed volunteers away from feeling a sense of unity. Most evaluators commented on an astonishing lack of connection felt by volunteers toward the agency and its goals of development. As one evaluator put it, "It is interesting to note that *esprit de corps* worldwide is not something held to a high degree by Peace Corps volunteers. In fact, in the conferences, it is revealed that it doesn't even extend to one's own country of service."[137]

Few felt much affinity for other volunteers or the Peace Corps as an organization, and most decisively rejected notions of togetherness. According to one report, in Nigeria, the volunteers had made "an explicit effort to avoid overidentification with the Peace Corps as an organization. They were anxious to be accepted on merit as individuals."[138] The same year, 1963, 62 percent of the volunteers in the Philippines claimed they had no feeling of esprit de corps toward the Peace Corps.[139] Two years later, an evaluator concluded volunteers in Peru felt "little connection between themselves and Peace Corps/Washington."[140] Report after report and evaluation after evaluation said essentially the same thing. Volunteers felt little loyalty toward other volunteers, even in their own country, and even less loyalty toward the Peace Corps as a government agency.[141] They sought to separate themselves from what they viewed as an inflexible, old-fashioned bureaucracy. This lack of connectedness reinforced the volunteers' individualistic ethos.

As we have seen over and over again, this individualism was explicitly not the traditional ethic of American frontier individualism, but something closer to independence. Volunteers had no desire to be categorized as one of many. Rather, they wanted to be viewed as individuals: "The volunteers have made, and seem to be in accord on the wisdom of, an explicit effort to avoid overidentification with the Peace Corps as an organization. They were anxious to be accepted on merit as individuals."[142]

Staffers believed that "insistence on individualism was almost universal among the young volunteers."[143] Evaluators, also, noted the volunteers' adherence to their own brand of individualism. In Peru, the members of one group who came into the country together expressed pride that "they had minimal contact as a group" and that the most successful aspect of the project was the "independence and individuality of the members."[144] The one thing that participants did agree on at the first national completion-of-service conference in Washington was that they did not want to start a national organization of returned volunteers. They refused to surrender any independence to such an organization, and they heartily endorsed a pamphlet circulated at the conference entitled "Lord, Not Another American Legion."[145]

Many Peace Corps staffers and leaders tired of this incessant defense of volunteer individuality. Staffer Vera Vinogradoff evaluated the beliefs of one returned volunteer: "His viva yo stance was disgusting; so was his involutional egocentrism, his lack of drive toward even his own stated goals."[146] Nonvolunteers often translated volunteer individuality as selfishness. One volunteer shrugged off a query as to whether or not he was contributing to world peace with the response, "World Peace? I contributed to *my* peace of mind. At least I tried."[147] Outsiders noted with surprise that the volunteers did not "think of themselves as a team. Each is his own individual. His individuality is his starting point."[148]

This individuality was not just a casually adopted characteristic. Many believed it defined them and their jobs as volunteers. They were always "wary of becoming a carrier in some ideological germ warfare, if that was what the Peace Corps had in mind. I felt an almost belligerent determination to maintain my individuality."[149] Many volunteers believed that individuality defined the Peace Corps, and without it, Peace Corps projects could not exist. From the start of training, they yearned for a chance to strike out on their own and prove themselves. As one volunteer phrased it, "We believed that once away in the barrio, away from all the training, we would be on our own, self-sufficient, and able to begin to move."[150]

Volunteer teachers clung to their independence in an especially tenacious manner. John Coyne, a teacher in Ethiopia, did not accept that all Peace Corps teachers needed to follow a prescribed method. Instead, he believed they should follow their individual instincts: "Teachers have to find their own style and their own techniques. Teaching is a discovery of one's own personality."[151] A teacher in the Philippines echoed that sentiment, believing that English teachers should stress "individual style rather than conformity."[152]

Lawrence Fuchs wrote a book revolving around the issue of individualism entitled *Those Peculiar Americans*. According to the forward by Peace Corps staffer and America's most prominent social scientist, David Riesman, Fuchs emphasizes the "near solipsistic individualism of Americans."[153] Riesman argued that this emphasis "seems right. Many of the Volunteers I have seen value their own independence and autonomy in an almost anarchic way." Fuchs went on to argue that this is yet another example of what he calls "the American cult" of individualism.[154] Whether Fuchs's conclusion about the history and society of the United States is correct, there seems little doubt that his findings about the centrality of individuality to volunteer ideology are correct.

This determined adherence to individuality and individual thinking, caused in large measure by the alienating training and operating procedures of the Peace Corps, opened the minds of volunteers to their experiences abroad. Because the volunteers felt little loyalty to the ideas of their leadership, they had the ability to craft their own opinions about the third world and how Americans should relate to it. They truly became independent ambassadors, believing themselves free to invent a new kind of American relationship with the world they were about to encounter.

5 The Realities of the Twentieth-Century Frontier

Living in the Third World

The first step in Sargent Shriver's plan for development was for volunteers to descend into the third world. Though the Peace Corps leaders respected the humanity of the less-developed peoples of the world, they still saw them as being stuck at the starting line in the race for development. This is why the frontier image seemed so apt to Shriver: people in the third world, like the historical actors on America's frontier, were just setting off on the road to progress. Volunteers were supposed to help show them along this road, which, though perhaps difficult and bumpy, was nonetheless straight.

For most Americans in the 1950s and 1960s, the third world remained very distant, primitive, and mysterious. In January 1959, staff writer Robert Coughlan wrote a two-part feature story for *Life* magazine intending to introduce the six million subscribers to Africa at the dawn of a new decade. Up to this point, Americans knew and cared very little about Africa. But after the Soviets launched the Sputnik satellite in 1957, the competition between the Americans and the Soviets took on a worldwide flavor. Development became one weapon in the world wide fight against communism.

Coughlan's article presents a detailed look at the Africa emerging from colonial rule during the 1950s. Though detailed in particulars, the story still presents Africa as a one-dimensional, mythical continent. Americans read, "It is the black Africa of apes and ivory, of Stanley and Livingston, of crocodile and lion, and of 125 million people still living in or at the edge of savagery." Until the Europeans arrived, Coughlan wrote, "almost all Africans were quite primitive," suffering from the "inertia of eons of ignorance." To live there was to live in a place of mystery, a place completely undeveloped and completely different from the United States in 1959. According to Coughlan, Americans had a role to help Africans "explode out of the Stone Age into the modern world."[1]

Coughlan's article exemplifies the prevailing attitude toward Africa and Africans in Sargent Shriver's world in 1961. Other popular magazines, such as *National Geographic,* echoed this depiction. This magazine, believed my many Americans to be the truest representation of life outside the United States, put a "sharp focus on the people of the fourth world as peoples of nature," and 75 percent of the photographs in the magazine during this period showed rural settings.[2] Africa was a place apart from the modern world, a place starting at the bottom that needed help getting to the top. Any American living there would have to begin at this bottom. Herbert Feis described this world in a book he wrote on foreign aid in 1964: "The area of destitution is vast . . . the dark, dank existence in the charcoal and fishing villages of Brazil; the shivering and dull faced Indians in the mountain towns of Peru, Bolivia and Ecuador . . . the teeming half-starved millions in the dirt and dung of the congested villages and city-slums in India . . . the teeming, ignorant millions in the tropical villages of Java."[3] By using terms such as *dark, dank, dull,* and *congested,* Feis is describing both a perceived economic weakness and cultural destitution.

Shriver accepted the arguments of *The Ugly American* that if Americans were to do any good, they couldn't live as modern refugees in a sea of Stone Age peoples. Rather, they would have to live like these peoples, "at the edge of savagery," as Coughlan put it, in order to help them learn of civilization.

Hence the famous, even clichéd, image of Peace Corps volunteers living in mud huts. Many lived in exotic, romantic, beautiful surroundings so different from the scene of their experiences in the United States that they had difficulties explaining or understanding them. Malayan agricultural worker Margaret Balfe outlined with wonder her "walk through the beautiful woods and river beds, and emerged to see the golden padi waving in the breeze, stretching ahead for miles and bordered in the distance by jungle covered mountains."[4] Moritz Thomsen, in Ecuador, described the jungles and bamboo houses as "pure Rousseau, and the pictures seemed to reflect a profound tranquility. The little village was going to be as romantic as hell."[5] Jaclyn Hyland poetically recalled one night in Liberia: "The murk of the frogs, squeak of the crickets and the pitter patter of the lizards on the zinc roof lulled us to sleep."[6]

One leader in a host country even joked, "Since we were Americans we would have preferred log cabins."[7] The volunteers reveled in the dramatic aspect of their life. In Sarawak, on the western shore of Borneo, "volunteers penetrate far into the jungle by longboat where the once fierce Ibans live in longhouses festooned with human skulls, grisly war prizes taken within living memory."[8]

Volunteers seemed most comfortable when their living conditions were the most primitive. Barbara Lorimer in North Borneo complained that she was tired, not from her hard work, but from "the throbbing of the gongs all night. They sounded like drums, actually."[9] She related with breathless excitement to readers of her article that these drums played a role in religious rituals. Drums were a favorite subject of volunteer commentary, due to their supposedly exotic and romantic nature. Roger McManus, in the Philippines, commented, "In the evening while I cook dinner, I can hear the tin-tin in the distance of the Moro drums."[10] Volunteers wanted to be shocked by their cultural encounter. They wanted the third world to present a strikingly different experience from their own.

In some countries, such as Nepal, volunteers did live in mud huts. Volunteer Jim Fisher proudly described his shanty to the *Volunteer:* "small doors and windows, the mud floors that crumble and sift down on the floor beneath, and the scarcities of meat and kerosene."[11] Carlos, in Brazil, preferred "to sleep in the traditional hammock instead of the bed the Peace Corps provided."[12] The conditions that some volunteers lived in frightened the pampered folk back home. The parents of one Nigerian volunteer visited her just after she delivered their grandchild. They were appalled at the conditions she lived in and found "the village to be squalid and unsanitary. They tried to persuade the girl to let them take the baby home with them."[13] She refused, of course, first because she did not want to part with her child. Yet she also wanted to reaffirm her belief in universal humanism, insisting she could raise her child as well in Nigeria as in the United States. If the conditions were primitive, she could justify her decision by pointing out that conditions on the American frontier were also primitive.

Volunteers also loved to relate stories about their exciting adventures and partaking in the strange customs of exotic lands. The more disgusting the story was, the better. Bob Siegal wrote in the *Volunteer* that on one trip in Nyasaland he ate a hamburger made out of hundreds of nkungo bugs.[14] Another article in the *Volunteer* discusses at great length a game in Afghanistan witnessed by many volunteers. The game, called *buzkashi,* resembled polo, except the body of a 150-pound beheaded calf served as the ball.[15] Jaclyn Hyland felt compelled to write home that she killed more than a dozen cockroaches the first night in her host country.[16] The volunteers and the magazine wanted to show that the Peace Corps operated in an area completely foreign to the United States, highlighting the need for development.

Some letters sent home by volunteers reveal two years of continuous adventure. One couple, the Pearsons, liked to begin their letters, "We have another adventure to tell about." They then proceeded to give their readers an intricately detailed description of one of their trips, neglecting to tell anything about their project in the meantime.[17] Some adventures were so exotic as to strain belief. Gena Reisner, in Togo, described how the local chief "blew into my house with the force and energy of a tropical storm," taking her all over the countryside, showing her all the local exotic customs and becoming her surrogate father.[18] Some volunteers wrote about local weddings, complete with gypsy bands, while others related stories about witch doctors and strange local sporting events.[19] Teacher Jack Magri, in Somalia, perhaps had the most exciting adventure of all when he saved a village by killing a rampaging hippo, in the process leaving "blood all over the place, and bloody tracks leading to the river."[20]

Some volunteers did live the life pictured on the pages of the *Volunteer.* But for the volunteers, the magazine and the image of the volunteer it portrayed served only as the butt of jokes. William Mangin, compiling evaluation reports from Africa in 1966, wrote after his visit with volunteers from Ghana, "As with the Togo group they laughed at the magazine *The Volunteer.*"[21] Some went beyond mirth in their disbelief of the stories and images in the magazine. One Philippine volunteer angrily wrote, "We are embittered by the facile self-congratulation and the persisting inaccuracies in depicting our experiences on which the public praise rests."[22]

The volunteers found that the third world did not fit their preconceptions. Living with the natives turned out to be more complicated than volunteers expected. They began their projects believing that their freshness and idealism would carry them to success: "We were young, blonde and democratic. Nothing ever happened to the beautiful people."[23] As beautiful and sensitive Americans, they came with faith in the universal goodness of humanity and the essential universality of the human spirit. They expected to find a vastly different, yet easily malleable environment in which to work. Instead they found strangely familiar environments peopled with cultures many could not relate to. Their living experiences soon challenged their preconceptions about the straightforward nature of their task and forced them to reevaluate their ideas about the third world and its people.

The shock hit many volunteers as they stepped off the plane. Jaclyn Hyland used a commonplace analogy to get across this point to her family:

Trainee Pat Cahill, from Seattle, learns the finer points of horseback riding, a critical skill for living on the new and old frontier alike. The picture-perfect cowboy in the background is instructor Don Corbin, who led the training for future volunteers deep in the heart of cowboy country, in Taos, New Mexico. Photo by Paul Conklin, courtesy National Archives.

"The sudden change from the cool, ever catered womb of the plane to an enormous shower room filled with steam is hard to feel unless you actually experience it . . . this is Liberia?"[24] Another volunteer used a different analogy to emphasize the same point: "It is something like not knowing how to swim and yet being thrown into a body of water."[25]

The Peace Corps appropriated a term to describe the stunned feelings of volunteers upon their arrival at their project: culture shock. The agency warned potential volunteers during training that this malady could affect them during their first few months in the host country. Many volunteers anticipated this condition with a mixture of dread and exhilaration. One wrote excitedly in his diary, almost as an afterthought: "Also, I have culture shock! It occurs from 2–6 months after arrival. I am depressed most of the time but not unhappy because I enjoy my work and friends both native and American."[26] Volunteers were trained to expect different customs and mores, and warned that, at first, these differences might cause a feeling of dislocation. After all, this fit in with the expectation that the third world was a place apart, a foreign atmosphere that volunteers were supposed to make more familiar.

But the shock they experienced was not necessarily the one that volunteers had been conditioned to expect. In a letter to his brother, David Wallendar complained, "The transition to this stage has been so incredibly traumatic as to defy conceptualization." But he felt it important to emphasize that this feeling "did NOT come because you are 'alone in the wilderness.'"[27] Many blamed culture shock not on leaving a complicated, civilized society for a simpler one, but on the host of complicated problems that third world countries had recently acquired. Despite claiming to realize that all cultures had intricate structures, many volunteers were still surprised to find the third world more complex than they had expected. Chad Bardone felt his "middle class background was not sufficient to enable me to understand people of other countries."[28]

Many volunteers realized immediately that their expectations about life in the third world were inaccurate. Richard Lazarus illustrated this in a letter home. As a newly minted volunteer in the wilds of Colombia, Lazarus thought he should get a horse and learn to ride it. "I adopted a nonchalant, knowing attitude and climbed aboard. At the same time I couldn't help giggling at myself because I felt like a parody on 'the Marlboro man.' I had no illusions about myself. I am at heart more the rocking horse type."[29]

Volunteers soon learned that much of the third world looked nothing like the kind of place Couglan described in his article on Africa. For example, on arrival in Cyprus, volunteers asked themselves, "What am I doing here? . . . Cyprus is in many ways a highly developed country . . . literate, politically minded, good roads, good communications, and excellent health care conditions."[30] Even those volunteers sent to the remotest locations, such as East Africa, noticed that the country and their projects were not as primitive as they had thought. Leonard Levitt felt compelled to comment, as other volunteers had, about "a drum, a native drum, from somewhere out of the blackness, almost as though to remind you—in case you were about to forget—that it was really Africa! Africa!" But Levitt continues by commenting how much of a contrast this presented to the "real" Africa he had seen the entire previous day, when he visited the school where he was going to teach—a clean, modern, "civilized" school that could as easily have been in Peoria as Africa.[31] Here the volunteer's universalist ethos is reversed. Whatever else he expected, Levitt expected the real Africa to be fundamentally different from the United States and had difficulty accepting the fact that in some ways, it really was not.

Some volunteers became so preoccupied with trying to deal with their country as a frontier that they couldn't deal with it at all. Carl Pope relates an anecdote to show how this happened to him in India: "At each station the Indians got off the train and leaned under the faucets, drinking in great gulps of fresh cool water. My wife Judy and I and forty-three other Americans nursed our lukewarm cups of disinfectant [boiled, iodinized water given them by Peace Corps staff]. No amoeba or bacillus would interfere with our getting to the real India."[32] Volunteers had been trained to be prepared for the harsh reality of the third world, and most followed their training, even if it defied normal life.

The third world was not a straightforward place, awaiting common-sense answers to unambiguous questions. For example, volunteers found the image many Americans, including President Kennedy, had of Africa as a battleground between Communism and Americanism to be muddled at best. On a trip he took to South Africa, Levitt explains that at first he accepted this worldview. While in South Africa he went to visit an opposition leader who was also a Communist. His trepidation was palpable: "A communist. A real communist. I've never met one before. What were they like, I had always wondered? Probably some dogmatic intellectual with glasses and long, un-combed, unwashed hair." This "communist monster" never materialized; a pretty blonde girl appeared instead.[33] "Communists" and "capitalists" became so mixed up in many areas that no one could tell them apart. In one village, the villagers branded any stranger a Communist. Naturally, that led them to believe that the local Peace Corps volunteer was a Communist, causing the government to attempt to remove him. Luckily, the mix-up was untangled, and the volunteer was allowed to remain.[34] Volunteers soon realized that Kennedy's Cold War rhetoric was overblown. One woman commented frankly about a village leader: "He really knows little about Communism except that it sounds a heck of a lot better than what he's got now." She hastened to emphasize, "We don't discuss politics with him."[35]

If the volunteers did not find a frontier and did not find the Cold War in the third world, what did they find? Many found an urban environment similar to the one they had left in the United States. According to Philip Cook in an evaluation on the Ivory Coast, "contrary to public belief, over

This image of the urban volunteer would have differed greatly from the image of the Peace Corps held by most Americans in the 1960s. African-American volunteer Jerry Page worked in the heart of big-city Caracas, dressed in a suit, and worked at the YMCA. Photo by Paul Conklin, courtesy National Archives.

70% of the Volunteers work in other than rural, isolated communities. Nearly a third reported they work in urban communities."[36] This fact required a "quick reversal of attitude," according to Chris Beemer, a lab technician in Rio de Janeiro. Many came in with inaccurate preconceptions gleaned from depictions of the third world in American culture. Training did not change these ideas. Volunteers need to "forget the skills acquired in training," Beemer argued, "everything from building water seal latrines to the treatment of snakebite."[37] Living and working in the city did not demand the type of pioneering skills taught in stateside training. Volunteer Judith Nordblom, in Ethiopia, argued that the "American of today is too far from the village situation economically and emotionally to comprehend it."[38]

Many cities that volunteers served in provided eerily familiar surroundings. In Maracaibo, Venezuela, Judy Thelen could get "*Time* magazine and any records" she wanted, and while shopping she could always spot a "Sears sign or an add for Colgate toothpaste" in a city infected by "the hustle bustle of modern oil capitalism."[39] In Ecuador, Paul Cowan could "always get the Rolling Stones on the jukebox, can always get a hot meal, plenty of flush toilets, plenty of good butter, Gerber strained babyfood, or a burger at 'the Reyburger.'"[40]

Volunteers worked on different types of projects in the city. They did not dig ditches or build schools, the two most common images of Peace Corps work. In Peru in 1963, most male volunteers worked construction jobs, while most women "ran kindergartens, gave literacy tests, and made door-to-door surveys of housing needs."[41] Even that might have sounded romantic to volunteers in Afghanistan who were assigned office work and constantly "complained of doing routine, boring work each day."[42]

City volunteers found themselves in societies much more complex than they had been led to expect. In the city, they felt "isolation and alienation that one has come to expect in a highly developed society, but that one is surprised to see here."[43] Because life in the city disagreed so completely with their expectations, many volunteers began to feel guilty that they were not a true part of the Peace Corps: "The city Volunteer is not without sensitivities on this subject, often finding himself beset with vague feelings of guilt over some unspoken apostasy or moral flabbiness that has caused him to end up in a 'soft' job."[44] Some felt compelled to write an article in the *Volunteer,* beginning with the query, "Has an urban assignment got you down? Do you crave the boondocks?"[45] This problem became so acute that by September 1966, the *Volunteer* devoted an entire issue to urban volunteers. Peace Corps leaders had realized by that time that "the folklore of the mud hut mainstream" caused problems for the many volunteers who did

Volunteers consistently commented on the strange transportation in the third world. Here volunteer Eugenia Lewis rides to her teaching job in a tricycle. Photo by Larson, 1969, courtesy National Archives.

not live the image.[46] The Peace Corps needed to "make . . . peace with the city."[47] The fact remained that volunteers were trained to "develop" the third world. This meant taking these areas from an undeveloped starting point through a perhaps difficult yet straightforward process to the promised land of "development." When volunteers found many areas to be in some ways already developed, confusion resulted.

One problem that seemed to surprise every volunteer was the difficulty of transportation in their new home. It seemed some even expected to get around by horse. Richard Lazarus got a rude awakening to what horses were really like on his arrival in Colombia. Instead of galloping away like the Lone Ranger on Silver, he remained stationary on "a nag related to don Quixote's horse. His head was locked at a 45 degree angle to the ground and he had but one gear and it was closer to reverse than low."[48]

Almost all volunteers were shocked by the types of transport they had to ride, perhaps because they had become so enmeshed in American automobile culture that they instinctively expected other cultures to revolve around the family car. Perhaps they expected busses, planes, and trains to exactly resemble those in the United States. Or, perhaps, they really did not think of it because their preconception of these places did not include mechanized transport. Whatever the reason, surprise at the types of transportation encountered probably ranks as the most written-about topic by volunteers just arriving at their project site.

Most frequently, the volunteers commented on busses. "Busses played a major part in the lives of the Volunteers," according to Lawrence Fuchs: "waiting for busses, dodging busses and squeezing into busses."[49] The first thing that struck volunteers about the busses was their quirky appearance: "They all look as though they had been designed by six year old kids; they are short, fat, and perky, painted in the primary colors, striped like a layer cake. . . . One thing they don't look like: they don't look like they'll ever move."[50] This superior tone runs throughout the descriptions. Richard Lazarus uses busses as a symbol for all of Colombia: "Learning to go where you want and when you want by bus has become a national sport and in some quarters elevated to the status of an art. . . . People are crammed into each bus beyond what any reasonable person would consider capacity."[51] Jaclyn Hyland noted an almost identical phenomenon in Liberia, where "oversized Volkswagen busses all had one thing in common. They all had a desire to squeeze as many people and animals uncomfortably in them as humanly possible."[52] The volunteers all seemed to forget that these countries were poor and could not afford brand new transportation systems. Instead, they focused on the strange, exotic preference the people had for this type of transportation. While volunteers virtually never criticized the people in the third world, they seemed to believe it was acceptable to frown on the bus service.

In Nigeria, they complained about a bus system they felt was "chaotic and uncomfortable." The evaluator sent to Nigeria sneered at the volunteers for this, because it meant that they were "weak" and could not survive the rough, frontier conditions. The evaluator also believed that carping about the transportation system was tantamount to disparaging the local culture. He did not accept the volunteers' apparent separation between their accepting views of people and their derogatory opinions about the busses.

Some volunteer writing varied slightly from this theme. In the Philippines, Margot Marrow complained about the "jeepneys," U.S. Army jeeps that had been converted for mass transportation and were "always jammed full."[53] Kevin Haverty traveled by truck in Bolivia and was "almost buried, crushed and nearly suffered a leg amputation" because the truck was so full of people and animals.[54] In Afghanistan it was a frightening ride in a cab and another on the national airline, "a pretty shaky outfit."[55] Another related that this same airline was known in the Peace Corps as "Inshallah (if Allah wills) airlines."[56]

Volunteers felt it especially necessary to comment on the quasi-modern transportation during their vacation time. In Niger, Mark Simpson survived "a harrowing, grueling trip on the remaining 120 km from In Gall to Agadez. The road is the worst I've ever been on—there were many swampy areas where we sank deep in the mud and crawled along at a snail's pace in 4 wheel drive, and 3 or 4 times we forded raging torrents."[57]

Arnold Zeitlin describes in a blur of detail a trip through West Africa, complete with lorry rides, ferry rides, and exotic food. At one point, he and his wife had their choice of two boats to ferry them across a lake. "At the lake shore," he recalls, "we rented a hollowed-log canoe, which a schoolboy propelled with a lollipop paddle. It was so much more African than the power launch with the frigid canopy also offered us."[58] Given a choice between something quasi-modern and a canoe straight out of a storybook, Zeitlin chose the canoe. Volunteers were not prepared for anything modern and had difficulty accepting that modern conveniences could be a genuine aspect of a third world culture. The canoe was more "African" because it reflected the volunteer preconception of the meaning of Africa. Here we see the tension over values played out in a different way. In effect, the volunteers rejected something that was African, because it did not seem African enough. They thought that by choosing the canoe, they were showing their preference for traditional African society. In order to appease their need to accept all culture, they rejected a modern African reality for a bygone African fantasy.

Leonard Levitt had a different kind of unexpected experience during his travels in South Africa. At the home of a white farmer, he relaxed and struck up a conversation: "Suddenly I didn't want to think about Tanganyika [where his project was] or think about its problems. It was too nice sitting there on the terrace." He made these comments even though he had to listen to the farmer telling him that the only way to treat Africans was to beat them. Sitting in the lap of luxury in the middle of Africa was so contrary to his expectations that he became momentarily dazed.[59] Of course, the moral of this story is that he eventually snapped out of it and returned with a greater sense of purpose to his job with the Tanganyikan students. But here we see a hint of a phenomenon common to many volunteers—they did not find a frontier world, only a vastly different world that they could not comprehend.

Living conditions surprised volunteers most of all. As we saw in examining their training, they had been prepared to live a spartan existence. Some found that living the rustic life sounded much better in principle than it was in reality. A volunteer in the Philippines described how a combination of nasty realities almost drove her home: "When faced with rotten teeth, foul breath, smells, sores, filth, rags, I couldn't take it. I was astonished to find my reactions were so diametrically opposed to my ideals. . . . I simply and truthfully hated it all, wanted to go home, and the only thing stopping me was pride."[60] Rather than finding Micronesia to be a primitive paradise, Nancy Caswell described it as "an incredibly dirty place" where "people defecated on the ground."[61] While believing in principle that they should accept all local customs, some volunteers could not accept them in real life.

Some decided they wanted none of these conditions and quit the Peace Corps. Julia, a volunteer in Guatemala, left because life there was "different from what she had pictured. She was alone, the food was poor; she had to draw water from a well. There was no bathing or shower facilities."[62] Another volunteer came close to leaving due to being "sick and hot and alone in the summer," but he was saved because of "endurance and a black sense of humor."[63]

Even many who never considered leaving barely recovered from the shock of their living conditions. Rachel Cowan commented, "The first community we visited was the most depressing place I have ever seen. . . . They were living in an actual garbage dump."[64] Volunteers found that poverty was not romantic, even strange third world poverty. Seth Tillman, a staffer for the Senate Foreign Relations Committee, found this to be the volunteers' opinion during a fact-finding trip in 1969. He wrote: "Wallowing in slums never was a very good idea; it was romantic, unnatural, unrewarding. There is nothing good about poverty. . . . The proper charge for the Volunteer is not to plunge into poverty but to help its victims climb out of it."[65]

Not only the sights of the area were depressing, but often the tastes were as well. Moritz Thomsen was so exasperated at the meagerness of his first meals that he wanted to "cry like a baby and later, if you are strong enough, begin stamping your little feet on the floor in baby rage."[66] Many realized that they could not escape these conditions. The weather, unchanged by air conditioning or even fans, took care of that. In India, "by the end of may the heat had obliterated curiosity. As the dry heat intensified, everything shriveled up—our bodies couldn't pump sweat fast enough."[67] In North Africa, the "howl of the harmattan blowing sand through the house" made life Hell for Michael Parrish.[68]

Even evaluators, expecting to find primitive conditions, occasionally found something so shocking as to jar their senses. Herb Wegner, while traveling through Peru, found a town that to live in "even for a period of a week would be an experience which would call for the depths of devotion to the Peace Corps ideal. Their living quarters are characterized by a fantastic aggregation of historical and contemporary filth."[69] The ideal he refers to is living a spartan life. In reality, people in the third world often did not live a spartan life, they lived a poor, exploited life. Their culture was not romantic, only depressed. Volunteers also occasionally got tossed into situations of uncommon deprivation or destruction, such as those serving in Nigeria during the Biafran civil war. Linda Muller traveled through the war zone and was shocked: "To see one killed child or a block of burned homes would have been depressing, but the unending damage was absolutely devastating. In some ways, I feel 10 years older this week."[70]

But most volunteers who viewed such carnage or lived in depressing conditions survived and even thrived. Volunteers had, after all, been trained to persevere in the worst conditions and help teach others how to persevere in them. Even if the beginning of the road to development was uglier than expected, it was still the starting point of a straightforward path with a more positive end point. Frederick McCluskey asked, "The living conditions depress us, but do they depress the people who live in them? How can we be of any use here if we are not here to introduce some of the niceties of American culture?"[71] McCluskey reveals here his inner tension over the question of imparting American values. In one breath, he argues that volunteers must not impose their opinions about living conditions on their hosts, while in the very next sentence he argues that it was his job to give the locals American niceties.

Living in outwardly familiar surroundings proved to be a more formidable obstacle. After arriving in Somalia, one volunteer immediately proclaimed that her living quarters were "a far cry from our original ideas of life in the Peace Corps," because they lived in a "beautiful house near the ocean in a grove of trees, with a view of the city and the ocean."[72] Many landed in the lap of luxury rather than in a mud hut. Lillian Carter raved over her situation: "A three bedroom flat (for two volunteers), kitchen and bath, and we have a balcony. The furniture is beautiful, the fabrics are handwoven and exquisite."[73]

Some volunteer descriptions sound more like real estate ads than descriptions of primitive housing. Arnold Zeitlin wrote: "The living room–dining room was 25 by 15 feet. . . . The garage had sliding doors. . . . Linoleum tiles lined the kitchen floor. The toilet flushed and the bathroom had sink, tub and shower with cold running water."[74] During their rigorous training, most volunteers would have been incredulous that they were going to live someplace with a garage, much less one with sliding doors! One volunteer in Nepal settled in the middle of a historic fantasy, in a house within a bazaar with "yellow mortar balconies; the middle one is mine. My neighbors have hand carved ones, possibly 13th or 10th century ones."[75]

Hilary Whitaker wrote an entire letter to her family describing her wonderful house. The only thing she could not decide, she confessed, was the type of furniture to put in it: "Most people have really simple Danish modern but I'm not sure I want that."[76]

The volunteers in these situations invariably described the positive attributes of the structure of the house. Whether "small but comfortable" or "bright and spacious," many lived in solid homes that often could only be described as "middle class."[77] One couple even lived in a "palatial" house that was "like living in a fortress."[78]

Most ironically, a great number of volunteers insisted they lived better on their Peace Corps assignment than they had back in the United States. Frank Brechin contended, "I live so much better than I did for those three years in Kalamazoo that there is no comparison."[79] College towns fared especially poorly in comparison to overseas assignments: "Often you live in accommodations that would be considered comfortable in most of America, if not luxurious compared with student apartments in Berkeley, Ann Arbor or Iowa City."[80] Volunteers had already lived a sparse lifestyle in college and were surprised to learn that life in the third world could be considerably more comfortable than their former Bohemian existence. One volunteer even compared her suburb of Acra, Ghana, to "Ardmore, Scarsdale, Lake Forest, Silver Spring, etc."[81]

Many volunteers came to believe that in outward appearance, their host countries were not very different from the United States: "The buildings are the same, the people dress the same, there are cars, bikes, busses, policemen, airplanes, etc."[82] Their complaints sound familiar to anyone who has lived in a big city. For example, one volunteer claimed, "Housing is nearly impossible to find in this city. . . . Some Volunteers here are too tempted to go to restaurants and get into debt."[83] Yet these same volunteers suffered culture shock, not because their surroundings were so different, but because they had been totally unprepared that they might be in many ways the same.

Guilt about their living conditions gnawed at volunteers. Many could not adjust to what one evaluator referred to as the "opulence shock" since it was so foreign to their conception of how a volunteer should live.[84] Christopher Wiles wrote letters home from Uruguay describing his comfortable living situation. "Not only has this brought on a few sarcastic comments from those at home," he lamented, "but it has also helped contribute to my own doubt of whether my Peace Corps service justifies itself."[85] Volunteers were conditioned by training and by understanding the Peace Corps dictum that they should live the stern life. When they did not live such a life, they felt like phony Peace Corps volunteers. Leon Weintraub, a teacher in Monrovia,

Volunteer Gail Egan shops at a Kenyan market in 1969. She seems to fit the stereotype of pioneering volunteer, but in fact, she lived in an "old English settlers' house," where her housekeeper did the cooking. Photo by Biddle, courtesy National Archives.

reported his dilemma: "How could I function successfully unless I lived in a mud and stick house with hot and cold running cockroaches? How could I be a successful volunteer unless I was in the bush?"[86]

Some volunteers had a bigger problem. Not only did they have a nice house, they employed servants as well. In the Ivory Coast in 1963, "all the Volunteers lived in European style houses with running water. Like many volunteers elsewhere, Volunteers have servants to wash and cook."[87] Ed Smith estimated that 90 percent of the volunteers in Ghana had a steward to wash clothes.[88] The evaluator in 1962 for the Cameroons claimed, "Every volunteer employs servants and in one case five volunteers have three servants, a cook, a houseboy and a small boy."[89] Bill Moyers was so shocked at this revelation that he scrawled a large exclamation point in the margin. The Peace Corps leadership did not envision their pioneers needing servants. They envisioned self-sufficient, egalitarian volunteers, and stooping to the level of needing servants was beyond the pale.

Outsiders could not reconcile the reality of servants with their image of volunteers. A photographer from *Time* came to Tom Livingston's village and insisted that he take a picture of Livingston drawing water from the town well. The photographer "wanted to show us roughing it in darkest Africa. But we weren't going into darkest Africa at all. It was highly civilized." Livingston refused to pose for the picture. He had two servants, one to draw water and do other household chores, the other to cook. He originally balked at the idea, but his headmaster convinced him that without them, he "wouldn't have time to prepare a lesson."[90]

Whether acceptable or not, many volunteers felt the need to hire a servant. One couple hired a servant to "cook, serve, clean, launder, market and iron."[91] Leonard Levitt's houseboy went to the market, went to the river to get water, did the cooking, and warmed up the water for his afternoon showers.[92] Volunteers did not hire these servants on a whim. Many believed that without a servant, they would spend so much time on chores that they could not effectively work on their project. A teacher in Sierra Leone "found carrying water, laundering, filling kerosene tanks, etc. from the village too much for me, so I have a man to do the chores."[93] They concluded that doing their job was more important than serving as an example of egalitarian American values.

Hiring a servant did not come easy to volunteers indoctrinated to be self-sufficient. Carl Pope asked himself, "What the hell are you doing with a cook? I did not want to identify myself with the people in Barhi who had cooks; they were the ruling class. I had not come to rule. But I had come to work. . . . To work we had to eat. The cleaning and sifting of rice . . . took two or three hours of labor. So we found ourselves plunged in a master servant relationship."[94] Pope did not believe in this relationship, but felt he had no choice. Some locals assumed that as Americans, the volunteers would want servants. They began to do work for them, even without asking. The Cowans faced this problem in Ecuador. When a local woman asked for a permanent job, wrote Paul Cowan, "it would have been cruel to refuse. . . . But I can't stand the relationship it suggests."[95]

The guilt caused by having servants eclipsed that of the volunteers who simply had nice houses. Some convinced themselves, as the Cowans did, that they were helping a host national and the host economy, and so no matter the relationship, having a servant was a good thing. A teacher in Somalia explained: "If our houseboy would save his earnings from us for two years, he could buy a donkey or a piece of land and go into business for himself."[96] Some leaders in the host countries also saw it this way, insisting that volunteers get servants. In Ghana, Arnold Zeitlin faced the firm orders of his counterpart that he hire a uniformed houseboy and fretted that he could not explain the "political dangers of a volunteer with a uniformed servant."[97] When a teacher in Togo refused to hire a houseboy, he was ridiculed by one of his fellow teachers, who asked, "What kind of a life is this you live without even a house boy?"[98]

Many were not prepared to be thrust into the position of master. Leonard Levitt explains how he felt the first time one of his servants did not do his job: "So how do you figure it? Be mean, treat them harshly? Or let up and find yourself in heaps of difficulty? They were almost like children. Or like slaves. Whoops, what am I saying?"[99] Levitt did not mention the word *slave* by accident. Americans in the 1960s could not accept slavery, even if it was an accepted relationship in the third world. Volunteers with servants were thus forced to deal with the incredible tension of how to effectively deal with their hires while at the same time respecting them as one of their hosts. Lederer and Burdick commented on volunteers in the Philippines who "were hesitant to exercise the proper degree of authority over their servants."[100] It's not clear how exercising authority would make volunteers anything but the type of ugly Americans Lederer and Burdick disliked, but they made this comment nonetheless.

The lives of some volunteers clashed with their expectations in ways beyond housing and servants. A few lived in what anyone would consider luxurious circumstances, while many concerned themselves more with material comforts than the image of a volunteer would suggest. Not surprisingly, many were "somewhat obsessed with the subject of food. It fills many of my conscious hours and most of my unconscious ones."[101] Whether living the spartan life or not, volunteers ate differently from what they were used to, and it had a great effect on some of them. Their letters home are filled with a stream of discussion about food, a common enough fixation of travelers but one not in keeping with the stoic and heroic Peace Corps image. Other creature comforts loomed large in the consciousness of volunteers. One in Iran complained about having to live with only bare light bulbs for light. Light bulbs "look better when you can't see them," he wrote, "but then, no one knows you have electricity."[102]

Medical care emerged as another central concern for volunteers. The agency insisted that each country have an American Peace Corps doctor at every volunteer's disposal. The volunteers always commented on the Peace Corps doctor at their end of service conferences, and medical care was virtually the only thing that all agreed was good about the Peace Corps.[103] If they had been pure pioneers, they would have been left totally alone out in the jungles of the world, fending for themselves whenever attacked by an exotic virus. If the Peace Corps leadership followed strictly the principles of universalism, they would have entrusted the health of the volunteers to local medicine. But in this case, practical considerations overcame philosophical purity. Many volunteers (to say nothing of their parents) refused to submit their well-being to a test of ideological integrity. So volunteers were given the most advanced medical treatment available, and for the most part they appreciated being well cared for, even at the risk of insulting their hosts.

Concern with material comforts went beyond necessities for some volunteers. As we have seen, transportation issues were crucial in the minds of some volunteers. One evaluator traveling through western Africa expressed with disdain that volunteers "defended their need for servants and good housing" and that "practically all of them felt that the Peace Corps should provide them with motorcycles or cars."[104] Many volunteers felt that to do their job, they needed motorized transport, or they would be spending most of their time traveling to and from their project.

Some volunteers became comfortable with amenities far beyond anything they would have ever dreamed possible for a third world country. In Afghanistan, "the Kabul Volunteers were preoccupied with the Peace Corps regulations about the use of swimming pools."[105] In Malaya, it was reported that "Jane is sharpening up her tennis eye and, bedecked in her tennis outfit, should stop something"; and John D., who complained about being off the beaten path, still managed time for plenty of swimming on his own private beach. In the same newsletter, another volunteer boasted, "They'll never top my cook!" and then complained about his "routine" life when he wasn't "playing golf a few times weekly."[106] Upon arrival in Tunisia, Philip Delfeld knew he would have to adjust his expectations, because rather than finding a country of desert nomads, he found "beautiful Mediterranean beaches, up-to-the-minute transportation facilities and good Arabic and French restaurants."[107]

David Schickele, in Nigeria, summed it up by declaring, "My life at Nsukka [a university in Nigeria] bore little resemblance to the publicized image of Peace Corps stoicism."[108] By 1966, even the *Volunteer* admitted: "In the early days of the Peace Corps, it was assumed that mere survival would be a major Volunteer accomplishment and that conditions of food, shelter and health would be the greatest problems. The report confirms that these problems were actually least among Volunteer worries."[109] Many wrote about the "fallacy of the self sacrificing volunteer" and took pains in letters home to point out how good their food, medical treatment, and housing were, especially compared to the life led by host-country nationals.[110]

Some seemed almost masochistic in their desire to tough it out: "Attracted in part by sacrifice, some volunteers have been made uneasy by the luxury of modest comfort. Life overseas is not necessarily a bed of nails."[111]

In fact, according to Jane Meleney, that life was "physically very easy." The difficult part for Jane was "the tortoise pace of life," because "many volunteers found it hardest to tone down their Yankee heritage of constant busyness."[112] For Jane, the outward similarities belied the cultural differences. Confused volunteers struggled to live in a world that seemed so much the same as their own yet was actually completely different.

In evaluation after evaluation throughout the decade, volunteers insisted that physical hardship did not overly concern them. For example, only 5 percent of the volunteers in the Philippines in 1963 said they had a problem with it.[113] In Ghana, their unanimous opinion on the harshness of the conditions was "less than I expected."[114] And in Guatemala, the only category on the completion-of-service questionnaire in which every volunteer answered "no problem at all" was physical hardships.[115]

Their letters consistently repeated that they did not suffer the expected hardships. Frederick McCluskey wrote, "The preconception I had of hardships, tropical climate, primitive conditions, pestilence, disease, starvation, etc., is false."[116] Volunteers were prepared for the worst in training. The Peace Corps gave them a medical kit, complete with snakebite kit and other paraphernalia to be used in remote conditions. Many either ignored this kit or found other uses for it. Wanda Montgomery used the little scalpel from the snakebite kit as a "screwdriver for that tiny screw in your transistor radio. . . . We don't see many snakes around here anyway." To make a doughnut hole, she continued, "Use the bottle of malaria suppressant pills." She said there was no other use for the bottle, since malaria was "well under control in this provincial town."[117]

Some volunteers, unable to relate to these strangely familiar yet different cultures, retreated into cultural isolation. Historian Gary May relates how volunteers in Ethiopia lived their lives exactly as if they were back in the United States. They "ate macaroni and cheese for dinner, after dinner the volunteers would play charades or bridge, eat popcorn or fudge, listen to the tunes of the Kingston Trio."[118] According to some observers, "parties, eating and drinking were more important to the lives of most volunteers than they had been in the United States" because there were fewer familiar diversions in countries isolated from much of American culture.[119]

Some volunteer parties were elaborate and extravagant. Volunteers felt comfortable attending parties held by other Americans, such as Frank Brechin, who looked forward to "Wednesday, when the Marines will have a real big party for just about everybody."[120] Esther Warber wrote enthusiastically of a jammed week of social activities: "Had two parties [in one week]—a house leaving on Friday for a young Peace Corps Volunteer couple and next night a hum-dinger of an apartment warming (my ex-roommate Grace), a 11th anniversary for our Peace Corps Representative and his wife and a birthday party for a Volunteer."[121]

The third world was not as remote from American influence as the volunteers had expected. Volunteer newsletters, common in many countries served by the Peace Corps, often read like social calendars. For example, in 1963 the Jamaica *Bullsheet* described a slew of parties, including one held by two volunteers described as "the party girls of 1962" in which the "food was superb, the music was divine, etc. Most of our bush-men attended."[122] Many volunteers did not give up the fast-paced social life traditional among Americans of their age.

For some, the relationships formed with other volunteers became the most important aspect of their Peace Corps reality. One wrote that she "really hated to leave the gang at Sokodé. The year just flew by. We had such wonderful discussions and danced the Charleston every night."[123] The Peace Corps leadership frowned on socializing amongst the volunteers. One evaluator criticized volunteers in Peru: "There was strong feeling on the part of the Representative that there was too much socializing among Volunteers."[124] Peace Corps ideology demanded that volunteers serve as lonely exemplars of American values, not ugly-American youths drinking and carousing on government pay. Peace Corps leaders actively discouraged social gatherings, and in doing so added to the bureaucratic wall that Shriver wanted so much to tear down.

Gary May has taken the fact that some volunteers brought with them the faults of American youth and expanded it into a critique of the entire Peace Corps idea. May's examination of volunteers in Ethiopia reveals that they were "ethnocentric" and "tended to Americanize their experience." In the end, the Peace Corps became just another example of American "cultural imperialism."[125] Yet it is not clear which values May is talking about. Some volunteers, as we have seen in this chapter, brought with them a materialistic mind-set. Others, as we have also seen, brought with them dreams of becoming a new American pioneer. May faults the Peace Corps for lacking a purified universalist ethic. Virtually all volunteers attempted to curb impulses toward cultural imperialism, even if they did not always succeed. As human beings, they struggled with inner tensions on this subject, rather than automatically forcing their culture on others or automatically accepting the culture of others.

Another aspect of volunteer life that surprised many was boredom. Leonard Levitt waxed poetic in his description of the doldrums he felt living on the Tanganyikan frontier: "I feel as though I have really come to the end of the world. And not just the end, but the beginning as well, where yesterday is today and today is tomorrow . . . day after day, month after month, year after year, generation after generation."[126] Boredom affected nearly all volunteers. According to an evaluation written by Efrem Siegal, "in Africa in general there seems to be a high incidence of boredom among the teachers."[127]

Many could not believe they were bored, even though they lived in surroundings that before arrival they would have considered exotic. According to another volunteer in Tanganyika, "If someone had told me I'd be bored sitting at the foot of Kilimanjaro with elands galloping around me, I would have said, 'You're out of your mind!' But believe me, I was bored."[128] Even the brightness and warmth of the tropics began to grate on volunteers, who complained about the "endless joyless sun."[129] No longer did serving in the most isolated place possible seem the most exciting assignment possible. In Ghana, Ed Smith prayed for a serious ear infection so he could travel the two hundred miles to Accra "just for some good company."[130]

Other volunteers felt depressed because they found no opportunities for intellectual stimulation. As Mark Simpson put it, "One of the biggest problems we have to face in this country is how to keep from getting bored."[131] The Peace Corps did not prepare the volunteers for this, assuming they would have plenty to keep them busy on the untamed frontier. Evaluations soon poured in suggesting otherwise, asserting, for example, that as many as "40% of the Volunteers overall" found lack of intellectual stimulation to be a problem.[132] The head of the Research Division, Dr. Joseph Colmen, declared that because volunteers lived "with limited sensory stimulation, one of the greatest problems faced by Volunteers overseas is the lack of intellectual stimulation."[133] The agency tried to ameliorate the problem by sending each volunteer a boot locker filled with books. Ironically, this unexpected program came to be one of the most successful aspects of Peace Corps work, since most of the books found their way into the hands of the host nationals and gave some libraries they hadn't had before.

Another reason for volunteer boredom came as even more of a surprise to both the Peace Corps and the volunteers. Some volunteers did not have enough work to do. In Somalia, they "discovered to their surprise that being a teacher was in many respects a tedious, tiring and humdrum round of activities, almost completely devoid of romance or adventure."[134] This runs counter to the frontier myth, for whatever else happened in the life of people on the frontier, they always had work to do. Some jobs were deliberately unstructured, causing volunteers to wonder, "What do I do when I start working? After breakfast in the morning what do I do? I find myself somewhat bored with the way things are going so far."[135] The Peace Corps expected that such volunteers, using their ingenuity, would invent things to do. Yet, unlike real pioneers, volunteers felt no necessity to do so. Their morale deteriorated accordingly.[136] Even when working, some found their work less than stimulating. One volunteer sighed, "My God, I was getting tired of talking about chickens."[137]

Even when they were surrounded by people, volunteers often felt isolated. They were so much the center of attention, they could do very little without being watched and evaluated. They were always on stage, and many chose to retreat from meaningful activity rather than have their activity become the object of discussion. Siegal illustrates his point by relating an anecdote about a volunteer who resigned because he felt like he was living in a fishbowl. Nearly every day "he was asked to marry someone's daughter and bring her to the United States."

His story was unique only in that the fishbowl existence led to his resignation. Raymond Stock, serving in Ethiopia, lamented, "After two weeks in Africa I am sick at heart. . . . Everywhere you are singled out as different and there is no privacy."[138] Even retreating into one's own room did not seem to help. Chad Bardone noted, "Physically, my room affords no corner in which I can shut myself from the rest of the world. People always want to know what a Peace Corps Volunteer is doing."[139]

Lack of work, lack of intellectual stimulation, and lack of privacy forced volunteers to focus on their isolation. Ed Smith tried hard to avoid "that deep down ache" that compelled him "to down vast portions of corn liquor and stumble drunkenly through more of Dunbar [the name of a book's author] until dawn began to sneak over the horizon."[140] Moritz Thomsen also believed that drinking represented "a real peak of excitement and release in a week of suffocating and crushing monotony."[141] Others, like Lillian Carter, became schizophrenic: "I have had four days of complete inertia caused by homesickness and no mail. . . . Nobody loves me, I am forgotten, I hate Mabel's [her roommate] guts, they push me too hard here, no food, no clothes. . . . Letter from home! I'm pepped up, everybody loves me, I don't have much to do, Mabel is sweet."[142] Americans in general and the Peace Corps leaders in particular did not expect volunteers to be drunk or crazy. The psychiatrists at training worked especially hard to prevent these problems, and very few volunteers suffered seriously from them. But many did have problems, many of which stemmed from a lack of understanding about what they were getting into. Few dreamed beforehand that every night they would have to deal with "terrifying boredom" and crawl "back to the pit and the mosquitoes and the worms and the deadly silence of another African bush night."[143]

The third world encountered by the volunteers failed to match their expectations. They came to develop an untrammeled, undeveloped frontier and move the third world along on the straightforward line of development. They ended up living in places that confounded their expectations and confused them about the mission of the Peace Corps. The scale of development in their host country, often completely at odds with their expectations, frustrated and confused volunteers. They faced a series of choices in living their lives overseas that challenged their assumptions on how cultures interacted with one another. A few retreated from these confusing, complicated, seemingly mixed-up places by dancing the Charleston or golfing every week. Most attempted to deal with this unique situation as best they could, learning from their unexpected predicament. As they left their not-so-humble homes every day, they found they had even more to learn at work.

"Which One Is Really the Underdeveloped Country?"

Working in the Third World

FRONTIER WORK

Many volunteers arrived at their projects bursting with idealism, hoping that training had readied them for the rigors of hard labor in the isolated outback of the third world. Others wondered if training had adequately prepared them for their specific job. Their living situations might have been confusing, yet all looked forward to improving the lives of people they might not have fully understood, but that they believed needed help. They were convinced that through unstinting effort, they could help their host country develop in a straightforward fashion. Work, they believed, lay at the heart of their Peace Corps existence.

But even more than living conditions, the work performed by volunteers led to disillusionment and frustration. Just as in the way they lived, volunteers learned through the way they worked that development was not straightforward and that they could not always produce the desired results. The work experience led volunteers to begin to develop a new theory of interacting with their hosts, not tied to ideas of national development, but rather to ideas of individual fulfillment.

The Peace Corps leadership intended volunteers to distill "American" values of flexibility and hard work into their jobs. Working with such values would have the dual advantage of showing people in the third world the American path of development and help the American volunteers themselves remember their hard-working roots. Again, development work would not be easy, but it would follow a time-worn and straightforward path.

Ironically, in asking volunteers to fill the prescribed role, the Peace Corps worked against some of the very values they sought to foster. Volunteers hoped to experience "individualism in the raw, working like silhouetted surveyors striding into Tanganyikan sunsets," but what they found instead was a not very glamorous job of mid-level technical assistance, becoming a "Borneo version of the All-American 'Organization Man.'"[1] Despite the leaders' desire for the Peace Corps to remain a loosely knit organization, most volunteers, from community developers to teachers, felt they operated under narrow bureaucratic constraints. These constraints did not translate into tightly focused job descriptions. Rather, volunteers were expected to meet specific requirements while working on vague jobs. They encountered a muddled agenda and tremendous confusion about whether they were supposed to change local values or leave them alone.

Many encountered jobs so nebulous as to defy description. Robert Gaudino wrote, "It seems entirely impossible for anyone to comprehend what type of work we have come to perform."[2] The Peace Corps did not make the mistake of proposing a single, coherent plan for dealing with the third world's problems. Rather, they elevated what they believed to be a quintessential American virtue, flexibility, into a supreme value for the Peace Corps volunteer. This approach frustrated volunteers, because if they could not describe what they were doing, they could not justify their work. How could they convince their friends and family that they were achieving their goals of helping the third world if they could not even describe their job?

Volunteers often questioned the purpose of their work. In India, one wrote: "It all depends on what we're here to do. Are we here to do a job? Are we here to make friends? Are we here to get a feeling for the Indian people?"[3] One group even joked at the end of their project that they believed their only purpose was entertainment, a sort of government-sponsored exhibit of rich Americans for the local populace to gawk at.[4]

Sometimes the volunteers had assigned work to do—they just were not sure what it was. Peace Corps Washington realized this was happening. One evaluation noted, "The Volunteers from the outset were thrown into jobs that did not exist."[5] Many project assignments lacked definition or structure due, at least in part, to a conscious decision by Peace Corps leadership. The *Volunteer* described how this worked for a group in Nepal. They were purposely put in jobs in which they had to "use initiative and imagination. Success of the Volunteer depends especially on flexibility, patience and effort. All Volunteers need similar imagination in developing their jobs."[6] In other words, Peace Corps leaders expected volunteers to use the ingenuity and resourcefulness inherent in all Americans and gained from their pioneering forbears.

The only rule that many volunteers felt they were supposed to follow in their jobs was to follow the dictates of this image. This meant hard, backbreaking work. When conjuring up the image of a Peace Corps volunteer at work, most Americans probably would have thought of volunteers digging ditches in the hot tropical sun. An evaluator claimed that for one group of geologists in Ghana, "a picture story of them in action would go well in the *National Geographic*. . . . Volunteers bringing up gold from the earth along stream banks in the rain forests of the Ashanti. . . . The work sounds exotic and exciting. And it is, when one considers the land, the people, the snakes and the animals."[7] One of the first groups of volunteers, working as surveyors in Tanganyika, had difficulty finishing their job because they were "occasionally driven off by curious elephants wandering too close for comfort."[8]

Even those who worked with their bare hands in the hard earth often found the jobs did not match expectations. Farming in the 1960s did not resemble farming on the mythic American frontier. One volunteer created a very complicated farming plan for his area involving "many agricultural techniques to which the people were not accustomed. It called for the use of nitrate and superphosphate fertilizers, which they had hardly ever used before. . . . Weed killers and disinfectants were also used to test their effectiveness."[9] Another volunteer boasted that the key to farming was not necessarily sweat and hard work, but "getting the strongest insecticide you can, preferably a spray. I use malathion. . . . At the first sign of insects or nibbling, spray heavily."[10] The volunteers worked with the most modern, developed farming methods, including heavy use of pesticides. Unfamiliar with Rachel Carson's *Silent Spring*, just gaining wide popularity and acceptance in the United States, the volunteers did not know what Carson had proved—that pesticide use might represent a step backward in human "progress," rather than a key step forward.

By the late 1960s, the Peace Corps leadership, always attuned to the latest political trends, tried to capitalize on the burgeoning conservation movement spawned in part by the publishing of Carson's book. But contrary to the goals of that movement, volunteers worked on projects more befitting the pioneer reality of exploiting resources than the new ethic of protecting them. One forester worked to change the view of forests in Peru from a preservationist ethic to the more American ideal of sustained use. While the Peruvians' old ethic aimed at the "protection of the existing forest resource,"

Volunteer Kirby Nichol supervises training for the Thai national track team, which he did in addition to his work as a college teacher. Volunteers filled many jobs that did not fit the popular "mud hut" image. Photo by Feldman, 1968, courtesy National Archives.

the volunteer worked hard for change, and by the end of his tenure, he declared: "We are now within two months of completing the most modern sawmill in Peru."[11] Other conservationist volunteers worked on increasing tourist visits to national parks and developing the tourist potential of newly designated wilderness areas.

Dirtying their hands in third world forests was not the only way volunteers were supposed to use American ingenuity. Another group of volunteers was assigned to work in a body shop, helping locals learn how to fix the busses of the new Kabul bus service. A letter from Frank Brechin shows that the work was not so simple: "Things at work are the same—terrible. I really don't know if I just can't take it anymore. . . . I want so badly to make it a good shop but I don't feel like I'm getting enough support from my Afghan superiors."[12] Peace Corps projects never existed in a vacuum, and the bureaucracy and politics many volunteers had to deal with often proved overwhelming.

Not all road surveyors had to deal with elephants, like the team in Tanganyika. Will Weiss was assigned to help build a system of roads in Malaya. Yet he was put in an office to do his job, where he remembered hot days working on surveying crews in his native Oregon. "Today," he thought to himself, "I operate my slide rule in the cool comfort of a modern, air conditioned office building. . . . Wait a minute, which one is really the underdeveloped country?"[13]

In fact, many projects involved working in offices. One volunteer, sent to Kenya to work on agricultural projects, expected to toil in the tropical sun. Instead, he ended up "setting up and running a department in the Ministry of Agriculture to produce educational materials—audiovisual aids."[14] One group in Jamaica worked as librarians at the Institute of Jamaica, a small-scale version of the Smithsonian. Because they were conditioned and trained to expect more vigorous work, office jobs caused a feeling of guilt. One of the Jamaican volunteers asked himself, "What am I doing living and working with middle class people who are not unlike those at home?" and admitted feeling self-conscious because of his "soft assignment."[15] Rather than always laboring with the poor or underprivileged, some volunteers found themselves working with the elite. One served as an athletics coach in an area where it was "difficult to imagine the need for any kind of community development."[16]

As in their living situations, many volunteers found the world turned upside down in their working situations. William Friedland describes a major breach of etiquette committed by a group of volunteer nurses sent to Tanganyika, a country situated in the heart of America's vision of deepest, darkest Africa. Upon their arrival at work at a hospital in Dar Es Salaam, the nurses failed to stand when the matron entered the room. "This behavior," according to Friedland, "understandable in the mores of American nursing practice, represented the apogee of bad behavior."[17] The Americans were considered uncivilized in this part of Africa, where people had retained certain cultural formalities from the British colonial past.

Volunteers may not have been able to describe exactly what they were doing, but they did know that they were not toiling like nineteenth-century American pioneers. Researchers from the Peace Corps Evaluation Division found this a nagging concern of all the volunteers they talked to. Jane Campbell, in a synopsis of a completion-of-service conference for Nigeria in 1963, wrote: "They were pretty cynical about the image of a Peace Corps Volunteer who is an adventurous, physically tough, inventive genius who lives abroad in romantic poverty changing the world into a model of American democracy. . . . They feel that far more attention deserves to be given the actual job they are performing in the host country."[18] Most volunteers worked at jobs that did not fit this image and resented feeling jealous of it. They were not "a bunch of self sacrificing pioneers . . . working our hands

Volunteer Bob Weiss's work experience could have been lifted straight from the pages of *The Ugly American*. Here he works with a Masai farmer in Kenya on an ingenious water pump. Photo by Biddle, 1970, courtesy National Archives.

to blisters but people with faults and weaknesses, as well as strengths and fine points."[19]

For the most part, volunteers just wanted to do their job and have a little fun while doing it. "Give me no tales of sacrifices," declared Mary Williams. "Despite momentary frustrations and loneliness, we're having a damned good time."[20] Many continued to believe that "the isolated rural village is a pleasant thought," but understood it was "not a realistic approach to the real problems with which we felt we should be dealing."[21]

The only structure that the Peace Corps idea put on the job, the image of the hard-working pioneer, was rejected early by volunteers, most of whom attempted to put an alternative structure onto their jobs. The specific jobs became more important than the overall image the volunteers were projecting, and they cared little whether they fit Shriver's frontier image. Strangely enough, this attitude confused some evaluators. Jane Campbell commented with surprise that in the Philippines, all four groups she interviewed were "decidedly job oriented."[22] According to Robert Gaudino, more than 60 percent of the volunteers in India believed the Peace Corps' biggest contribution was "specific contributions of specific jobs."[23] Although some hankered after "something more than doing well [their] mundane professional duties," all seemed to believe that doing those duties well came first.[24] Volunteers also came to believe that educating themselves was important to their jobs. This was first a means to an end—volunteers could do a better job working with the locals if they understood local culture. But education also became an end in itself as volunteers learned the weakness of development as a reason for their work and the reciprocal importance of cultural awareness. Volunteers in the two most widespread job classifications in the Peace Corps—community development and teaching—rejected liberal development ideas and replaced them with ideas of task-oriented work and cultural awareness.

COMMUNITY DEVELOPMENT

One job that seemed to fit the structure of the Peace Corps image was community development. We saw earlier how the goals and philosophy of this idea meshed so well with Shriver's goals for the Peace Corps as a whole. Community development was designed to foster frontier qualities in the host nationals. The Peace Corps seemed the perfect vehicle for this, the volunteers leading by example, showing the locals how an American conquers frontiers so they could do the same. Community development also dovetailed nicely with the leaders' squeamishness about forcing American values on other peoples, since nothing could be done without the active approval of the locals. In sum, community development provided a microcosm of the entire Peace Corps idea of development in the third world.

Because the fit seemed so perfect, most analysts at the time believed "community development is probably the most exciting field of Peace Corps endeavor."[25] Analysts found anecdotal and empirical evidence that the connection worked. For example, Morris Stein told a story of a volunteer who walked to and from his project, a distance of 10 km, every other day, meeting and prodding the junta to accomplish tasks, and who had time to teach English on the side. Here is the hero volunteer, living the image by working hard and stretching himself to the limit. According to Stein, such volunteers were common in community development in Colombia, where they built forty-four schools, twenty-seven aqueducts, two hundred miles of rural road, and over one thousand latrines in the first four years of work.[26] Such accomplishments coincide with the Peace Corps of popular imagination and Shriver's expectations.

Frank Mankiewicz, who helped invent the concept, served as the agency's point man for community development. Like other Peace Corps leaders, he thought in big terms: "Our mission is essentially revolutionary," he wrote. "The ultimate aim of community development is nothing less than a complete change, reversal—or a revolution if you wish—in the social and economic patterns of the countries to which we are accredited."[27] Community development would change the political, social, and economic relationships in the third world and make them more like those in the United States. Volunteers were taught the "hope that North American efficiency would quickly conquer the Latins' more convoluted form of bureaucratic behavior." They could accomplish this because, as volunteers were told, "These people will follow the example you set."[28]

This idea was not unsophisticated cultural imperialism. Community developers were trained, almost brainwashed, not to force their ideas on the locals. Self-help keyed the entire concept. One community developer in Colombia summed up the creed that became a mantra for so many: "Our objective is to improve their capacity to think and act for themselves, to recognize and deal with their problems. Community development is guiding the people in the villages to become self-reliant."[29] Volunteers carried this philosophy to extremes. Kirby Jones told the story of a house that almost did not get built. The volunteers in the area, believing that "the house *must* be built by the people,"[30] could only act as a catalyst for the construction. As a result, it took almost two years to build the most basic of houses.

Even though volunteers did not practice cultural imperialism in the strictest sense, community development theory taught them that through their shining example, volunteers would convince the locals to act like Americans. The theory was that if they did so, they could also develop as Americans had. Logically, all the locals had to do was follow the lead of pioneering Americans and they could conquer their frontier as well. Americans would not force the natives to follow these ideas, which would be followed because they worked. Living the image would show the locals how to be pioneers.

Unfortunately, the realities of community development work in the third world of the 1960s did not match the expectations of the Peace Corps leaders or the volunteers. Some found their assigned job completed before they arrived. As community developers, they were supposed to convince the locals to organize themselves, adding structure to a chaotic society. But many of the societies were not chaotic. Paul Cowan noted with discouragement, "There were, if anything, too many organizations in the suburbios" when he arrived.[31] Fred McCluskey was surprised to find that "all the ingredients of good community development theory are [already] present—widespread community participation, democratic organization, cooperation of agencies outside the community." Before he even began to work, then, he realized "what appears to be a model self-help project is actually a rather lame duck."[32] As with their living conditions, volunteers did not find the third world mired at some early stage of underdevelopment. Rather, they found an odd and confusing mix of "developed" and "undeveloped" institutions and cultural ideas.

McCluskey also commented on an aspect of community development that would have horrified Mankiewicz and Shriver. Community development theory required the locals to help themselves. But nothing substantial could be built, not a house, not a school, not a road, unless large numbers of locals agreed to help themselves. As when any group project is attempted, arm-twisting occurred. According to McCluskey, this caused problems: "People resist being regimented into work squads to work for community action just as the Chinese and Russians resisted working in the national communes."[33] Communist communes were the antithesis of what Shriver and Mankiewicz had in mind, but the reality of the third world did not always coincide with the ideas of the Peace Corps leadership.

Lack of structure permeated Peace Corps projects, but none struggled more with a lack of structure in their jobs than community development volunteers. After all, what was their job? To be an example? To show the locals how to think for themselves? In the best of circumstances, this sounds nebulous. Development was a clear, linear concept, but no theorist was ever able to show volunteers how to apply this linear concept to a three-dimensional world. Some groups stumbled from the beginning, never realizing what they were supposed to do. The volunteers in Peru "came expecting fairly well defined jobs, and found the government and community agencies they were to work with not expecting them. Although nominally trained in community development, they underwent some unhappy first weeks trying to find a job they could structure themselves into."[34] Apparently, this problem never went away and may have even worsened, because two years later, also in Peru, evaluator O. M. Scruggs noted, "This group was trained (if this is the word) to find out the tools, or distribute the tools, or be the tools (who knows, the group apparently never learned) in a project of rural community development."[35]

Assorted odd jobs provided the main tasks on many projects. Richard Lazarus described some of his typical duties: "I always seemed to be on the run visiting communities, talking to groups and individuals, teaching Junta presidents how to run a meeting, and teaching them how to write a solicitous letter to an organization, etc."[36] This motley collection of mundane tasks frustrated volunteers, in large part because it contrasted with the image of doing big things to help the third world. The glacial pace of progress gnawed at the conscience of some. David Nelson, in a letter to his parents, complained, "This last week I've done nothing (or so it seems). I just got a little more done on the smokeless stove and just about finished the well (the hole that is)."[37] Expecting that they could steadily move the locals along the scale of progress, volunteers had doubts when they could not observe this movement. Many Peace Corps projects lacked structure or a grand design, failing to live up to the dramatic expectations of the volunteers.

For some, the problems became acute because the Peace Corps decided that community development was the perfect place for volunteers with no technical expertise: the B.A. generalists, who had no special training in foreign development, teaching, building, or anything else. In an issue of the *Volunteer*, Louis Rapoport discussed the implications of being a B.A. generalist in community development: "No one really knows what community development entails, and who is better qualified for an undefined project than an undefined person?" Rapoport readily admitted that he "could do absolutely nothing of a practical nature." Far from being a pioneering jack-of-all-trades, he claimed to be a clod around the garage. Nonetheless, he was assigned to a construction project and "tried to fake his way by dropping words like hammer, cement, and wrench." In the end the project failed, in part due to his incompetence.[38]

Sending B.A. generalists to work on vague projects was a recipe for failure. After their service, many community developers concluded, "Attacking a specific problem with a concrete program would be much better than the haphazard approach that often seems to be used now."[39] After the 1960s, one Peace Corps staffer admitted, "The Peace Corps hurled thousands of BA generalist volunteers, like infantry storming a beachhead, into its own murky and ill-defined version of CD [community development]."[40]

As with Peace Corps jobs in general, community developers endured frustration over the slow pace of their work. At one point, Fred McCluskey ended a letter to his family, which he decorated with sad and angry self portraits, with the lament, "I bet you all feel better than I do." Five months later he continued to languish because "the work, community development, continues to go slow and has many frustrations. We are plagued on the one hand by lack of contact with technical and material aid and on the other by an indifferent attitude among local people."[41] His last point stands out as the most incongruous. How can a community developer survive if the locals don't care? Volunteer community developers failed to anticipate this. They expected the people to be eager to learn ways to conquer their frontier. Volunteers had trouble realizing that for some locals, the frontiers, such as they were, could not be conquered in any teachable way by American volunteers.

Despite these obstacles, the Peace Corps leadership often demanded concrete results from community development jobs. One report recorded that the group "objected strongly to what they called a continuous pressure to produce projects for the sake of projects."[42] Many volunteers felt that the Peace Corps wanted to tabulate completed projects to prove to the world that the agency was helping these countries civilize and move along the scale of development. Some volunteers felt guilty if they did not live up to the goals they felt pressured to accomplish. Fred McCluskey, in another letter expressing his disappointment in himself, described his life as "pretty dead." He explained: "It's true, we are living the way the Colombians live and we are living with Colombians. But we haven't started any revolutions or community development projects. In short, we have made lots of visits and speeches and acquaintances but no action—no schools built, roads built or agriculture improved."[43]

In reality, community development did not provide the vehicle through which volunteers could live the pioneer image. No matter how hard volunteers worked at it, they could not always convince the locals to act to help themselves. Or, as Chad Bardone put it, "Unfortunately, a lot of programs fall on their face as soon as the Peace Corps Volunteer leaves."[44] The host-country nationals did not automatically accept everything the volunteers wanted to impart. One couple in Peru finally came close to giving up because of the intransigence of the "Directora" of the school. They believed she was "incapable of running a school. She is a tired old woman who needs a rest. We are trying to organize and push a stronger PTA who will take more interest in the problems of the school—including a new Directora."[45] They wanted one of the classic tools of community development, a local organization (the Parent-Teachers Association), to act to eliminate one of their own. Many volunteers believed the community development model would not work because it did not attack the real problems of the host country. In Guatemala, "the volunteers were of the opinion that the present techniques we use to promote social mobilization tend to be naive and ineffective."[46]

The locals, volunteers complained, were immune to change. Community developers working in agriculture found the going roughest. One volunteer introduced concepts to local farmers that seemed eminently logical to both the volunteer and the farmers. He then planted and cultivated the crop himself, showing them it was possible. But, even though "the farmers of Monte Plata told us they thought it would grow, they have never tried it and they—like a lot of farmers everywhere—were reluctant to try something unfamiliar."[47]

Other volunteers convinced some locals to change their ways, only to find they had unleashed a new series of problems. Moritz Thomsen tells of one local, Ramón, who followed his instructions and examples more closely than anyone else in the town. Ramón was rewarded with a modicum of financial success. Yet he was also rewarded with a new way of thinking that was not necessarily "more developed" than the old. "Before you came," Ramón whined, "well, you know how poor I was; I had nothing. But I was happy; I lived without worries. But now. My God, I am half crazy with worry."[48] Thomsen had made Ramón into a petty capitalist, complete with stress and anxiety. No matter how the agency and the volunteers tried to disguise it, community development still involved trying to change the mind-set and cultural values of the local people. The program provided the ultimate expression of the pervasive tension over this question, because volunteers worked to change their hosts but tried as hard as they could to deny they were doing so. Even the weather seemed to conspire against Thomsen in Ecuador. He brought with him a community development idea to have everyone in town start their own garden. But the idea never was successful, because "the basic problem still remains: If it is too dry in the dry season, and too wet in the wet season, just how and when does one make a garden?"[49]

Urban community development programs exemplify most clearly the host of problems encountered by volunteers. The *Volunteer,* along with Sargent Shriver, confessed that the urban community development programs had "the highest failure rate, and some have questioned Peace Corps effectiveness in this sphere."[50] The Peace Corps leadership had difficulty figuring out why volunteers in the city found little success. Many failed because community development theory required the host country to be an undeveloped frontier, and by definition, an urban area could not fit this requirement. Alex Zipperer, who worked on an urban community development program in Santiago, Chile, pointed out that the training he received was "irrelevant." He continued by arguing, "The complexities of the urban environment warrant a method of operation entirely distinct from that employed by the Peace Corps in rural areas," supporting his contention by pointing out that urban dwellers already had connections to government and many agencies working for them. These facts countered community development mythology about undeveloped areas.[51]

Another favored community development idea that did not always succeed was the idea of the cooperative. According to Moritz Thomsen, "The aim of the co-op was to move a whole group of people out of poverty right into the middle of the middle class."[52] This was another straightforward, linear concept of development that seemed to fit the American experience but was more complicated than it seemed. The theory behind the co-ops sounded attractive. Volunteers would help poor peasants band together, and the power of the group would defeat the entrenched oligarchies of the area.

A variety of cultural attitudes conspired against this admirable idea. One volunteer wrote of his discouragement when the "almost magical sort of cure all" of credit cooperatives failed in his part of Ecuador. They failed because credit made little difference in his area, where many of the peasants lived on a barter economy.[53] In Thomsen's area of Ecuador, cooperatives failed for a different reason. He found the villagers "fiercely individualistic," quoting one as saying, "You know we've never worked together, and I don't think we ever can."[54] For American volunteers, working together to reach a common goal seemed like an important cultural value to impart to the local peasants. But the peasants clung to a different value, ironically one associated with pioneer individualism. Some co-ops worked, but for the most part this idea did not fit the Ecuador of the early 1960s.

Volunteers found community conditions in the third world much more complicated and confusing then they had expected, and consequently, they often rejected the liberal ideas of development so central to the specific idea of community development and to the Peace Corps idea in general.

Peace Corps leaders believed the agency was important because it fostered "the open mind, which proclaims that all things are possible; it can only insure that a gung-ho try will be made, and its failures are often as glorious as its successes."[55] The key to this thinking is the "gung-ho try," which brings up images of young, white, male athletes diving into the line at a college football game on a crisp afternoon in New England. It was a foreign concept for many volunteers.

The volunteers rejected the liberal programs of their leaders. As Paul Cowan put it, "The liberals based their decisions on ideas they had developed in the libraries of Harvard, not on anything they had ever experienced."[56] He went on to discuss exemplars of the most progressive kind of liberal ideas from the 1950s, such as Al Lowenstein. As Cowan understood it, Lowenstein "tried to appeal to the moderates, the freckle faced descendants of Tom Sawyer, the cashmere coeds."[57] Cowan rejected the leaders for not being progressive enough, while self-styled conservative volunteer John Freivalds criticized them for being too progressive. As Freivalds saw it, the Peace Corps was successful up to a point: "It is a good agency with plenty of enthusiasm and liberalism. What it often lacks, however, is a professional focus to get this enthusiasm working in the right place and the right time. Rebels are needed, but competent ones."[58]

Commentators sometimes claimed that this anti–liberal-establishment feeling really meant that volunteers had become anti-American. Some volunteers would have agreed. Paul Cowan, after all, called his book *The Making of an Un-American*. One evaluator declared, "The most mentioned attitudinal change as a result of Peace Corps service is a tendency to be more critical of U.S. society and foreign policy."[59] According to one poll, 43 percent of the volunteers who served in Colombia returned from their projects with a more negative view of the United States.[60] Volunteers were not the only young Americans to recoil from their country in the 1960s. Such an attitude was prevalent, if not common, among American youth at the time.

But whatever their opinions about the United States, most volunteer community developers did not throw up their hands in despair and abandon their posts. Rather, most decided to invent specific projects that might do some specific good for a specific community. As one volunteer put it, "If we're serious about community development, we should stop treating it like jazz—you can't explain it, you have to feel it."[61] Volunteers forced themselves to be concrete in their work, rejecting grand theories of development. One enterprising evaluator in Guatemala even took a poll of exiting volunteers, asking whether the Peace Corps should be promoting economic development. The proposition lost, 21 to 8.[62]

As volunteer Frederick McCluskey put it, "Community action is not a panacea to cure all the ails of an underdeveloped world. It must be used with discretion; in the right circumstances and under the right conditions."[63] Karen Clough, a volunteer in the Dominican Republic, provides a prime example of how a volunteer reinvented community development. The Peace Corps gave her "a volleyball and told me to go play with the children in order to ingratiate myself in the barrio."[64] This was supposedly the beginning of a master plan for local development. She rejected this lack of clear guidance, discarding the volleyball along with the vague instructions. She eventually decided that the community needed a music instructor, and so she taught music for two years.

Patrick Mertens underwent a similar experience in Colombia in 1966. According to his account, his first year was a disaster. Disillusioned, he concluded, "The Peace Corps was not designed to accomplish anything in the host countries." He then decided, as he put it, "to get serious," and took a course at the local agrarian institute in preparation for specific crop-planting projects. "I didn't tell the peace Corps anything. I just did it," he proudly proclaimed. Mertens had replaced the grand scheme of community development with a specific job requiring a specific task.[65]

Volunteers understood that they did not necessarily know how to create a "better community." Volunteer Tom Newman wrote a letter to the editor of the *Volunteer* in 1965 insisting that Americans had no special knowledge about how to create or develop a community.[66] As a matter of fact, most volunteers believed the most important task they could accomplish was learning how their hosts created communities. As Venezuela volunteer Robert Sebring phrased it, "We did not join the Peace Corps to teach the 'American way' or to preach the 'Christian way.' Rather we came to participate in an exchange of ideas and to learn the customs of our host country."[67] Volunteers working in community development invented a two-pronged focus for their work. First, they would do whatever specific tasks they felt might help their community. Second, and most importantly, they would actively learn about the host culture while living within it. The real development in community development became the development of the volunteer, rather than that of the host country.

TEACHING

None had more difficulty dealing with the Peace Corps image than volunteer teachers. The majority of volunteers during the 1960s were teachers. But their numbers never changed the image of the Peace Corps volunteer as a

In the Philippines, volunteers served as teachers' aides to well-qualified Filipino teachers. However, the agency often depicted them leading the class, as in this picture, where Peter Weisbrod demonstrates an ingenious home-made "story box," while the full-time teacher fades into the background. Photo by Larson, 1968, courtesy National Archives.

sweaty, bare-chested ditchdigger. The number of volunteer teachers who used precisely this image for a foil is surprising. According to one group, "The Peace Corps experience is always depicted in terms of a volunteer surrounded by naked children or grateful, toothless turbaned villagers for whom he had just completed a cistern."[68] Another group of teachers used similar imagery, grumbling that the Peace Corps leadership was "trying to make a teaching program as exciting as digging latrines."[69]

Many volunteer teachers felt that the Peace Corps leadership and staff created this feeling that teaching did not qualify as real Peace Corps work. Some "complained of the displeasure, lack of interest and the half hearted attitude with which their work had been received by the Peace Corps staff."[70] Social scientists who studied the Peace Corps in the mid-1960s found this to be a problem. Arnold Deutchman, a returned volunteer and graduate student in sociology, noted, "The Volunteer teacher has his own perception of his role. His perception does not necessarily coincide with Peace Corps/Washington's expectations."[71]

Volunteers did have foundation for this belief. If not prevalent at Peace

Like most volunteer teachers, Lauren Hale taught English. She is seen here in a modern-looking classroom in the Ivory Coast in 1968. Photo by Pickerall, courtesy National Archives.

Corps Washington, the belief that teaching was not a worthwhile volunteer pursuit was at least common. Evaluator Philip Cook made his feelings on this score clear in his evaluation of the teaching projects in the Ivory Coast in 1965. Cook complimented "the determination of the current Peace Corps representative to ease the Peace Corps out of the generally unsatisfactory task of English teaching and into roles which promise greater satisfaction to the Volunteers and more practical significance in the development of the Ivory Coast."[72] Part of the disdain toward teachers stemmed from the tension over forcing values on other peoples. By definition, teachers are proselytizers. They can't help pushing one set of ideas, because that is their job. Teaching made Peace Corps Washington and the volunteers uncomfortable because of its nature as well as its image.

Volunteer teachers also felt pressure from family and friends to conform to the image. Every time Bennett Oberstein explained his project to a friend, the response was, "You're going to the Peace Corps to teach drama? You mean they need this?"[73] Friends and Peace Corps staff alike seemed to hold a grudge against volunteer teachers. One report argued, "In actual fact, the image is used *against* the Volunteer. It makes him feel guilty when he's placed in a situation which does not fit the preconceived global image produced in Washington."[74]

Peace Corps evaluators and leaders found guilty teachers everywhere they went. Seth Tillman, in the Evaluation Division, described the feelings of one group of teachers: "Like so many of the other Volunteers I met, these teachers were full of doubts about their usefulness and prospective success."[75] Another evaluation describes a group that suffered from a "major collective guilt complex." The same evaluation noted yet another volunteer teacher who compared himself unfavorably with those who built outhouses, muttering, "I couldn't enjoy my teaching because I felt I should be digging a latrine."[76] William Mangin argued that these feelings endangered the whole Peace Corps effort in Ghana. "I think," he wrote, "that Peace Corps should give a lot of thought to the gap between the 'Peace Corps image' and the reality in West African teaching projects. . . . The combination of guilt and resentment over the nature of 'outside work' of the Peace Corps and the living standards, etc., seems more disruptive than it has to be."[77]

Guilt caused many teachers to feel as if they were not doing enough in their assigned project of teaching. In Nigeria, each member of a secondary education project felt "he was regarded as just another teacher." According to the evaluation, most volunteers in this group were "not happy."[78] These feelings pushed many volunteers to devalue the work they did as teachers. A group in Ghana came to a unanimous decision that "secondary school [where the volunteers taught] is a luxury that was not relevant to Ghana's current needs."[79] Peter Deekle, teaching in Iran, would have agreed. He wrote in his diary, "My job in Iran must exceed the bounds of the classroom if Peace Corps is to have much meaning here."[80]

The Peace Corps leadership made it clear that the way to alleviate this guilt was for teachers to get involved in secondary projects, because teaching by itself was not enough. According to Arnold Deutchman, Shriver insisted on such involvement because he believed "the school does not exist apart from its sociocultural matrix."[81] In 1969, the Peace Corps Evaluation Division circulated a memo arguing that volunteer teachers could not allow themselves to live in "self imposed isolation from the culture and people around them." The memo emphasized the importance of this issue for the Peace Corps hierarchy: "There is no issue that the office of evaluation has discussed at greater length than the persistent failure of Volunteer teachers to become involved in the lives of the communities in which they teach."[82] The evaluators believed that teachers had to have secondary projects to be effective volunteers. In other words, they believed volunteers should feel guilty for not living up to the image, because teaching was not sufficient in itself to be a Peace Corps project.

According to William Haddad, one of the leaders of the Office of Evaluation, those volunteer teachers who thought "solely of doing their teaching jobs well . . . tend to drift into expatriate ways of thinking." As an example, Haddad pointed out that teachers in Ghana "constantly compare themselves with contract teachers . . . and speak of their 'pay' and 'salary' rather than their living allowance. . . . They wonder why they shouldn't get the same pay as other expatriates."[83]

The Peace Corps staff and leadership asserted that volunteers were volunteers first and teachers second, and remained consistent on this issue throughout the 1960s. Teaching by itself was not enough, and they reported in surprise and dismay that volunteers disagreed with them. Robert Lystad, writing in late 1962, reported, "Volunteers regard the principal aim of the project to be that of teaching in the secondary schools. Their desire is to do the job as well as they can. They do not regard the 'people to people' aspect of the Peace Corps as realistic."[84] Shriver and the other Peace Corps leaders, of course, felt the "people to people" idea was of central importance to the Peace Corps mission.

Five years later, evaluating a different project in a different part of Africa, Richard Lipez reported with disdain the "cries" of volunteer teachers: "We're teachers, not Community Development workers. . . . We're here to do a job, and that's the main thing." Lipez commented that he did not think it possible for volunteers to teach effectively without "immersion" in the culture through a secondary project.[85] Another evaluator, visiting Ghana, believed volunteer teachers "tended to overemphasize the importance of the job in the classroom and to de-emphasize any extra-curricular involvement." He wrote, "There was unanimous resentment in the group over what they believed to be a basic tenet of Peace Corps philosophy—that the classroom work of the teacher is important—but only as a means of bringing the Volunteer into contact with the community outside of his school." This staffer, whose evaluation was written anonymously, rejected these opinions in favor of the image created by the Peace Corps leadership.[86]

Some teachers tried to follow the official ideal by initiating secondary projects. A group of university teachers in Nepal, while still working on their primary project, went as far as building "a smokeless chulo (mud stove), an oven, a bamboo-pipe system for water, and a 50 gallon drum complete with spout to store the water, a pig pen, a bamboo chicken house, a rabbit coop, beds, closets, benches, sofas and tables."[87] Another volunteer took it upon himself in his spare time to clean up a local prison. He proudly asked himself in retrospect, "Did John Kennedy suspect, when he started the Peace Corps, that Volunteers would have experiences like this one?"[88]

Even if they did not work on secondary projects during the school year, many volunteer teachers felt compelled to do so during their summer vacations. After returning to the United States, Samuel Abbott wrote about the intense pressure that volunteers felt to work on summer projects. According to Abbott, the Peace Corps staff believed "that the Volunteer teachers were out of step with the rest of the Peace Corps, and somehow not true blue until they used their teaching job as an excuse for community development."[89] Hence, many volunteers struggled to conform to these expectations. In Nigeria, some teachers built a health center, while others built an incinerator.[90] In the Ivory Coast, they volunteered for work at a leprosarium and at a hospital.[91] Many volunteer teachers worked, in effect, two jobs: teaching and community development.

The most common secondary jobs for volunteer teachers involved extracurricular efforts at their schools. Fewer objected to these since they seemed integral to their primary teaching job. Arnold Deutchman noted one school in which "school libraries and newspapers have been started. Softball has been introduced. Music and handicrafts clubs have been started. Teams have been coached to victory. Scout groups have been formed."[92] Volunteer teachers tried to create American values in their students by pursuing American activities. They wanted to help and knew no other way than following a route they believed to be successful in the United States. From the perspective of the Peace Corps leadership and the volunteers, they were using the excuse of their teaching position to do the real work of the Peace Corps. Some managed Herculean efforts, inventing a complete extracurricular program for their school. Paul Gilbert wrote an entire history of Somalia, in English, for use in his school.[93] Richard McManus staged plays at his school in the Philippines, including *Cinderella:* "We worked like slaves and have created a thing of beauty. The children are darling, especially the ones who are mice and who do the cutest dance. They are in mice costumes from head to toe, with big tails and ears."[94] This comment sounds like the comment of any proud American drama teacher at a Christmas play, and it reflects the idea many Peace Corps leaders had of volunteer teachers.

No group of volunteer teachers felt the contrast between their jobs and the Peace Corps pioneer image as keenly as university teachers. The host country decided the nature of the projects according to the needs they felt, but Shriver and his colleagues could, and often did, suggest possibilities for projects. In the end, it was the host country that decided, and often they picked projects that seemed antithetical to Shriver's chosen image, such as

university teaching. The popular image of the university teacher—intellectual, contemplative, effete—contrasted sharply with the rough-and-tumble
volunteer image cultivated by the Peace Corps leadership. In the end, these
volunteers had the most difficulties coming to grips with the gap between
image and reality.

Alan and Judith Guskin described their difficulties with university
teaching in Thailand in an article in the *Volunteer*. They begin with the
obligatory nod at "the image," asserting that they were "not who we thought
we would be: a pick-and-shovel type with callused hands." Instead, they had
come to Chulalongkorn University because it was "one of the best places to
use our skills, and because these were very important students to teach."
They had what some Peace Corps staffers might have considered lowly goals.
They had no desire to "save Thailand. We didn't come to fill all its needs."[95]
Most university teachers felt the same way. In Nigeria, teachers were "all
sufficiently busy preparing their lectures, marking papers, that they have
little or no time to spend off the campus."[96] In Venezuela, they realized that
"giving a university lecture obviously demands a different style than teaching
campfire songs to half naked youngsters who have never been to the first
grade."[97] In order to do their job right, they felt, they had to devote their
entire effort to the job, rather than living the image. They felt that other
volunteers, the ones dealing with half-naked youngsters, might live the
image, but university teaching did not blend with being a pioneer.

Yet even the teachers of ill-clad children insisted that succeeding in
the everyday tasks of their job was more important than chasing after the
elusive image of the heroic volunteer. Most of the problems volunteer teachers faced every day didn't remotely resemble the problems they expected or
had been trained to deal with. They were trained to survive long treks in
the wilderness, to deal with communist opinions and to expect exotic local
customs. But they encountered problems similar to those faced by teachers
in the United States in their everyday jobs. Leonard Levitt described the host
of difficulties he faced at his school. He had to endure interminable, useless
staff meetings; the headmaster disrupted his after-school sports program
and argued with him over methods of discipline; and he got caught in the
middle of a dispute between the headmaster and a fellow teacher, who was
often drunk.[98] In their daily work, most volunteer teachers did not live
romantic, exciting lives. They worked as teachers, with the problems of
teachers and the concerns of teachers.

Volunteer teachers looked "at themselves primarily as teachers—not
as Peace Corps Volunteers." They felt there was a clear separation between
the two. The Peace Corps concentrated on being "clinical, fatherly, imagey,

munificent; too rarely is it concerned with the professional job of teaching."[99] Volunteer teachers, on the other hand, were "very job oriented" and spoke negatively "of the Image that Peace Corps/Washington sent out, and felt it was grossly inaccurate."[100]

Most volunteer teachers clung tenaciously to the belief that the job of teaching was central to their work. A teacher named Tom, about to start his job in Ghana, declared, "I plan to go to Ghana to teach, not to answer questions [such as on U.S. race problems, Castro]. I hope the Peace Corps has the same idea. If not, I don't want to be in it."[101] A staffer in Ghana could not understand this attitude and asked Arnold Zeitlin about Tom: "Why did he join the Peace Corps? Why did he come to Ghana?"

Volunteer teachers could not shake the pioneer image. Some, such as Gwynne Douglass, contrasted their everyday life with this more romantic image: "No, I didn't build any bridges. I don't know anything about culverts or soil conditions. I didn't organize any clubs and haven't started any libraries. I just go to school every day and try to do my job."[102] Volunteer teachers insisted they had little time for anything but teaching. Jaclyn Hyland's diary is littered with entries like "wrote lessons all day and night."[103]

Teachers were almost always succinct in their statements on the issue of their responsibility as teachers in the Peace Corps. One in Ghana simultaneously dismissed directives from Washington and summarized the feelings of his fellow teachers in a single sentence: "Our primary aim—sometimes ignored by Peace Corps policy—is to fill a job."[104]

Just like the community developers, many of the teachers were B.A. generalists. Partly from necessity and partly by philosophy, the Peace Corps leadership decided that teaching would be a good project to assign volunteers with little specific training. They reasoned that volunteers, by definition, had to be adaptable and so could easily fit into the role of teacher. Also by definition, volunteers were supposed to lead by example. In effect, all were asked to be teachers, with the host nationals as their students, learning how to better cope with their world from the image set by the volunteer.

Many volunteer teachers decided that being assigned to teach did not make them teachers. "It is said," wrote English teachers David and Kathie Miller, "that some people have the personality for teaching and others do not. All of us know from experience this is true. . . . *But* a classroom manner is no substitute for mastery of the subject matter."[105] The Millers feared that without a concrete grasp of the subject matter, volunteer teachers could flounder. A math teacher in the Philippines agreed. After his group of teachers was hastily introduced to the concepts of the "New Math," he feared that "the whole math program could explode. The volunteers know very little about the devices they're working with."[106] Seth Tillman, a congressional staffer sent to Asia to evaluate the effectiveness of the Corps, found similar attitudes. After eating dinner with three teachers, Tillman wrote, "All three are firm in their insistence upon technique and training. . . . One of the Volunteers said that he sees little value in the dispensation of pure 'love' (he stressed the word with mocking intonation)."[107] Questions about the teaching competence of B.A. generalists led to one of the biggest controversies in the first ten years of the Peace Corps. The leadership, knowing they were assigning B.A. generalists to teaching positions and believing the job to be secondary to the image, insisted that volunteer teachers be treated as amateur, temporary teachers. The volunteers, heavily involved in their daily work as teachers, felt like professionals and wanted to be treated as such. Yet this countered the entire ideology behind Shriver's volunteer. The beauty of volunteers, according the philosophy, was that they were adaptable, just like the uneducated but innately intelligent mythic American westerner. Too much education might stifle creativity, and too much professionalization in a volunteer might smother the ability to be a new frontiersman.

Professional educators objected to this theory in regard to teaching. John Lunstrum, a professor at Indiana University and an educational consultant to the Peace Corps, decried the Peace Corps' "faith in amateurism" and "preoccupation with image building," because it tended "to cast the Volunteer teacher in the role of an evangelist proselytizing for democracy" and was "tantamount to pouring out the baby with the bathwater."[108] Thorburn Reid, in an evaluation of an education project in Senegal, wrote: "Reckless expansion and frantic scrambling . . . seem to have taken on the qualities of absolute virtue. Careful planning, definition of policy, concern with standards—what I would call professionalism—is censured as creeping bureaucracy, an epithet."[109]

Volunteers and observers alike outlined many potential solutions to what they considered the amateur nature of Peace Corps teaching. Many campaigned for more effective training. Linguist William Marquardt argued that English teachers should be trained for nine months before going to their projects, triple the amount of training they actually received. Failing that, he wrote, "They should be under the supervision of experienced teachers wherever possible and assigned a series of tasks that will give them the competencies they failed to get in their formal training." Marquardt presented a four-page list outlining what he thought every volunteer English teacher should know.[110]

Some staffers contended that the solution was to create a systematic method of assessing the performance of individual volunteers. They frowned on the volunteers who were only "liberal arts generalists postponing an uncertain future."[111] In part, their attitude stemmed from changes in the U.S. government as a whole during the middle part of the 1960s. Deriving at least in part from the ideas of Robert McNamara, the secretary of defense, these ideas became known in government jargon as the PPBS (Planning-Programming-Budgeting System). This system was designed to quantify the results of supposedly nonquantifiable government activities, thus making them more efficient. McNamara became famous for using such a process in the Defense Department in an attempt to systematize the understanding of the mysterious war in Vietnam. The Peace Corps did not escape this change in focus, especially since it represented a new, cutting-edge direction for government.

Psychologist Jesse Harris Jr. outlined how the Peace Corps could adopt such a system. He argued that the agency could accumulate a "systematic organization of data" about volunteer performance rather than "loose tangential associations or commentaries." Harris suggested the leadership create a set of performance criteria, and he gave an example of some he thought would work. In pages of charts and graphs, he argued that collecting large amounts of numerical data about each volunteer and then subjecting these data to "nonstepwise discriminant analysis" and "F-ratios" would give a clear picture of the success rate of each volunteer. This, Harris argued, would help the Peace Corps become more professional.[112]

The Corps never adopted these suggestions. The leadership never accepted the fact that the pioneering traits that made a good volunteer could be measured. They successfully defended the agency from such change by insisting that the anti-bureaucratic impulse stood at the core of Peace Corps beliefs. If nothing else, the PPBS represented the cutting edge of bureaucratic management, and as such it rubbed too many Peace Corps leaders the wrong way. That it was even considered attests to the power of creeping bureaucracy, even in an environment explicitly designed to prevent it.

Some in the leadership thought the answer to professionalization was to recruit more professionals. Though they did not have the romantic allure of the jack-of-all trades B.A. generalist, they could be trained in the same manner as previous volunteers, to become pioneers and professionals. Dr. James Robinson, the director of Operation Crossroads Africa and a member of the Peace Corps National Advisory Board, suggested such changes as early as 1966. According to Robinson, "The future will demand that the Peace Corps make a much larger effort to recruit more skilled and seasoned personnel to serve its aim and objectives."[113] Chester Bowles, a foreign policy wise man for both Kennedy and Johnson, called for "wholly new organizational concepts" in the Peace Corps. Such concepts would include sending generalist volunteers off to projects only if teamed with more technically skilled partners.[114] Some volunteers, such as Frances Hopkins, agreed: "As the Peace Corps goes about defining itself, there will be demands of ever greater skill—professional and social."[115]

Many other people in the Peace Corps leadership worried about making the Peace Corps a professional organization. They believed the Peace Corps essence demanded volunteers be qualified to do many things but not eminently qualified to do anything. After touring the Philippines, Maureen Carroll and Gardiner Jones of the Office of Development expressed Peace Corps Washington's feelings on the issue. As they put it,

> The pressure for more highly skilled, experienced Volunteers is likely to grow. . . . How far can the Peace Corps move in this direction and still be the Peace Corps? Whether the organization can retain its uniqueness as it shifts closer to technical assistance may well be tested in the Philippines. . . . There is an ill defined longing for the good old days of scatteration and lack of structure, when a Volunteer was more of a free spirit, albeit less effective on the job.[116]

During the 1960s, the Peace Corps never moved away from wanting the volunteers to be scattered free spirits. Some on the staff might have wanted it, and some volunteers, especially volunteer teachers, might have viewed themselves as professionals. But Peace Corps Washington viewed them as frontiersmen, albeit in the unfrontierlike job of teaching school.

As we have seen, the volunteer teachers themselves always valued their professional duties more than the image. Yet as they set about this specific work, they encountered a slew of differing cultural concepts about the purposes and meanings of education. Teachers arrived with beliefs about their role and the role of education that differed from the locals'. They derived these beliefs from American cultural ideas about how to best educate "modern," "developed" individuals. Volunteer teachers expected to blow in, with their relaxed, informal, charming teaching methods and sweep the native students off their feet. Ironically, the volunteers turned out to be more wild than the mythic noble savages they expected to teach. In Ethiopia, for example, the students told the teacher, "Sir, you must not joke with us"; being "chummy" created an "un-Ethiopian relationship to students."[117] The students expected their teachers to be more formal and academic, quite the opposite from the personable character volunteers were trained to assume.

Many volunteers encountered systems of discipline they felt uncomfortable with. Jaclyn Hyland commented that in her school, "The discipline is done as we did in America in the colonial days. The switch is the constant reminder of the desires of the teacher."[118] This, of course, fits the mythic expectations of the volunteers that they were living on a frontier and that things were being done just as they had on the American frontier. The volunteers, for the most part, refused to use the switch and lobbied to change the disciplinary practices at their schools. One teacher in Nigeria complained bitterly about corporal punishment at her school: "I hate it. I know it's traditional in British public schools, but I think it is a form of punishment that only arouses resentment and is totally inappropriate in today's world."[119] She recognized that "today's world" differed from the world of nineteenth-century America, mythic or real, and she would not repeat mistakes of the past.

More surprising to some volunteers was dealing with the spoiled children of the elite. An Ethiopian volunteer commented about one of her students, "Her father is wealthy, as most of the girls' parents are."[120] Arnold Zeitlin taught an elite group, one of whom wore his uniform not "to eliminate difference in wealth and station. He wore it to distinguish himself as a rare and special Ghanaian."[121] Betsy Lebensen taught the "princess, the prime minister's daughter, and other children of the elite" in Afghanistan.[122]

In this situation, the pioneer image had a negative effect. These students were certainly not the half-naked children envisioned by the university teacher. Many of them challenged volunteers' credibility and had trouble accepting that the ill-housed, sometimes ill-clothed volunteers had much to teach them. Leonard Levitt described this belief perfectly: "Because we taught at Ndumulu, because we lived next to them, because we lived the way they did—because of this our degrees were suspect."[123] Education meant something different in their country than it did to the volunteers. It meant training future leaders, not in an abstract sense, as in American educational ideology, but in a concrete sense. The volunteer teachers felt a persistent tension between their views of education and the views of their hosts. They wanted to accept the views of their hosts but at the same time wanted to change them.

In rare instances, discipline problems ballooned into more serious incidents for volunteer teachers. In one case in Korea, a volunteer complained that for him, things had "gone sour. The kids know it and I know it. Sometimes I am nearly sick after I leave class."[124] Others had to deal with student strikes, something unthinkable in the United States but much more common at this time in the countries in which volunteers were teaching. Polly Kirkpatrick related one of the strikes in a matter-of-fact fashion in her diary: "Only one interesting thing today—the students decided to go on strike. They were yelling and writing 'vive le Togo' and 'greve' (strike) on the board. Apparently, they were sick of sitting without anything to do several periods each day."[125] The strike was nothing very exotic, and Kirkpatrick expressed sympathy for it. Because these students considered themselves part of the elite, they believed they had a right to a superior education, and hence went on strike whenever they felt cheated.

The central incident of the narrative in Gary May's "Passing the Torch and Lighting Fires" is a strike by Ethiopian students. According to May, the students went on strike because volunteers called them "'lazy, goofy, dogs, animals,' and 'wild black beasts.'" The volunteers denied the accusations, insisting the students misunderstood and confused some words for others. The result of the strike was severe disillusionment among this group of volunteers, who, according to one volunteer, felt "the strike was . . . a real kick in the face. . . . I thought things were going fairly well and that we had established a good rapport. . . . We were almost in shock that this could happen." They were in shock because they had expected immediate acceptance. In cases such as this, volunteers did not understand the students' world, even though they thought they did. May tells the story as an example of the failure of the Peace Corps. Yet this was a unique incident. It can serve as a general example of lack of understanding but not of cultural imperialism.[126]

The entire system of education overseas seemed to conspire against the values of volunteer teachers. Many believed that the formal attitude students had toward school mirrored a formalistic and old-fashioned style of education. Jim Bain, a teacher in Nyasaland, described the accepted method: "The students dutifully copy everything into their exercise books. As exam time approaches, the painstaking job of committing to memory every bit of copied material assumes top priority on the student's schedule."[127] David Nelson was shocked when he first saw a class at work, commenting, "The way they read orally their lessons is enough to make Dewey spin in his grave. A monotone with absolutely no meaning whatsoever."[128] John Halloran compared it unfavorably to his experiences in a parochial school, saying that in classes in the Philippines, "There is more memorization and a learning ritual that is followed. . . . It reminds me of catechism classes with kids saying things you're not sure they understand."[129]

The freshest American creative teaching methods filled the novice teachers' minds. L. Gray Cowan, a consultant to the Peace Corps and a professor of government, wrote, "One of the most common, and strongest, urges among volunteers is the urge to innovate."[130] They soon found that they could not adapt these methods to a rigid educational system. Dennis

Shaw found out immediately that "habit and tradition have tied my students to an educational system based on copying, memorizing and repeating." He tried to rectify that with a learning game, but had to watch his "creative teaching idea sink into ignominious failure."[131] Most volunteers tried to use a few creative methods, and not all failed. John Halloran wrote in a letter, "The longer I am here the more informal I become in handling classes. I am doing more with games and songs."[132]

The Peace Corps even published instructional materials to help volunteers better utilize their creative abilities. One such brochure, "From Rote to Reason," describes how volunteers could best use games, puzzles, and songs to teach English as a foreign language to the host nationals. The irony of this system was that many educators believed that the only way to teach English as a foreign language was by using memorization techniques. In other words, they believed volunteers should have been using the "old-fashioned," "British" system all along. One evaluator called this irony "the Peace Corps' longest running gag."[133]

Most staffers, as well as most volunteer teachers, continued to believe that the main purpose of their teaching was to introduce concepts of reasoning to the host countries. This was one area where volunteer teachers, otherwise feeling guilty for living comfortable, non–Peace Corps lives, felt they could make a genuine contribution to the welfare of their host country. Jaclyn Hyland describes the beginning of the process: "So we began to introduce a thing called reasoning. This was foreign to them and as of yet they are still not sure of its meanings and implications."[134] Naturally, reason was not foreign to the American volunteers. In fact, volunteers and Peace Corps leaders alike would have agreed that reason stood out as a central part of the American character, but not of the cultures of many host countries. For example, some volunteers in Afghanistan felt frustrated because "the Middle Eastern student has 20 centuries of rote learning and memorization behind him."[135]

Regardless of the accuracy of these cultural generalizations, volunteers soon learned that the realities of life in their host countries in the 1960s worked against the volunteers' educational innovations. As Fannie Shaftel wrote of one such system, volunteers had to deal with "the very grim reality of the examination system which is the gateway to higher education in Malaya."[136] Volunteer teachers throughout the world learned quickly that their students were "very reluctant to study anything which is not directly connected with the examination."[137] No matter what games they played in class, no matter how kind they were to their students, volunteer teachers could not be effective unless they helped their students pass the national exams.

This could only be accomplished by following the detailed syllabus provided by the government. "The syllabus is truly a sacred document in Malaya," asserted teacher John Thayer, "as it is in all British founded school systems. I have come to like this word [syllabus] so that my life seems more or less to center on it."[138] Arnold Deutchman, speaking for many Peace Corps leaders, argued that such adherence to the syllabus was "inappropriate" and volunteers should "become agents for social change" by discarding it and following their more creative instincts.[139] Many agreed with him, but others cautioned against too hasty a change. David King, a teacher in the Philippines, argued, "Perhaps we don't fully understand the problem. We say 'free the child from traditional forms. Allow him to be imaginative, creative, original.' This just doesn't work with Filipino kids. The social structure places children in a position of complete dependency."[140]

Teaching children to be creative seemed to be the right thing to do from the volunteers' perspective. But the countries they taught in were not like the United States, neither their America nor the mythic America of the nineteenth century. The system of national exams and rote memorization might have been relics from the third world's colonial past, but they were also realities of the students' present. Volunteer teachers wanted to work to eliminate the old system but understood that doing so meant ignoring the students' needs. The dilemma of how to teach their students baffled volunteer teachers more than any other. Most firmly accepted the importance of creativity, yet few agreed to ignore the realities of the educational system they taught in.

In the end, some teachers believed that their job provided the answer to the tension they felt over accepting local values while at the same time promoting change. The volunteers learned about third world cultures through their daily teaching chores. This world was both similar to and different from the world of America, and it was this knowledge that became the central revelation and ideology of the volunteers. Many of their students were excited participants in the volunteers' work. Alicia Teichman wrote in pleased surprise: "It's very nice adjusting to the enthusiasm these boys have about education."[141] These are exactly the kind of students Leonard Levitt found in Tanganyika, who "literally knew nothing about anything," but they "were bright. But more than just bright, they were eager. They weren't afraid to speak up."[142] David Schickele wrote in the *Volunteer* that for him and his students, "Literature became the line of commerce between us as people, a common interest and prime mover in the coming together of white American and black African. Ours was a dialogue between equals."[143]

Episodes between teachers and individual students provide impressive testimony to the potential satisfaction in the job of teaching for volunteers. One teacher described an occasion in which she felt she finally got through to a student: "The student in the fourth row who never smiles and never works (I wasn't even sure she breathed) smiled at me today. Then she handed in a very well-written assignment. If she did it herself, it is very good. Suddenly everything seems worthwhile."[144] For Angene Wilson, a teacher in Liberia, her job was worthwhile because she could teach something and accept local values at the same time. According to Wilson, the value of teaching was encapsulated in the "glow in an 18 year old fifth grader's eyes as he talks about Sir Roland who died for his leader Charlemagne. 'My grandfather told me about Gola warriors like him. So brave, he says admiringly.'"[145] This teacher reached across cultures and across generations, teaching the student something as well as helping create a bond within a family of host nationals. Though the episode had nothing to do with conquering the frontier or building a nation, it seemed to have a lot to do with what Peace Corps volunteers were trying to accomplish.

Even if volunteer teachers could introduce just one of their students to the greater world, they would consider their project a success. Arnold Zeitlin taught a student named Grace that made his teaching worthwhile. As he put it, "If we see no other result of our work in Ghana than Grace's continued education, it will be sufficient for us."[146] Margaret Elberson started a kindergarten that seemed like a failure. But as time went on, she believed it had become a success: "The children's shining faces, as well as Ricardo's words (I don't want to go home. I had fun here today) attested to their happiness in their new experiences."[147]

The work experience changed the view most volunteers had about issues of development. The work was supposed to allow the volunteer to use his or her frontier ingenuity to show the host nationals how to conquer their own frontier and develop in the straightforward manner that had worked in American history. Volunteers were supposed to help the natives learn new values, but in a way that recognized the validity of traditional values.

Many volunteers and observers of the Peace Corps in the late 1960s noted that working conditions overseas did not meet expectations—a change often attributed to a loss of the Kennedy idealism. Volunteer John Freivalds wrote, "Little is left of idealism after two years of frustrations."[148] An anonymous volunteer stated bluntly at a completion-of-service conference, "My idealism regarding the Peace Corps is gone."[149] Samuel Abbot, just back from Nigeria, "mourned the failure to translate the initial Peace Corps ideal into action."[150] Most volunteers, through their work, developed new ideas about what was important in their relationship with their hosts. They developed a philosophy based on their individual relationship with peoples of the third world rather than any preconceived ideas about linear, straightforward national development. This philosophy, the subject of the next chapter, also differed from early notions about how the American volunteers would interact with peoples of the third world.

7

Encountering the "Other"

Relationships in the Third World

The greatest hope of both the Peace Corps leadership and the Peace Corps volunteers was that the Peace Corps would make friends, both for individuals and the United States. Many hoped they would be loved by the locals because they were going to be working hard for their benefit. None expected difficulty in getting to know the local people. Their living and working conditions had proved to them that straightforward development was a mirage. Their work experience began to point them toward developing a new philosophy of their relationships with their hosts. The intricacies of these relationships would push them even farther away from their earlier ideas about straightforward development and making friends in the third world. Rather, the volunteers' relationships with their hosts created new, more complicated ideas of respect and egalitarianism in the volunteers.

From the beginning, volunteers were shocked by how strange the local people seemed to be. Although they "had been trained in the Peace Corps to see through, a little way at least, that cultural veneer to the common humanity that binds us together," they could not help wide-eyed commentary about their strange hosts.[1] One volunteer in the Philippines related a discussion with some Filipinas revolving around the topic of "how many of us had urinated in the water while we were swimming. We discovered that one of the girls had urinated three times."[2] The volunteer had difficulty understanding this behavior because American girls would never bring up such a question in mixed company. Leonard Levitt described an even more shocking situation: "Then one of them swung her baby around in front of her and suddenly, without warning, she reached her hand down into her dress and pulled out a big black breast and began feeding her baby right there, in front of all of us . . . as casually as if she was powdering her nose."[3]

Local ideas sometimes elicited disdainful commentary. William Martin, a health volunteer in Brazil, wrote an article in the *Volunteer* pointing out some of the "silly superstitions" followed by Brazilians. He noted that "going to sleep after eating goat tripe was particularly fatal."[4] John Halloran described the Filipinos in his village as "very simple in their living and thinking and there is much superstition. . . . We have been told many stories about fairies that appear. . . . All in all it is like going back a century or two."[5]

Some volunteers could never understand the people they encountered. They might have been prepared for "primitive superstitions" but were rarely prepared for the odd combination of primitive and "modern" that they found. One report mentioned that "drinking on and off the job by host country nationals and seeing the most respected man in the village drunk in the gutters was a bit shocking and distasteful to many [volunteers]."[6] After sending letter after letter home describing the strange customs in the Philippines, John Halloran concluded, "Mentally it is a very mixed up country."[7]

Ignoring local foibles fit the Peace Corps philosophy of universalism. The volunteer was supposed to enter the third world with an open mind about how, in the end, humanity is all the same. Most tried to adhere to this attitude, but as we have just seen, some did not succeed.

Most volunteers did not expect to find a world even more complicated than the one they left. When they heard far-off drums, they expected it to be part of a primitive ritual, rather "than a group of half dressed natives, half drunk on their pombe, celebrating an afternoon the way we would take in a ball game or shoot a round of golf."[8] David Nelson found a society in Ecuador riddled with complicated but rigid class distinctions. Most surprising to him, he found himself interacting mostly with the upper class: "Although the upper class is notorious for its neglect of all the classes below it, nevertheless it goes out of its way to make the foreigner feel at home."[9] Others found racial tensions that they did not expect. A teacher in Ghana sheepishly admitted to a roving Peace Corps evaluator that she had joined an all-white club. She insisted that she had to, because all of the white teachers at her school also belonged, and when she didn't join in her first year, these colleagues ostracized her.[10]

A wide range of unexpected problems with the locals cropped up for the volunteers. One group in the Philippines found their biggest difficulty

The image most Americans thought typical of the Peace Corps: working closely with locals, using local materials to build thatched structures, and, in this case, improving sanitation by building a latrine. Photo by Pickerall, 1968, courtesy National Archives.

to be "excessive social demands by host country nationals."[11] They were not prepared to land in the middle of a social world, expecting instead to be able to do their work in frontier isolation. Many volunteers, such as the group called El Salvador VII, complained that no one in the host country appreciated their work and the host country government gave no support to it.[12] Volunteers expected that their work would be viewed as positive, and were surprised when it seemed to be ignored.

The Peace Corps did prepare volunteers to deal with the host-country counterpart, a local resident chosen by the host country to work with Peace Corps volunteers. The idea of the counterpart was central to the Peace Corps leadership's thinking about exactly what volunteers were supposed to do in the host country, that is, use their American know-how to teach the counterparts how to be effectively develop their own country. Volunteer training reflected this idea, because volunteers were given just enough language instruction to deal with their counterparts. The Peace Corps volunteer would not force the local to follow his ideas, but the learning would take place through a symbiotic relationship. Richard Ottinger, a Peace Corps staffer who later became a congressman, believed the central merit of the

Third world nations asked the Peace Corps for drama teachers, university professors, and, in the case of Bolivia, ballet dancers and symphony musicians. Usually members of the Bolivian national symphony, these volunteers took time to bring their skills to the frontier town of Swapi. Courtesy National Archives.

agency to be "coming to a foreign community as an equal rather than as an adviser."[13] This is how Lederer and Burdick depicted the relationship in *The Ugly American,* when the native "Jeepo" learns American-style ingenuity through the patient effort of prototype volunteer Homer Atkins.

In practice, the relationship between many volunteers and their counterparts was not nearly this uncomplicated. As one volunteer phrased it, "You cannot imagine the gulf between East and West, and it makes me laugh now to think that I expected to bridge it with a smile and a handshake."[14] They expected to find diamonds in the rough, pure exemplars of the perfect human spirit, who only needed polishing to reach their full potential. Lederer and Burdick, who of course helped create the image of the perfect counterpart, noted in an evaluation, "Before his arrival the Peace Corps volunteer tends to cast the native in a somewhat heroic mold."[15]

John Freivalds found that in Colombia, the "noble savage was not to be found. . . . Everyone had a skeleton in his closet."[16] One of his counterparts was a cattle rustler, and another enjoyed swapping wives with his village friends. Most counterparts lacked such apparent vices, but many lacked commitment to the development work. "The Indian counterpart," one local official wrote, "is not there because of his choice and, perhaps, in many cases it is against his wishes."[17] This stunned the volunteers. They had come all this way to help a foreign country, and the locals did not always want to help themselves. Volunteers had difficulty understanding that some of their counterparts had no desire to change their life. In Thailand, they found the locals "proud of an ancient and highly traditional society. They see this traditionalism, combined with religious influences, as creating a lack of desire for any significant change."[18]

It was hard for volunteers to understand that the locals had to do development work their entire life, and it may not have been their first career choice. Many counterparts who were educated urban dwellers frowned at what they considered the "dirty work" of working in poor villages. Arnold Zeitlin quotes one Ghanaian as saying, "I guess I've lived in the city so long I have lost touch with the customs of the village."[19] According to a local in India, "The village is properly an object of development, but it is not a living place for educated people."[20] In other words, many counterparts shared assumptions of superiority and straightforward development with the volunteers. And just as with the volunteers, these assumptions caused confusion and disillusionment.

Some host-country nationals distrusted the volunteers, adding another difficulty to their relationship. Those who had struggled their entire lives to break free of "the frontier" in their country often could not understand how volunteers could revel living in it. One local student showed that he thought more like a materialistic American than his volunteer friend did: "Why should I study English? Look at you. You speak English. You went to school. You have a degree. And what have you to show for it? You can't even buy a motorcycle, to say nothing of a car."[21] According to one volunteer, "The people here don't respect us for hardship living. They think that every American is filthy rich, and it is his standard of living they admire, nothing else."[22] In Ghana, the locals seemed to care only about "any and all *things* American. American music is extremely popular, especially rock and roll and the twist."[23] In Ecuador, a native named Wai "could never understand what the Peace Corps was all about. It went against everything he had learned in life; there was something preposterous, something dangerous about a rich white man living in this town and talking about working with him, helping him make more money—for nothing."[24]

The unease that many counterparts faced working with people they considered to be rich and powerful pushed some into a position subservient to the volunteer. This, perhaps more than anything else, infuriated volunteers. They wanted to work on an equal footing with their counterparts and could not cope with the situation if they were made to feel superior. In India, Carl Pope immediately became the "Sahib." He tried to shed the title, but it "stuck to my white skin like beggars at bus stops." After a few months on the job, it became apparent to Pope that "our small house had become the Big House."[25] Here again is the volunteer as master, a relationship abhorred by volunteers, but one expected by some locals.

Volunteers serving in Latin America frequently commented on this phenomenon. In Ecuador, Moritz Thomsen fell into this relationship over and over again, despite attempting not to. "It was a relationship that almost every poor Latin sought," he wrote, "to be subservient and protected by a powerful father figure. . . . It was the subtle relationship of master and slave."[26] In Africa, volunteers found an almost identical situation. Arnold Zeitlin's experience in Ghana taught him that for many Ghanaians, "white men were potential patrons, to be cultivated hopefully and carefully."[27] In East Africa, Leonard Levitt believed the people were "so easily swayed, so easily led, just like a group of little children."[28] Whether or not the people actually acted like this is immaterial. The point is that volunteers believed they did, which is surprising, considering that volunteers so wanted to be involved in the perfect volunteer-counterpart relationship as conceived in Peace Corps philosophy.

Some volunteers became so frustrated with this situation that they began to group their hosts together into an undifferentiated other, rejecting the universalism that they had previously embraced. Robert Gaudino relates how he was warned against doing this in a letter that his group read and discussed during training: "A great problem that I've found myself and many other Volunteers facing is actually losing respect for the Indians, as a group. . . . I've found myself lapsing into the use of the generalized 'they.'"[29] These generalizations often took the form of stereotypes, often ugly ones reminiscent of epithets conjured up by other masters of a previous era.

Perhaps the most common stereotype used by volunteers to describe host nationals is that they were uneducated. This was an easy one, since it did not imply that there was anything wrong with the natives, just that they had not yet been given the light of civilization. As Myron Gildesgame put it, "It's really kind of easy to place blame for things that go wrong on the uneducation of these people, their unawareness and their humility."[30] (Perhaps he was unaware of the irony of using *uneducation*.) Richard Lazarus believed that in Colombia, "the Campesinos who make up the vast majority of the population are uneducated and have neither the necessary under-standing of government nor the will to change things."[31] Some believed that even those who considered themselves educated did not qualify as educated in any absolute sense. In Brazil, one volunteer reported with horror, even the "educated mothers" were "forever making booties and bonnets for their babies when the temperature never drops below 65 or 70."[32]

Some volunteers vented their frustrations by insisting that their counterparts had a character flaw. One raved about the stupidity of Indians, noting an instance in which there was "a dead sacred white cow in the middle of the street in front of the airlines office with people just doggedly stepping around it."[33] One volunteer in West Africa complained, "There is no tradition of the Puritan work ethic there—there never has been. . . . I suppose there are thoughtful students there, but I can honestly say that so far I have met none."[34]

The most common complaint about the character of the counterparts was that they were lazy. Sometimes, volunteers attached specific facts to their complaints. Mark Simpson wrote home that his counterpart would "work for two days, then [take] off for a month."[35] A volunteer in Ethiopia referred to the Ethiopians "as a lazy, seemingly useless people."[36] Myron Gildesgame in Ecuador called the Indians "an unbelievably passive group."[37] Afghans, according to Betsy Lebenson, had "no work ethic. Their ideal was to sit on their rumps and drink tea."[38] After compiling questionnaires from volunteers in Peru, David Pearson concluded, "Laziness, or lack of the real values of pride, combined with the machismo (you can't teach me anything) attitude stumped these Peace Corps Volunteers throughout the two years."[39]

Volunteers in Latin America seemed especially fond of attributing their difficulties to local character traits. In order to assuage the tension within themselves about sneering at their hosts, many played amateur sociologist to explain the antecedents of aberrant Latin behavior. Fred McCluskey discussed the issue with his fellow volunteers in Colombia, trying to figure out why "they do not strive; they are apathetic; seek no change."[40] Kirby Jones, a volunteer and then program operations officer for Latin America, hypothesized that historical oppression made campesinos "fatalistic concerning their future, suspicious of neighbors, and reluctant to attempt anything new."[41] Colombians believed, according to John Freivalds, that "fate will take care of tomorrow."[42] Whether because of religion, history, or a stubborn nature, peasants in Latin America seemed to be especially difficult for volunteers to work with. Regardless of whose fault this might have been, it was a different relationship than the volunteers had expected or hoped for.

Sometimes, though not often, the volunteers rejected all semblance of respect for the locals. Paul Cowan relates an incident in which a fellow volunteer proclaimed, "I can't wait until the wrong Ecuadorian hits me at the wrong time so that I can beat him up." Another volunteer declared: "I can't wait until I get home and into the army. I want to go over there to Vietnam and shoot some of those Viet Cong. It will sure feel good to pretend they're the Ecuadorian campesinos I've been working with."[43]

Even more surprising was a failure to establish any relationship at all with the locals. Volunteers assumed they would be welcomed with open arms and that, as isolated individuals living in a sea of host nationals, they would forge some strong friendships. Volunteers in Nigeria told evaluator Timothy Adams that they "assumed Nigerians would welcome them enthusiastically."[44] Many found that not to be the case. "Most of the Volunteers," wrote Dr. William Gaymon in an evaluation of the Nigeria program, "reported dissatisfaction in relationships with Host Country Nationals. They contrasted what actually developed with expectancies upon arrival and were disappointed."[45] Many thought that their most exciting experience would be meeting and getting to know their hosts, but they soon learned "the disappointing reality that they just were not readily accessible."[46] Evaluation after evaluation noted that volunteers did not meet very many host nationals, at least not at the level that provided "stimulation, easy social relationships or first hand understanding of Nigerian society."[47]

This lack of contact bitterly disappointed some volunteers. After eight months of trying to build friendships, Esther Warber concluded, "All in all I'm a bit disappointed I haven't gotten further in my friendly relations."[48] Combining this disappointment with the frustration many felt working with uncooperative counterparts soured some on their experience. One volunteer in the Dominican Republic came to believe, "90% of the people seem to have their hands out. Two weeks ago I hit a little girl with my jeep. I didn't hurt her, but the police, her parents, and the district attorney wanted a bribe."[49]

Others tried in vain to learn why they could not connect with the locals. Volunteers in Ghana concluded that the Ghanaians became suspicious due to "overenthusiasm on our part."[50] Another group in Ghana believed, "It's nice to talk about getting to know Ghanaians, but when you have nothing in common, it's darn hard."[51] Some thought it impossible to ever get to know the local population because not only did they have nothing in common, but they never could due to vast cultural differences.

This lack of understanding, mixed with the frustrations many volunteers had with their counterparts, occasionally created a volatile concoction. Volunteers in training would have been horrified to think that *any* volunteer could argue or fight with their hosts. Volunteers gave little thought to the possibility that any human beings living together in close proximity might, on occasion, come into conflict. Such a possibility belittled the image volunteers had of their jobs. In the image of Americans helping these countries develop in a straightforward way, there was no room for conflict with those in the developing country.

For David Nelson, this possibility became reality. He wrote home that soon after his arrival he was "jumped by locals who were a little too high after visiting a bar." Of course, such an incident could have happened anywhere in the world and for any reason, but Nelson's letter reflects amazement that anyone would have done this to a Peace Corps volunteer.[52] In Korea, one volunteer described the "Koreans throwing rocks and spitting at us." These Koreans viewed the United States with contempt, and "taunted us with chants of hello, hello, monkey."[53]

Volunteers liked to consider themselves apolitical, and most did not consider themselves Cold Warriors. Nonetheless, some found they could not escape the Cold War world they lived in. David Nelson insisted that Ecuadorian students thought "the U.S. is exploitation personified. We steal their oil, their tuna fish, their bananas and their money—as profits which leave their country."[54] In Ethiopia, volunteers were "simply the most visible sign of American support for the emperor." This led to a student riot in 1970, in which, according to volunteer Craig Johnson, "the students behind us pinned our arms back and began to pummel us with stones, sticks and fists."[55] In Colombia, Freivalds received threats from host nationals who termed themselves "Colombian Viet Cong."[56]

A few volunteers lost their cool and attacked their hosts. Carl Pope attempted to calm his anger at the overwhelming bureaucracy he had to deal with in India, but finally "blew up and screamed 'It's god-damn illegal to do your job in this system.'" Frederick McCluskey wrote of a remarkable altercation with a host national. In a letter home to his parents, he described his feelings of frustration after a long day of dealing with uncooperative locals. While walking down the street, he was stopped by a dirty boy in rags, begging for food or money, and McCluskey hit him: "There I was, an American, a Peace Corpsman, 23 years old and supposedly cementing relations between us and Latin America and I went and slugged a poor street urchin."[57] Surprisingly, McCluskey reports, nothing much came of the incident, except the tarnished image he had of himself. For McCluskey, this incident represented the ultimate denial of the Peace Corps universalist ideal, for if he could not accept the annoyance of a foreign child, how could he live with the cultural differences of an entire society?

Many women volunteers felt most keenly the dissonance between their expectations of relationships with their hosts and their actual experiences. An incident described by Carl Pope illustrates this problem. At a dinner with Indian villagers, he was invited to go out on the porch with the men, while his wife Judy was supposed to go into the kitchen with the women. What happened next sounds like a scene right out of *The Ugly American:* "Once inside the house, Judy found that she could not communicate. We had learned Hindustani, the lingua franca of Northern India. The local dialect was quite different. Hindustani was the language of merchants and traders; it was learned in the bazaar, so all the men knew it. We had not learned the language of the kitchens and bedrooms."[58]

Women volunteers often had to deal with cultural barriers stemming from differing definitions of femininity. At times, their jobs seemed to fit cultural ideas well. Leslie Hanscom, a nurse in Afghanistan, wrote that she succeeded at her job because it had "an almost startling effect upon the Afghans to see an American girl in white uniform appearing to take their troubles to heart."[59] The volunteer nurses were usually not specialists and had to be prepared to work on a variety of problems. Volunteer nurses Nancy Crawford and Catherine Abitz worked on a multitude of different chores. In one day, they treated an eye wound from a fight, assisted in a birth in the back of the jeep, examined patients for tuberculosis, and gave a weekly prevention clinic.[60] Volunteer nurses taught proper sanitation and cleanliness. In India, Lila Schoenfeld wrote that after trying for months, "through demonstration, repetition, nagging and dramatics, the light finally dawned and the word clean began to mean what I wanted it to."[61] Volunteer nurses were literally in charge of cleaning up the world and making it safe for democracy.

Volunteer women sometimes faced a challenge to their femininity from their hosts. Some staffers took this into account when they placed women in jobs that fit the feminine image. Sally Yudelman, a Latin American program officer in Peace Corps Washington, thought the agency should "learn to live with the problem" of women not being accepted in certain jobs. According to Yudelman, the only acceptable jobs for women in Latin America were education, social work, health and home arts/nutrition."[62] Lawrence Fuchs agreed, arguing, "There are few things more strikingly peculiar about American culture than the assertion of independence and equality of unmarried females."[63] He insisted that women volunteers tone down their independent nature or face the brand of sexual looseness.

Volunteer women did occasionally face unpleasant situations when they strayed from the local standard of feminine behavior. One volunteer in Korea reported, "Principals and teachers were upset by female Volunteers smoking and drinking. . . . Practically all Koreans believe that the only girl who smokes or drinks is a bar girl."[64] Women in Latin America, more frequently than in other parts of the world, reported this kind of problem. In Brazil, the Peace Corps staff and local leaders warned Joan Marasciulo not to go into the local slums, known as *favelas,* because "only two kinds of single women live in favelas—nuns and prostitutes."[65] But she reported success, arguing the people she worked with cared little for the conventional feminine image.

In Latin America, justification for subordinating women centered on the supposedly macho culture. Gaile Nobel acknowledged this problem. Of course the macho culture of Latin America was an obstacle to women, she wrote, but it was "not insurmountable if a woman has some maturity, common sense, initiative and intelligence." She was proud that she and her peers "did not lose our femininity," even though they "worked primarily with men."[66]

One area in which female volunteers felt they could contribute without compromising their feminine image was in personal encounters with host women. Nancy Galvin Petty, in Morocco, insisted, "We Volunteer women have a distinct advantage. The men are limited for the most part to getting to know male Moroccans. They know Moroccan girls only through the man's ideas on them."[67] The women, on the other hand, could develop a special connection with their female hosts. Nancy Scott, in the Ivory Coast, believed that this connection could transcend any other division between her and her hosts. She wrote in the *Volunteer:* "There are between us fundamental bonds of womanhood: feelings for maternity, for home, and for family. There is no barrier of race or tradition meeting one another on these planes. Watch an African mother bathing her baby; watch her hands. She may not be doing things just as you did them, but if you have bathed a newborn baby you can fairly feel your hands in hers."[68] Naturally, this belief reinforced the feminine image of volunteers. The women volunteers were fundamentally different and served a different purpose than the men. At the same time, this belief was empowering, because it gave them a feeling of purpose separate from male volunteers and distinct from the image of the new pioneer.

Some volunteer women felt that they needed to break out of all the images and teach the local women how to be liberated. One group in Afghanistan felt their greatest contribution as volunteers was "unlocking the locked places in the minds of the people" regarding the treatment of women. All the volunteers, men and women, decided that this success "depended a great deal upon the example set by Peace Corps girls working in these same places and demonstrating to Afghan men that women can think and stand by what they think."[69] Many Peace Corps women felt this way about their projects. In India, one declared, "I want the women to have a break. I think the Indian women are really neglected. . . . They feel humble in the system, they're afraid."[70] This attitude was more didactic than many volunteers were comfortable with. Some women believed that trying to change local attitudes about women overstepped the bounds of their role.

Women volunteers had trouble reconciling pressures to remain aloof and their need to develop personal attachments while overseas. As George Sullivan put it in *The Story of the Peace Corps*, "Girl Volunteers find the problem much more severe than do the men,"[71] partly because men faced fewer restrictions than the "girls." Some women completely changed personalities because of the pressures. They suffered from loneliness, and "as the loneliness deepened, the need to have someone hold your hand, put his arm around you, maybe kiss you, was very strong." Because such behavior was often taboo, "some girls invented fiances in the US. Most became circumspect in drinking, smoking and dress."[72] Others discarded their feminine personas and buried themselves more deeply in the image of the new pioneer. One male volunteer in Somalia noted, "In their work, the girls more often than the men act the part of pioneers." He believed this was so because the girl "begins to realize that she is twenty seven and single, and the prospects for two years are exceedingly dim."[73] In other words, the only reason he could think of for a girl to reject her feminine image and don that of the pioneer was that she realized she had failed to live up to the feminine image.

The Peace Corps generally encouraged volunteers to discuss issues peripheral to their jobs, but in the early years, birth control was not among them. Lynda Edwards, a community developer in the Dominican Republic, got around the problem by being "discreet" about sexual relations: "If the Peace Corps told me to stop, I don't think I would have and I might have been sent home." She succeeded, ironically enough, because, as a single woman living alone, the local women thought she was a prostitute. They asked her why she never got pregnant, and she took advantage of the opportunity. It seems odd, though, that in a job of community development, volunteers were not allowed to discuss birth control. How did Peace Corps Washington expect to "develop" these areas without some control on the growth of the population?[74]

Volunteers from minority groups also faced unique difficulties relating to people in the host countries. The Peace Corps leadership believed minority volunteers had a special role in building friendships and hence building nations in the third world. In an attempt to prod more blacks to join the Corps, C. Payne Lucas wrote: "To me it is sadly depressing that so

Volunteers Andy Falender (right) and Wayne Kaufman (center) worked as city planners in the Philippines. Here they enjoy a Coke in front of a Filipino-American menu with their counterpart, symbolizing the complex cultural mixing experienced by volunteers and hosts alike. Photo by Larson, courtesy National Archives.

few black Americans are ready to meet the African on his own soil; that too many would rather borrow or buy a supposedly lost identity than invest two years or more in working with Africans towards their self-made goals."[75] This was a thinly veiled criticism of the burgeoning black nationalism movement and the Black Muslims, whom Lucas accused of phoniness, while insisting that the only way to meet and help "real Africans" was to join the Peace Corps. This message became central in recruiting black volunteers, and the prospective volunteers understood it clearly. Carolyn Gullat described how she was recruited: "He talked about how I, as a black person, could get 'home' and join with the Brothers and Sisters abroad where people have grown into Black pride naturally. Black power is the status quo and Black Action is the working reality."[76]

Historian Jonathan Zimmerman shows how this initial hope was soon dashed by the reality of life in the third world: "The handful of African-Americans who visited their ancestral 'home' found it less than hospitable." Volunteers did not find an Africa unified by the American concepts of black empowerment. Instead, they found a diverse, complex, foreign continent, filled with difficult-to-understand cultures. As volunteer David Closson put it, "From Senegal to Somalia, Black volunteers were alternately amazed, confused and inspired by the wide range of ethnicities they encountered."[77]

The story of one volunteer, Ed Smith, portrays this idea most clearly. Smith joined the Corps believing he could combine his strong beliefs with the goals of the Peace Corps. Even before he volunteered, he felt himself "chained to an active program of aggressively asserting his and his people's right to be."[78] He described himself as a Pan-Africanist and thought the Peace Corps would give him a chance to get to know his fellow Africans and help them "be" at the same time.

After his arrival in Ghana, Smith immediately became frustrated. He applied to work at a school with a European principal but was rejected because the principal believed the Europeans there would not appreciate a black teacher. He felt "bitter and disillusioned" when he saw Ghanaians "begging the forgiveness of a white volunteer because the lorry had no room for him" and felt "hostility when I heard Ghanaian girls begging white male volunteers to give them white babies."[79] Not only did he believe Ghana suffered from a racist system, he became disillusioned with the Peace Corps. He wrote that he was called a racist by the white volunteers: "I'm so reserved and make no effort to be friendly with our white element. . . . Were I white and aloof, I'd be just another odd ball."[80]

Before the completion of his project, Smith renounced the ideals of the Peace Corps. First, he insisted on being transferred from his isolated and rural assignment. The more rural the assignment was, the more appropriate the image seemed to be, and hence the less Smith liked it, because the image had nothing to do with his goals. Then he began to wonder why he should be in Ghana at all. He asked himself, "Why should I waste another year out here? The real struggle is elsewhere, closer to home—the seat of Whitey's real power. The black man worldwide is politically, economically and culturally bankrupt." The Peace Corps and its philosophy seemed useless to Smith. He ended his account with the declaration that he had burned the last two months of his diary because they would be seen as too subversive: "I'll be damned if I wasn't going to include the full text of the speech Malcolm X made at the University of Ghana." Smith had joined the Peace Corps believing his activist beliefs could be merged with Peace Corps ideology. His failure to reconcile the two shows how far from understanding young black America the Peace Corps leadership was.[81]

Smith was not alone in finding racism in his host country. Another black volunteer, Calvin Sparks, wrote in the newsletter of his country, Malaysia, that "most of these people just don't dig black skin. They may eventually consider you a person (lower form), of course, but not the skin. And as for me, if you don't dig the skin, you don't dig me."[82] Willie Hankins, a teacher in India, described his first haircut as chaotic because his curly hair attracted so much attention: "The first strands never hit the floor, as there was a mad scramble for souvenirs."[83] In the Philippines, blacks often met with the salutation "nigger" before Filipinos learned their names. Lawrence Fuchs thought black volunteers "showed extraordinary resiliency and strength in dealing with the frustrations of intercultural conflict."[84] An evaluator of the Philippines projects agreed with that assessment: "Several Volunteers commented that the color consciousness of the Filipinos—who attribute the greatest beauty to the lightest skin—had rubbed off on them, that they were probably *more* color conscious after two years in the Philippines than before they left home."[85]

Not all black volunteers believed their host countries to be racist or that they themselves suffered from racism. Ann Covington was told that as a black, she would be less accepted as a teacher in Ethiopia. She believed that was not the case: "With the Negro there is no initial wall of color. The sameness of color opens the door."[86] As with all categories of volunteers, African-Americans tolerated a wide variety of experiences, some positive and some negative, and these experiences differed from most of their expectations. The Peace Corps leadership gave them little idea of what to expect because the image they had of the volunteers, black as well as white, was static and shallow.

African-American volunteer Anita Quick enjoys a conversation with two women in the Ivory Coast. African-Americans and women faced unexpected complexities in their relationship with their hosts. Photo by Pickerel, 1968, courtesy National Archives.

Some volunteers found neither racism nor racial solidarity—only fundamentally different concepts of race than they had expected. As Willie Mae Watson found, "This is the first place I've ever been where I've been called so many different colors or taken for anything but Negro." Some of her students described her as white but admitted she had an "African nose."[87] As Jonathan Zimmerman notes, some black volunteers in Nigeria were referred to as "white Black," while another in Cameroon was known as "black white woman."[88] Many of these volunteers came to Africa straight from the civil rights movement, complete with the Afro hairstyle so symbolic for many of them. Yet they soon learned that "there was nothing particularly African about the Afro at all," and some of their African hosts "expressed polite amusement at their unkempt 'bushes.'"[89]

The experiences of volunteers from other minority groups resembled those of African-American volunteers. The Peace Corps was sensitive to their problems, and the *Volunteer* even devoted an issue to the unique difficulties of being a minority volunteer. Nonetheless, minority volunteers were vexed by their unique problems. For example, all minority groups were most surprised that they were seen by the host nationals not as minority groups, but as Americans. Ed Smith, the radical black nationalist and Pan-Africanist, found this out to his disappointment. He came to the realization after an especially difficult day of miscommunicating with his Ghanaian students: "Well, it is about time I faced facts: I am *not* one of them, and never can be. I am not one of them, with the same problems, but am an American, even though a black one, as different from them as ole' bos [his nickname for another volunteer he thought was especially racist]."[90] Arnold Zeitlin noticed the same phenomenon in Ghana: "The students were interested in Negroes. . . . A Negro to the students was an alien, an American with dark skin."[91] Even the leadership belatedly recognized this, as Frank Mankiewicz wrote in 1967: "Volunteers, whatever their position in society, whatever their color, whatever their national origins, are Americans—gringoes—and, therefore, powerful and influential."[92] This did not necessarily fit with the original Peace Corps ideology, which taught that fundamental humanity was far more important than race, class, or nationality.

Many minority volunteers felt confused about their role and the part their race played in it. Some felt their "dual status" helped, while others felt hindered by it. In Peru, one volunteer from Puerto Rico who was "completely bilingual" became "well accepted in the community, and is doing an excellent job in a quiet, unobtrusive way. . . . The children worship her."[93] Another volunteer of Latin American descent believed he had an advantage: "I drink like they do, I sing like they do, I feel and dance (almost) like they do." But he appreciated his dual existence, because despite his Mexican heritage, he was also perceived as a gringo. He wrote, "Being a Gringo has clearly expedited my work when I needed to cut red tape for appointments, etc."[94]

This dual image also caused problems. In Colombia, Dolores Trevino tired of the refrain, "When will a Gringo Peace Corps Volunteer Come?" and became angry when the locals added, "You're a Mexican and Mexicans don't know as much as gringoes."[95] This made her job all the more difficult, because if her hosts viewed fellow Latins in this way, how were they to succeed in a self-help project? And why did they believe that white gringos were smarter than Latin American gringos? She believed part of the problem was the image of a volunteer created by the Peace Corps. She said her work was more difficult because she did not "fit the nice, all-American, U.S. standard that had been set up."[96]

Asian-Americans faced the same problems in their work as volunteers. Robert Ishikawa decided, "The problems usually revolve around one fact: complete disbelief that I could possibly be an American. Some Indians think

I am a Russian or a Chinese communist."[97] Ishikawa and other Asian-Americans first had to live down their image as non-Americans before they could live up to their Peace Corps image. Toshi Watanabe found her life in the Philippines even more complicated, because she had to live three images: that of a Japanese-American, that of a female American, and that of a Peace Corps volunteer. In an article in the *Volunteer,* she related how difficult it was for her to constantly hear the question, "What part of Japan do you come from?" In the Philippines, with the history of the Japanese occupation, this question was usually asked in a negative tone. Her life was even more difficult because she was a woman. She believed she was "looked on as a brazen sort of female for attending a cockfight or hitching a ride on a cargo truck, while the 'real' Americans receive indulgent smiles."[98] Real Americans were not only white, but also male, and this made Watanabe's life and work difficult.

The confusion could reach chaos when Asian-American volunteers were sent to non-Asian countries. Glenn Tamanaha, a Japanese-American sent to Colombia, felt helpless to say who he was, and being called a "chino" made his job all the more difficult: "I can't play billiards without being harassed by bystanders. . . . I can't enter a restaurant without hearing chino jokes directed at my presence."[99] The Peace Corps gave little special preparation or training to these volunteers, because they thought they had created a universal volunteer and did not consider what would happen when the looks did not match the image. Dave Matsushita almost attacked a Colombian who called him a North Vietnamese. Then he began to wonder about the purpose of the Peace Corps and its connection to the American government. He wrote about how confused he became when he thought of what the volunteers were trying to accomplish. He wanted no part of promoting American values, because he understood the dark side of America's past: "I have held the feeling up to this day that the United States is not a democracy but a hypocrisy. I was born in a concentration camp where my family had been sent by our government simply because we looked different from most Americans. Is that democracy? . . . I think it can happen again."[100]

Even if the Peace Corps had been better able to include minorities, the agency worked in an American society that was ignorant at best and racist at its worst. William Mercer, the only African-American on his project, believed he encountered more difficulties from his fellow volunteers than from the host nationals. He "had to face their queries as to how I managed with the indigenous people, why Negro men wear mustaches. . . . My peers perceived me not as an American but rather as a Negro."[101] Paul Cowan describes a scene of ethnic insensitivity from his training. The group viewed a movie, and at one point they broke out in uproarious laughter as an

African carpenter stuck nails in his hair while building a school. At this point, Cowan relates, "Never had I felt so keenly aware of biased remarks directed at Jews."[102]

In the end, then, most volunteers learned that their original hopes about making friends in the third world were overly simplistic and superficial. A common humanity did not always guarantee cultural understanding, nor did a common sex or a common racial identity. Just as in their living and working experiences, volunteers learned in their personal relationships that the third world was a more complicated place than they had believed before joining the Peace Corps. Their experience in dealing with the locals did reinforce a belief in the egalitarian ideal, however. Although many gave up on the idea of making real friends overseas, and many others admitted to never understanding the "mixed-up" cultures they experienced, almost all volunteers clung tenaciously to a fundamental belief in the cultural equality of their hosts.

One core belief of this ideology was a commitment to some kind of democracy. In his study of volunteer effectiveness in Colombia, Morris Stein found that volunteers left the Corps with "slightly more democratic attitudes."[103] Many who started 4-H clubs did so for the stated purpose of increasing knowledge among host nationals about democracy. John Briscoe insisted that he designed his 4-H club in India to democratize the operation of local farmers.[104] And a group of volunteers created a 4-H club so the members could belong to "a group which is self-organized and which makes decisions democratically."[105]

Some volunteers believed bringing democracy to a country also meant bringing American political institutions. Robert L. McAndrews, a teacher in Kpaiyea in western Liberia in 1962, provides an example of this attitude. While there, he witnessed the investigation of one of his students for a crime the student did not commit. The student was convicted, not necessarily because the investigators thought he did it, but because he challenged his elders about the matter. McAndrews found this disturbing: "I was trying to teach some democratic principles to my students and the whole tradition of the society was geared to a different set of principles. Much of the proceeding of the trial seemed illogical to me." McAndrews thought the student needed to "have a trial by American standards,"[106] but in the end, he accepted the situation in order not to confuse his students. For him, though, democratic principles meant American standards.

Most were more specific about what they meant by "democratic principles." While conducting his survey, Morris Stein was also concerned with defining what the search for democratic values meant. So he sent some

non-American interviewers into the villages to find out from the host nationals what the volunteers emphasized. Stein found out that two of the most
important beliefs stressed by volunteers were the "belief that all men are
equal" and how important it was for people to be "more informal with each
other."[107] A central aspect of volunteer philosophy was that "the Peace Corps
exists as a vehicle for acting out your fantasies of brotherhood."[108] According
to Alan Guskin in Thailand, "the Volunteer is by ideology an egalitarian."[109]

Outside observers and Peace Corps staffers alike noted the dogged
attraction to egalitarian ideas on the part of volunteers. John Lunstrum, an
Indiana University professor hired by the Peace Corps as an educational
consultant, complained about "the zealous, dogmatic application of American egalitarian values in the field."[110] Mankiewicz tried to answer
Lunstrum's charges about the shortcomings of this egalitarianism but did
not deny its existence. The volunteers trumpeted their egalitarian actions at
every turn. Edna McGuire relates an incident in which volunteers "were
shocked when the students first came as their guests to have them go in the
back door. This, it seemed, was a custom established in colonial days. The
Peace Corps Volunteers promptly ended that remnant of colonialism and
taught a lesson in democracy by assuring the students that they expected
all their guests to enter through the front door."[111] Here the Peace Corps
triumphed over antiquated colonialist values. In India, because of the caste
system, volunteers felt the need to promote their egalitarianism most keenly.
Carl Pope recalled feeling morally superior to a Brahmin host because unlike
the Brahmin, he could interact with the untouchable cook.[112] Many came
to the conclusion that the biggest obstacle to progress in their host country
was a lack of egalitarian values. For example, John Freivalds argued that the
real problem in Colombia was the "pretentiousness of townspeople." The
poor having to call the rich "your highness" and co-op managers wearing
their "best suits to work and addressing the poorer customers with disdain"
caused a rift that doomed Colombian society.[113]

This almost religious dedication to egalitarianism caused a severe
tension within the volunteer philosophy. A strict belief in equality might
mandate a fundamental respect for the beliefs of other cultures. What if, as
in the case of Pope in India and Freivalds in Colombia, the host culture
rejected egalitarian ideas? Some volunteers solved this problem by stressing
the importance of universal human egalitarianism over the specific beliefs
of other cultures.

Other volunteers might have called themselves cultural relativists,
because they felt it most important to accept the views of other cultures,
even if they seemed unjust to Americans. David Szanton wrote that this

"kind of primitive egalitarianism" predominated in the Philippines, where volunteers admired all things Filipino.[114] In a book on the Peace Corps, author and evaluator Mark Harris tells a story about a dinner he had with some volunteers, during which he mentioned the difficulty he was having with the bad odors of the host country. The volunteers immediately cut him off, arguing that mentioning the odors, bad or not, was "not good democratic form."[115] Peter Deekle, living in Iran, ruminated over this question in his diary. He agreed that some customs in Iran, such as restrictive laws aimed at women, might seem nonegalitarian to Americans. But he believed that even though Americans might see such codes as "Victorian," they actually were a "very comfortable set of behavioral codes—built up over the ages."[116] Consequently, he had difficulties with the Shah's programs to make Iran more like the egalitarian West.

Volunteers sensed this internal strain in their philosophy. While in training, Grant Farr and his fellow trainees "agreed that it is ethically wrong for one culture to impose its values on another culture." After serving for a time in the field, he was not so sure. As he put it, "In theory I still agree but now I realize that giving technical assistance implies changing social values. Simply by being in Afghanistan we are examples of a different culture."[117] Farr put his finger on a central contradiction in Peace Corps and Peace Corps volunteer philosophy. Just by being there, volunteers were a living implication that they knew how to do things and they were there to teach the locals, who did not.

The idea of community development suffered the most from this difficulty. Many volunteers involved in community development accepted its tenets because they seemed so egalitarian. Volunteers accepted the fundamental equality of the locals by stressing self-help, rather than ordering them to do something. Tom Carter, a community developer in Peru, insisted, "A corpsman has to be careful and not become too much of a leader." He cites as a prime example putting a roof on the local school: "It would be a ten dollar project and one days labor for two or three Peace Corpsmen to build that roof. Yet we don't do it. If we gave my school a roof, it would always be that, a gift, a gringoe's roof. If it takes me a year to talk my neighbors into putting on that roof, it will be worth it."[118] The problem arose when volunteers understood that even the act of "talking them into it" implied a contradiction of their egalitarian ethos—that the Peace Corpsmen knew best what was good for the host national. Lawrence Fuchs noted this inconsistency in the Philippines. The volunteers "wanted very much to help the Filipinos but mainly for the purpose of promoting self-help." Fuchs saw that they "were caught in the dilemma of trying to promote self reliance in a culture which did not value individual initiative in the first place."[119] In other words, volunteers promoted egalitarian values and American individualism in a society that did not accept these as important values.

Despite this internal contradiction, many believed their heightened sense of egalitarianism to be the most important aspect of volunteer philosophy. According to a study conducted by social scientist Robert Doerr, the most important thing volunteers got out of their experience was an increased sense of "human mutuality, defined as reciprocity with other Volunteers and host nationals."[120]

These new ideas colored volunteers' perceptions of American society upon their return. Many came from families and towns that were not only insensitive, but also openly racist. After meeting and dating a local Catholic girl overseas, David Bentley wrote home, anxious about the reaction of his family: "I'm pretty sure I know how you'd react to my bringing a negro home [to marry]—I believe we went through it once but I was just wondering what would be your reaction to a Catholic."[121] Some volunteers, especially those from the Deep South, realized right away that the Peace Corps differed from their insulated, racist society. Lillian Carter, from the heart of Georgia, relished the reaction of her town to her training program. "Its so different here," she wrote, "because I don't think there is a segregationist in the whole group. . . . I'm getting used to being taught the facts of life by a young black man. Lord, the folks in Plains would have a fit!"[122]

This new attitude contrasted sharply with the opinion of locals held by other American diplomats abroad. One United States Information Service official in Ghana reportedly complained, "The poor people here are like animals. They should never be allowed to come to the city." His answer: create a strategic hamlet system, as in Vietnam, and herd them into it. Paul Cowan reported an AID official in the same country saying that giving Ghanaians birth control without sex education would be like "giving the niggers the right to vote and not teaching them how to use it."[123] The Peace Corps came from a cultural milieu that made true equality of minorities virtually impossible. Shriver and other leaders thought they had created the first color-blind governmental agency, but the culture and their own image making prevented them from succeeding in this effort.

Peace Corps leadership and white volunteers alike prided themselves on their progressive, liberal view of race issues, regardless of how minority volunteers might have felt. One volunteer commented, "There was one black in our midst and because he was there we all felt like integrated, liberal, nice people."[124] A white southern volunteer named Dan Boucher experienced an epiphany on race relations while in the Corps: "I was one of those white southerners that had to go out of the country to really become enlightened on the problems of race in the south and so I feel it is my obligation to go back to the south and do something about it."[125] Lillian Carter declared, "I have simply become color blind. I've become as dark as most of my friends, and the little black babies are no longer afraid of me."[126] Volunteer Jim Crandell believed, "Our time in Africa has really opened our eyes to many problems." [127] Volunteers believed they had a better outlook on race relations than any other Americans.

Some white volunteers took their new beliefs to such an extreme that they felt ashamed and depressed about their white skin. Polly Kirkpatrick complained, "It begins to grate when you are always addressed as 'whitey' and everyone wants to touch you."[128] David Schickele, serving in Nigeria, wrote about an incident where he and his Nigerian friends were joking about their respective colors. Soon, he wrote, he "felt ashamed" of his "chalky, pallid skin against the splendor of the Africans."[129] Arnold Zeitlin described how his relationship with a black volunteer soured because Zeitlin envied him.[130] Many volunteers wrote of their embarrassment over being given special status as whites. In every story Zeitlin told about his vacation time, he mentioned that the locals wanted him to travel in a first-class compartment, but he refused because he wanted to ride with the locals.

Other white volunteers declared that the only way to be effective was to suppress these feelings of difference vis-à-vis people of color. Kitsie Ewer, a teacher in Nigeria, wrote a paper with the argument that "the initial feeling of guilt on behalf of one's white skin and over privileged background must be dismissed."[131] Instead, she believed that volunteers must strive to pretend the colors don't exist. Socially, this might be difficult: "Moving in African circles will require your really bearing down and learning the language and being prepared to face suspicion from both the Europeans and the Africans." [132] But many volunteers and Peace Corps leaders believed this to be one of the central missions of the Peace Corps.

The volunteers were bred to believe they held a superior position on issues of race. John Rex referred to American southerners as those "ignorant, stupid, prejudiced bastards in the south."[133] When they returned home, white volunteers found a society that did not live up to the ideal standard they thought they had lived with abroad. They "were disturbed to return to a society where 'invisible barriers' are ever present."[134] Because of this, many became involved with the civil rights movement after their return home. Just before his return, one volunteer asserted: "The race problem back home will bother me a lot. I will be much less patient now. You might even say we're radical now."[135] This political stance is ironic, since Shriver and the other

Peace Corps leaders were the very definition of liberal, rather than radical. But their rhetoric on race had spurred the volunteers in different directions. This rhetoric could not effectively recruit black volunteers. The image behind the rhetoric repelled minority and women volunteers. But the words themselves helped spur volunteers, on their return, "to take a much firmer and more active position in the field of Civil Rights than ever before."[136]

Novelist James Michener, a strong proponent of the Peace Corps idea, described what he believed happened to the volunteers' sense of egalitarianism while working on their project. "People who go into the Peace Corps come back with some imagination," Michener wrote. "They aren't frightened when a Negro runs for sheriff or something. They've seen Negroes run societies. They've seen Polynesians do just about as well in medicine as we do. People who have this experience are set free by it."[137] This is precisely what happened to most volunteers. They were set free from previous ideas of the third world, set free from previous ideas of the straightforward nature of development, and set free from previous notions of America's role in bringing this development to the rest of the world. This new philosophy, set free from the mind-set of American liberal development in the 1950s and 1960s, would present a new, more educated and sophisticated, way of dealing with the third world in the final years of the twentieth century.

Breaking free from liberal ideas of development also set volunteers free from traditional liberal political beliefs. Many volunteers might have come into the Peace Corps following the liberal ideology of their leaders. Kennedy's charisma attracted them. So did the energetic, visionary ideals of Shriver, Wofford, and Mankiewicz. But by the time they left the Peace Corps, volunteers had developed a disdain for the liberal ideology of their leaders. Their experiences had been too different from the expectations given them by the liberal leadership.

The experiences of most volunteers forced them to rethink their attitudes toward American culture. As one critic put it, they had "begun to see the cultural load they carry as Americans."[138] One volunteer, serving in Latin America, came "to feel that we North Americans are on a treadmill of accumulating possessions and conveniences."[139] Some mirrored the attitudes of radicals in the United States, rejecting American culture for something as unusual as possible. Myron Gildesgame commented that his best friends, Tim and Tom, had "been talking of Zen and meditation." Gildesgame's reaction: "I am really far away, so far, from that kind of thinking."[140] In general, most volunteers agreed with him, accepting materialistic American culture, foibles and all. One volunteer in Ghana said in a bemused tone, "We could look with fond tolerance at the absurdities of American living."[141]

The established power structure also drew their ire. Volunteers felt "shaken about U.S. blunders overseas" and were "less optimistic about the future of the U.S. as a great democracy."[142] Black volunteers, especially, believed that the Peace Corps sought "to superimpose American attitudes, methods and ideals on cultures and ideologies that are different."[143] The problem was not so much the attitudes themselves, but the fact that volunteers believed the Peace Corps leadership was trying to superimpose them throughout the world. We have seen that Shriver and the other leaders would have vehemently denied this sort of charge of cultural imperialism. But we have also seen that their idea of the new pioneer, while not forcing American ideals on the third world, tried to convince the underdeveloped country of the merits of these ideals. Many volunteers mistrusted their leaders and their government. In Guatemala, volunteers left feeling "deeply suspicious of American foreign policy in Guatemala, which they fear is secretly committed to maintaining the current power structure."[144]

Volunteers were egalitarian to a fault, not only respecting the cultures and viewpoints of their hosts but occasionally adopting them as well. After returning from his teaching job in Nigeria, Donald Sher insisted that for any given volunteer, "his loyalties during his stay abroad shift."[145] After discussing American policy in Southeast Asia, a group of volunteers in Thailand decided it would be best if the United States removed its military from there, even if it compromised American policy. The evaluator commented, "It was the hallmark of this group that their primary concern was not for their future or the future of the United States but for the future of Thailand."[146] Again and again, evaluators and commentators recorded this phenomenon. One evaluation in Guatemala noted a trend that some governmental officials might have found sinister. The volunteers made it plain, the evaluation reads, "that they now feel some loyalty to people and places beyond the borders of the United States, and they cannot be expected to automatically side with the United States on every issue. . . . A number said [given a revolution opposed by the United States] they would work actively against the American position."[147] Many rejected American government policy, and all of them seemed to reject government ideology and the official Peace Corps ideology during the 1960s.

Yet the volunteers did not leave the Corps following a single, cohesive, antiliberal political ideology. Just as it is difficult to generalize about them in any way, it is difficult to generalize about their political beliefs. They did not reject the liberal ideology of their leaders to take up the conservative banner, nor did they all become stereotypical student radicals. Instead, their ideology represented an eclectic mix of beliefs gleaned from their background and their experience. Buried deep in the prose of an evaluation from a completion-of-service conference in the Philippines, Jane Campbell and Thomas Scott may have put their finger on a way to understand this subtle yet enigmatic ideology:

> At the end of two years in the Peace Corps, the Volunteers in these groups appeared to have a rather unique combination of the views of the 19th century liberal and the mid-20th century middle-class housewife. They're strong on civil rights, laissez faire and less government control—but they also think the PTA and little league baseball sound like pretty fine institutions after all.[148]

Campbell and Scott don't discuss this idea any further, but it provides us with a suggestive framework for understanding volunteer ideology.

It is easier to come to grips with the ideas and attitudes attributed by Campbell and Scott to the mid–twentieth-century suburban housewife. Paul Cowan believed the ideology stemmed from a class basis: "Most Peace Corps Volunteers come from the much larger middle class to whom democracy and freedom mean the sacred right to buy a second car or build a new home."[149] But, according to a study done by Robert Gaudino, volunteers could not be so easily categorized in purely socioeconomic terms. Gaudino found that for one group serving in India, half of their fathers had no more than a high school education, more than half came from families with incomes that would be "lower middle class" at best, and half came from households in which the mother worked.[150]

Yet even if they did not come from the middle class, most adhered to middle-class cultural ideology. One volunteer in Brazil wrote in her diary about how she inculcated these values in local children: "I have three big boys that come every morning to eat. I tell them tomorrow you go after wood before you get any food here. They are learning many lessons, please, thank you, etc. . . . They must come with clean faces. If not I send them home. That way the mother learns too."[151] She believed it was critical to teach them American middle-class etiquette. Volunteers in Costa Rica also brought customs straight from Main Street, USA, of the 1950s. Debbie Graf organized a prom complete with decorations resembling a local volcano.[152] Such superficiality could not be more stereotypical of 1950s middle-class American high school life. In the Dominican Republic, Wesley Stewart and Jon Fosdick "started a Baby Ruth league. They had seventeen baseball uniforms and some equipment sent in by friends in Toledo, Ohio."[153]

These institutions of American suburban culture were intended to infuse the values of that culture. Although related to pioneer values, these were not the romantic values of myth, but the values volunteers thought important for survival in 1960s America. Fran Brewer helped start a YMCA in Colombia because it could use "the competitiveness of boys to help them learn games with rules."[154] James Oliver and Will Prior also helped a local YMCA, because they felt it important for the children to play games so they could "learn respect for property by handing their gloves to the next player."[155]

Another favored organization for volunteers were 4-H clubs. The Peace Corps leadership liked volunteers to be involved in these clubs because they could work with animals and live like new pioneers, but most volunteers saw their importance in other terms. Ann Weir, in Brazil, believed they helped teach "leaders how to lead, members how to participate, and everyone how a club functions."[156] With 4-H clubs, volunteers promoted family values that were central to American culture during the 1950s and early 1960s. They were horrified to find children "living without parental love," children who had "the beautiful but empty and expressionless eyes which reflected the obvious lack of a warm family environment."[157]

Volunteers often wondered what to do with the ideas they believed in strongly. Were they supposed to ignore them in the two years they lived as a volunteer? Or, even if they didn't try to coerce their hosts into attaining these ideas, shouldn't they at least live by them themselves? John Rex, a teacher in Ethiopia, struggled with exactly this dilemma. As he put it, "When we work within a system which is foreign to our own ideas, should we be forced to compromise our basic ideals concerning honesty, truth and honor?"[158] Seymour Greben, the director of the Office of Public Affairs in Washington, believed that volunteers in Peru chose to stick with their own ideas, rejecting those of the host culture. As he viewed it, "They had apparently not, in their two years' experience, come to any real understanding of relative cultures."[159] Greben, imbued with the liberal ethos of the Peace Corps leadership, could not understand this viewpoint of the volunteers.

These conservative, traditional ideas also popped up in the more strictly political views of many volunteers, most of whom could not be categorized precisely as conservative or liberal. Richard Lazarus is a good example. As the heir to a wealthy retail family in Ohio, his family had generally conservative instincts. Also, he had difficulty following the lead of the liberal Democrats, because he disagreed with their leadership of the Peace Corps. But, as he mulled over his decision in the upcoming election in 1968, he wrote: "I hope it doesn't sound naive but the idea of the Republican party being represented by Richard Nixon in 1968 is frightening. It's almost as if they were asking every thinking member of my generation to vote Democratic. The least they can offer is a positive alternative."[160] Most staffers at Peace Corps Washington accepted the belief that volunteers came from the "broad center" of the political spectrum.[161] The political tastes of most volunteers seemed to mirror their traditional, middle-of-the-road ideology, the ideology of the mid–twentieth-century suburban housewife.

Outsiders often found themselves surprised at the mild beliefs of volunteers. The first conference for all returned volunteers, held in Washington in 1965, provides a perfect illustration. Nonvolunteers were invited to the conference as "special participants." The idea was to expose leaders from the corporate, political, and academic worlds to the new American, the Peace Corps volunteer. According to the report from this conference, "Some of the special participants complained that among the Volunteers were more doves than hawks. 'Where are the revolutionaries?,' asked a corporation executive. Volunteers in one workshop seemed to think the solution to most problems was talking to PTAs."[162] The tone of this comment, written by Harris Wofford and other Peace Corps leaders, suggests the disdain and surprise that the volunteers' conservative methods held for the leadership.

The volunteers' political views might have surprised the liberal Peace Corps leadership. Every letter David Nelson wrote home to his parents discussed the importance of governments balancing their budgets. He also consistently discussed his disapproval of labor unions and his desire to write his congressman in support of antitrust legislation against big labor—this from a volunteer who in other matters might be considered radical.[163] Robert Attaway, in a letter to the editor of the *Volunteer,* told what he thought of the student radical movement in the United States and its applicability to the agency: "Flower power and love strike me as erroneous and revolting words to describe both the Peace Corps and the people in it. If there are passive idealists in the Peace Corps, the Peace Corps should get rid of them. Such pompous, self deluded piety does more harm than good; it makes cloud high what should be down to earth."[164]

This is not to argue that Peace Corps volunteers were an army of clean-cut, conservative youth. Part of their philosophy might have been that of the mid–twentieth-century suburban housewife, but most volunteers would have still called themselves liberal. For the second half of the volunteer puzzle, the Campbell and Scott evaluation presented the idea of the "19th century liberal." It is not at all clear what this refers to—American liberals in the nineteenth century? Traditional British liberalism as expressed by the leading intellectuals of the time, such as John Stuart Mill? It appears the evaluators meant it to describe a democratic, open-minded ideology, something akin to what they saw sweeping American campuses in the late 1960s.

Many volunteers considered themselves to be in the center of the radical movements of the late 1960s. Because of the new and inspiring rhetoric of the leaders of this movement, many thought they ought to be revolutionaries, even though the Peace Corps leadership explicitly discouraged revolutionary thoughts.[165] The liberal leadership often worried that their charges were becoming too radical, and in the Philippines, they commissioned a survey of volunteers' political beliefs. The results must have been sobering to them: "Our survey clearly shows a 'left-ward drift' among Peace Corps Volunteers after they arrive in the Philippines. The real and immediate danger here is that a professional Marxist or communist organizer, without revealing his identity, will 'take over' the Volunteer. We saw at least three Peace Corps Volunteers who were in a psychological condition to 'defect.'"[166]

Some volunteers did defect. Linda Muller told her Nigerian students a story that exemplifies how radical some became: "Many people, old and young, had come to Chicago to demonstrate against the war in Vietnam. They had no place to stay, so they had to live in the city park. Now, the police of Chicago liked the war in Vietnam and hated the people who were demonstrating against it."[167] The moral of her story turned out to be that violence against the people was bad no matter where it occurred, whether in Chicago or in Biafra. Whether or not this is the version of events that ends up in history textbooks, in 1970 it represented a relatively radical interpretation of the events outside the Democratic convention in 1968. At least one other volunteer must have agreed with this heroic interpretation, for after hearing of the difficulties in Chicago, she decided the first thing she would do upon returning to the United States was to go to the SDS office in Chicago and volunteer her services.[168]

After their return, some radical volunteers kept in touch with other volunteers of similar persuasions. Some of them created underground newsletters, intended mostly for their small group of friends and other like-minded people. One set of returned volunteers from Africa called themselves "The Group" and published a newsletter in West Virginia called *Tidbits—Nkwantabisa*. They proudly touted an increase in subscriptions, even though they had received "a smattering of rumble that our bias is too left."[169] The newsletter contained articles decrying U.S. policy in Vietnam, for example, written by former volunteers and culled from various national newspapers. They were most interested in exposing the conservative tendencies of the American aid establishment. For example, they published one article excoriating the USIA's conservative book list and mocking its conservative editor, who claimed that one book contrasted "the myths of the communists . . .

with their record of famine, terror, secret police and concentration camps."[170] The Group definitely fit the pattern of small, radical groups that cropped up all over the United States in the late 1960s to protest the war in Vietnam and civil rights abuses.

Another organization fitting this category was the Committee of Returned Volunteers, or CRV, organized to protest injustices such as the war in Vietnam. When it first formed, outsiders considered it "a new young pressure group . . . sort of a liberal American legion."[171]

But volunteers were a different sort of radical. They did not fit the stereotype of "flower power" radicals so frowned upon in Robert Attaway's letter to the editor. Other radicals sneered at volunteers, considering the agency and anyone attached to it "part of the Establishment and . . . irrelevant."[172] And, as we have seen, the ideology of the volunteers can not be so easily characterized.

One aspect of the volunteer mind-set that did not mesh so easily with that of the 1960s radical was a desire for discipline. Some of the more politicized radicals, such as those working in the FSM in Berkeley, believed in the importance of discipline. But for the more stereotypical "hippie" from the Haight, nothing could be more of an anathema to his or her belief system than control.

Throughout the 1960s, volunteers consistently complained about a lack of discipline at the Peace Corps. Outsiders noticed this immediately. Morris Stein, in his study of a group of volunteers in Colombia, noted with surprise that one of the biggest changes experienced by volunteers' attitudes was an increased need for order in their lives.[173] While in the Peace Corps, they sneered at confusion and had little patience with disorderly volunteers.

Virtually every report from volunteer completion-of-service conferences mentioned this disdain for chaos. In Peru, "the Volunteers definitely felt that transgressors of vacation rules, social conduct rules, etc., should be disciplined or sent home."[174] It seems strange that the very same volunteers who complained about the rules also complained that the rules were not enforced. Many volunteers sounded draconian in their desire to punish offensive colleagues. One group from the Philippines insisted the Peace Corps was "not a goddamn rehabilitation center."[175] A volunteer in Nigeria quipped, "Do the Peace Corps reps get points for not sending Volunteers home?"[176] Apparently, this belief was not confined to a few disgruntled volunteers. The Philippines II project volunteers were "fully united and adamant" against the Peace Corps' "too permissive atmosphere."[177] These are not the stereotypical radicals of the 1960s, pushing for freedom to experiment.

The evaluators who reported what one volunteer referred to as "the coddling problem" were not concocting this story so Peace Corps Washington could increase its control over wayward volunteers. Volunteers themselves consistently referred to this difficulty in letters and journal entries. Mrs. Frances Cunha, a teacher in Brazil, wrote home about the "big flops," "the boys" who "don't behave well, not mature enough for this work."[178] Admittedly, she was seventy-three years old at the time and might have believed anyone in their twenties to be immature. But she was not alone. In Ecuador, Myron Gildesgame wondered whether the "Peace Corps in general is like it is in Ecuador as I've seen it. So many people here are doing minimal work or just hanging around."[179] Further north, in Colombia, Richard Lazarus wrote, "The Volunteers quite frankly need an occasional well-placed and well-timed kick in the old 'gluteus maximus.'"[180]

Volunteers were not traditional conservatives, nor were they traditional radicals. They certainly saw themselves as different from the liberal leaders of their own agency. They had been set free to create their own ideology, their own view of the world. The result was a subtle, complex, and rarely well-articulated ideology.

Volunteer ideology was a puzzle. Volunteers seemed equally comfortable with being a mid–twentieth-century suburban housewife and a nineteenth-century liberal. They believed many different things at once, as long as these beliefs could be called their own. Perhaps this enigmatic ideology showed that the Peace Corps leadership succeeded despite itself. Peace Corps Washington set out, in part, to educate American youth to become more thoughtful about the world. Yet they tried to do this by creating a cadre of like-minded volunteers. Luckily for their initial goals, the volunteers rejected the indoctrination and in so doing opened their eyes and minds to the world. They found a world filled with mixed-up people and mixed-up cultures—a revelation that challenged previous ideas about the third world and yet one that described this world in much more accurate terms.

Conclusion

From Development to Multiculturalism

American foreign policy makers began the 1960s with straightforward ideas about what they called the "developing world." American technology and hard work would help third world nations "develop" themselves. These countries could then reach the ultimate "stage" of "economic take-off," eventually reaping the benefits of the modern industrial age. Sargent Shriver's Peace Corps, as we have seen, became the ultimate flower of this liberal developmentalism. Shriver and his agency advanced these ideas to their most sophisticated, thoughtful, mature level. They would use the Peace Corps as their tool in this pursuit of development. The volunteers in the Peace Corps were to be molded into twentieth-century pioneers, helping countries in the developing world to conquer their frontiers, just as America had at an earlier time.

As this book points out, Shriver's plan faced huge obstacles from the beginning. From their very first contact with the Peace Corps in training, volunteers lost connection with their leadership and the goals of developmentalism. The content of the training disillusioned them, and the physical and psychological testing during training alienated them. Many volunteers found that this adversarial relationship continued while they were overseas, and conflicts over everything from motorcycles to politics sapped the volunteers' commitment to the idea of development.

Despite these problems, most volunteers arrived at their posts ready to at least try to move their third world country along the line of development. What they found on their arrival immediately shattered their beliefs and forced them to reevaluate their preconceptions about the third world. They willingly lived among the natives but found this to be a task completely at odds with their expectations. The third world was not universally primitive, and in some ways the people there were already "developed." In the work they did and in the relationships they pursued, volunteers learned that they had been wrong about the third world, causing them to reject their earlier liberal ideas of straightforward developmentalism.

Volunteers as a whole did not replace this idea with a coherent ideology. Rather, they developed a complex, often contradictory definition of this part of the world, the people in it, and their role as volunteers. They clung to their own definitions of individualism, egalitarianism, order, and progress. This ideology helped them survive their two-year stints abroad. More importantly, it gave them a completely new perspective and understanding of the world. They had learned that "other" cultures were dynamic and complicated. Their job had educated them and helped them develop new ideas about how American culture might interact with other cultures in the post-Vietnam world.

We can better grasp this ideology if we explore the work of anthropologist, historian, and philosopher James Clifford. In *The Predicament of Culture,* published in 1988, Clifford put together a collection of essays on a wide variety of topics, including surrealist art, early twentieth-century anthropology, and a late twentieth-century court case about the Mashpee Indians. Clifford saw these disparate analyses coming together to answer questions about how Western societies deal with "exotic" non-Western cultures. As he put it, "What are the essential elements and boundaries of culture?"[1]

Clifford's answer resembles that reached by Peace Corps volunteers in the 1960s. "This book," he argues, "makes space for specific paths through modernity. . . . People and things are increasingly out of place."[2] Clifford finds that many early ethnographers, modern artists, and art collectors came to the same conclusions that volunteers did about the incompleteness of Western cultural definitions of the third world and the need for development. In an argument that exactly describes volunteer feelings after arrival at their posts, Clifford concludes, "One no longer leaves home confident of finding something radically new, another time or space."[3]

Clifford's most compelling story lies in his final essay, about a civil suit brought by some Mashpee Indians in a Massachusetts court in 1976. These were "modern Indians, who spoke in New England–accented English about the Great Spirit."[4] They were suing to be recognized as a tribe, and the trial revolved on cultural and historical definitions of "tribalness." The Mashpee eventually lost their suit. For Clifford, however, the story shows how ideas about culture came to be contested in the American culture of the 1970s. No longer did Indians fill the "pathetic space" of "only survivors, noble or wretched." The trial forced Anglo-American culture to look deeply at the idea of culture and change its previously simplistic view. No longer could "stories of cultural contact and change" be viewed by a "pervasive dichotomy." "What if," Clifford queries, "identity is conceived not as a boundary to be maintained but as a nexus of relations and transactions actively engaging a subject?"[5]

This is precisely the conclusion reached by Peace Corps volunteers during the 1960s. They traveled to the third world holding firmly to the "dichotomizing concepts" of the "West-rest split" so central to liberal ideas of international development.[6] They found these ideas did not explain reality and were forced to reformulate their way of thinking about this area of the world. The resultant ideology, though never complete and well articulated, nonetheless "actively engaged" the other cultures and resulted in a new "nexus of relations," more mature and informed than the previous cultural boundaries.

Peace Corps volunteers served as de facto ambassadors of American culture during the 1960s. For many people in the developing world, volunteers served as the only direct contact to the United States. As such, volunteers helped create American foreign policy in these areas, whether or not they were recognized as traditional policymakers. But did their new mindset, this new, more informed and mature way of looking at the world, filter up into the area of traditional foreign policy making? What effects did the day-to-day experience of the Peace Corps have on the overall story of American relations with the world in the post-Vietnam era?

Volunteer thought and action during the 1960s had very little connection to John F. Kennedy's original ideas of how a Peace Corps might serve as a tool of foreign policy. In the end, the Peace Corps was not another tool in America's Cold War arsenal. As far as the volunteers were concerned, it made little difference whether the host nationals became socialist or communist. Volunteers worked to achieve their own individual goals, which often related to middle-class culture, but which did not necessarily preclude more radical political or economic ideas.

What about the idea of nation building? Intellectuals of the Kennedy administration, such as Walt Rostow and Arthur Schlesinger, believed this was the central purpose of the Peace Corps. Yet they never defined what they meant by the term. Shriver, Wofford, Wiggins, and the other Peace

Corps leaders did provide a method by which nation building could be translated from an abstract principle to a concrete project. They intended to build other nations by letting the people of those nations follow the mythic American example. New pioneers would fan out across the globe, helping the people of other countries conquer their frontiers as America had conquered its own.

But the reality of Peace Corps work did not match this ingenious plan. Volunteers rebelled at living like, working like, or acting like new pioneers. The plan did not stand the test of reality. Instead, volunteers took certain ideas and values and crafted their own view of the world. In the end, they probably did not succeed in "building nations." Other studies will have to evaluate the success or failure of the Peace Corps in this arena. As P. David Searles has pointed out, "Virtually no comprehensive effort has been undertaken to understand how the presence of the organization has affected a country."[7] In *The Peace Corps in Cameroon,* Julius Amin gives a generally positive appraisal of Peace Corps volunteer effects. But a cursory look at some of the other countries in which volunteers were heavily involved— Somalia, Iran, Liberia—might lead to different conclusions.[8]

For the most part, the upper echelons of American policy making remained unaffected by the experience of Peace Corps volunteers. One of these policymakers, Robert McNamara, began the 1960s as one of the leading proponents of the idea of liberal developmentalism. As David Halberstam put it, "He was a man of force, moving, pushing, getting things done, *Bob got things done,* the can-do man in the can-do society, in the can-do era," a man thoroughly imbued with "the American certitude and conviction."[9]

In his recent memoirs, designed to show the world how his thinking has changed, McNamara shows just how his thinking has *not* changed on issues of development: "To this day, I see quantification as a language to add precision to reasoning about the world. . . . It is a powerful tool too often neglected when we seek to overcome poverty, fiscal deficits, or the failure of our national health programs."[10] McNamara believed, and still believes, that American technology and hard work applied in the developing world would help these countries progress in a straightforward fashion. The scale of development was quantifiable, and McNamara believed it possible to measure the progress of this development. McNamara applied these same formidable analytical/rational ideas to solving the puzzle of Vietnam. The failure of this strategy is well documented, a misunderstanding far more tragic than the cultural disconnectedness suffered by many Peace Corps volunteers originally imbued with McNamara's can-do spirit.

It is no accident that after the debacle in Vietnam, McNamara was "kicked upstairs" into the post of director of the World Bank. Usually viewed by historians as a meaningless assignment earned because of Lyndon Johnson's wrath at his dubious accomplishments in Vietnam, McNamara apparently viewed his new role as critical to American ideas of liberal developmentalism. At least he tackled his new job with extraordinary vigor. Yet he attacked it as if he had learned nothing from his experience dealing with Vietnam or with the reality of development as learned by Peace Corps volunteers.

One of McNamara's first tasks at the World Bank, as he proudly noted, was to formulate a "development plan for each developing nation."[11] In other words, he applied some of his standby mathematical formulas to assist in the straightforward development of these nations. Aid could work, McNamara argued, only if the "performance deficiencies of the poorer nations" could be avoided.[12] Always the Rostowian disciple, McNamara diligently worked at the World Bank without looking to the lessons learned by workers in these foreign countries, such as Peace Corps volunteers. Without American aid, these countries faced "certain disaster."[13] Like all liberal developmentalists, McNamara's motives were admirable. As he put it, "Development is about people. The only criterion for measuring its ultimate success or failure is what it does to enhance the lives of individual human beings."[14] Yet, as we have seen with Peace Corps volunteers, good intentions did not suffice. Only a new understanding of these areas of the world and a new definition of ideas such as development could enhance the lives of people on both sides of the development line.

Whereas the volunteer view of the developing world had little effect on American foreign policy in the early 1970s, it is not too far-fetched to imagine that this sort of philosophy contributed to the broader push for human rights half a decade later in the Carter administration. After all, as we have seen, Carter's own mother had served as a volunteer. Many in the Peace Corps believed Carter to hold sympathetic views. After he was elected, Peace Corps staffers, many of whom were returned volunteers by 1975, unfurled a banner outside the Washington headquarters proclaiming, "We won."[15]

Perhaps most suggestively, many returned volunteers served in the foreign policy establishment during the Carter years. Hundreds of AID staffers were returned volunteers, and the director of the Immigration and Naturalization Service had served in the Philippines as a volunteer. Carter's administration is well known for its unique push for "human rights." According to political scientist Martha Cottam, this focus represented the "best example of diversity in images" in dealing with the third world, a policy contrasting sharply with the "extreme simplification" that other administrations had been guilty of. Cottam argues that except for the Carter administration, all American policymakers since World War II have viewed Latin American countries as "weak, childlike, inferior and inept." Only a small group of Carter advisers and legislators in the Carter years broke the mold and viewed countries in the third world as "sophisticated and complex." This view sounds very much like the one reached by Peace Corps volunteers in the 1960s. This is no accident. Two of the leading five legislators initiating this view, Christopher Dodd and Paul Tsongas, were former volunteers. One of the two leading point people in the administration's Bureau of Human Rights and Humanitarian Affairs, Mark Schneider, also served as a volunteer. (The other agency leader, Patricia Derian, was a Mississippi civil rights leader for twenty years before joining the foreign policy establishment.)[16]

Carter's personal view of the third world was fraught with tensions on how to deal with different cultures, how much to respect local values, and how much to work for change. On the one hand, he "believed we needed to correct an injustice" by giving Panama sovereignty over the Panama Canal. The United States needed to respect the rights and culture of a third world nation. At the same time, Carter believed American foreign policy should "induce our more authoritarian allies to change their repressive policies." He sought to "improve" the third world through a firm stand on human rights.[17] Carter, just like a volunteer, attempted to articulate a fresh approach toward the third world but could not choose between contradictory goals of respecting the cultures of others and pushing others to change.

Ronald Reagan's election represented a firm rejection of the Carter foreign policy. Reagan portrayed Carter's ambiguous feelings as indecisiveness and called for a return to a simpler foreign policy toward the third world. He rejected the subtle, nuanced understandings of these parts of the world that had been formulated by volunteers. As Cottam argues, the Reagan policy was guilty of "obvious simplification" resulting in "policies that required an equally simple reality."[18] From Nicaragua to Afghanistan to Angola, the third world once again became a battleground in the struggle with the "evil empire," and American leaders never saw the third world as containing anything more than primitives or, as Reagan's United Nations ambassador, Jeanne Kirkpatrick, phrased it, "butchers."[19]

George Bush followed in his predecessor's ideological footsteps in his policy toward the outside world. When the Berlin Wall fell in 1989, it seemed that all impediments to world development fell with it. Not only could the ideas of liberal developmentalism be spread into the third world, now they could help to develop the Eastern bloc as well. The Peace Corps served as one tool for the spread of this ideal. One former volunteer who wrote on this new Peace Corps task referred to these areas of the world as "a new breed of 'developing country.'"[20]

All too predictably, volunteers in the reformed Eastern bloc faced the same types of snags and cultural misunderstandings that their volunteer forefathers had thirty years earlier. Mary Lou Schramm, associate Peace Corps director, explained the goal this way: "When we arrived here [in Russia], we were supposed to start helping with small business development. Except there was no small business to develop." Everything was more complicated than the business volunteers expected. The Russians were "loathe to put anything on paper" or they would be exposed to up to 80-percent tax rates. Yet the American businessmen could not figure out how to "develop" these businesses without detailed accounting records and business plans. Just as volunteers in the third world of the 1960s had found, these volunteers found that in the new third world of the 1990s, cultural differences destroyed the meaning of the development idea. In the end, even though the volunteers "thought they were coming here to change Russia . . . Russia ended up changing the Peace Corps."[21]

Although the Peace Corps volunteer experience has had little effect on foreign-policy making, American cultural beliefs about the third world appear to have shifted since the 1960s. The Peace Corps volunteer experience is by no means the only or even the central reason for this shift. Obviously, America's most profound experience with the developing world in the 1960s took place in Vietnam, and that experience, more than any other, shaped American images of this area of the world.

Over 150,000 Americans have served in the Peace Corps since its inception, and their experiences clearly jolted many of their fellows upon their return. Jonathan Zimmerman relates the story of one African-American who wore a Malawian wrap given to her by a friend from the village in which she had worked. Her African-American friends chastised her for not wearing the "*de rigueur* dashiki" worn by American black radicals.[22] They did not see her as being African enough—yet she was wearing the "real" African dress. She brought with her a new, complex and confusing understanding of culture, an understanding that by the 1980s was steadily reflected in American popular culture.

Many Americans felt confused and frustrated by the changing terrain of cultural understanding. This confusion, augmented by the painful failure of Vietnam, caused many Americans to reject any sort of cultural interaction whatsoever. As historian Elizabeth Cobbs points out, this shift is reflected in a central premise of the hugely popular television series *Star Trek*. The "prime directive" for the Star Fleet mandates a lack of intervention in the "cultural" affairs of alien species, even if a lack of intervention might result in great harm to the aliens involved.[23]

Other Americans seem to cling to stereotypes of third world peoples as diametrically different "others." Movies such as Arnold Schwarzenegger's (Sargent Shriver's son-in-law!) blockbuster hit, *True Lies,* depict Middle Eastern culture in overly simplistic, stereotyped terms. In a study of comic books, culture critic Jack Sheehan found that "not a single Arab heroine or hero was featured." Instead, Arabs were consistently depicted as "bestial, demonized, dehumanized" or even "uncouth, unclean and unkempt." Sheehan's study shows very little difference between the comics of the 1990s and those of the 1950s. Even Disney got into the act: only "horrible" Arabs appeared in a comic entitled *Uncle Scrooge.*[24]

Yet such stereotypes no longer occupy the field of cultural understanding in isolation. Disney's full-length animated feature *Aladdin,* a far more important cultural artifact than *Uncle Scrooge,* features both an Arab hero and an Arab heroine (as well as, of course, a despicable Arab villain). Many movies since the mid-1980s present other cultures in a more complex light, the most famous of which is Kevin Costner's *Dances with Wolves.* In that movie, Costner's character resembles a 1960s Peace Corps volunteer much more than the Civil War soldier he is supposed to be. Perhaps more interestingly, a well-publicized movie starring megastar Harrison Ford entitled *Mosquito Coast* depicts a series of surreal cultural confrontations in Central America, highlighted by the construction of a gigantic ice machine by an American bent on helping the natives improve their steamy lives. The movie was based on a book written by the man many consider to be America's premier travel fiction writer, Paul Theroux, a former Peace Corps volunteer. Theroux himself, obviously never sure of the positive effects of volunteers' actions overseas, was always convinced that Peace Corps volunteers did change *American* culture. As he put it in an op-ed piece in the *New York Times,* "America is quite a different place for having had so many returned Peace Corps Volunteers."[25]

We can see just how different a place it is by examining the bombing of the federal building in Oklahoma City in May 1995. In the fearful aftermath, many Americans quickly fit the atrocity into their overly simplistic stereotyped view of Arabs. Importantly, however, even in this situation of maximum duress, American culture and the American government "showed uncharacteristic restraint in avoiding a rush to judgment." Two culturally mainstream news magazines, *Time* and *Newsweek,* published editorials in the week after the bombing discussing how complicated cultural understandings had become. As Jonathan Alter phrased it, "'John Doe' is not an Arab name:

It's part of a Frank Capra movie title, resonant of everything American." The "depravity of this crime" could not be proven to be "the product of another culture unfathomably different from our own." Rather, the crime came right from the heart of supposedly sophisticated, developed America.[26]

Looking at Peace Corps volunteer ideas also gives us a look at the controversial idea of "multiculturalism." The complicated, often contradictory ideas that reflected a more mature, educated understanding of other cultures resembles the better impulses behind the 1990s drive for multiculturalism. Peace Corps volunteers never formulated the answers on how best to deal with the third world, but they did successfully identify many of the problems. For example, volunteers quickly abandoned the terms *third world* and *developing world* and the terms *native* and *local* to describe the people living there. The Peace Corps leadership became an early leader in the movement for cultural sensitivity, later branded by critics as "political correctness," by replacing in 1966 the term *Far East* with *East Asia* in all agency discussions of the area.[27] These terms reflected an overly simplistic view of these places and peoples, a view that helped create ineffective, sometimes dangerous, policy. Volunteers never came up with a useful replacement term—the best they could do was the awkward "host country nationals"—but their work had successfully reshaped their thinking.

In a similar way, by the mid-1990s, many Americans found their thoughts about other cultures remade. Other Americans failed to accept this rejection of older, easier to understand ideas about culture, resulting in the "culture wars" of the 1990s. Ideas developed in part by returned Peace Corps volunteers swirled at the center of this battle, as Bill Clinton proclaimed in his 1993 inaugural when he argued that the Peace Corps "defined a generation of Americans." This generation of Americans rejected long-held views of other cultures and began an important reshaping of American cultural understanding of the rest of the world.

Notes

INTRODUCTION

1. James N. Giglio, *The Presidency of John F. Kennedy* (Lawrence: University of Kansas, 1991), 158.

2. Gerard T. Rice, *Twenty Years of the Peace Corps* (Washington, D.C.: Peace Corps, 1981), 18.

3. As this book goes to press, historian Elizabeth A. Cobbs's book *All You Need Is Love* (Harvard University Press) is also scheduled to be published. See also the article by Jonathan Zimmerman, "Beyond Double Consciousness: Black Peace Corps Volunteers in Africa, 1961–1971," *Journal of American History,* December 1995.

4. Stephen Thernstrom, *A History of the American People* (San Diego: Harcourt, Brace, Jovanovich, 1989), 833.

5. Thomas G. Paterson, *Meeting the Communist Threat: Truman to Reagan* (New York: Oxford, 1988), 200.

6. Elizabeth A. Cobbs, *The Rich Neighbor Policy: Rockefeller and Kaiser in Brazil* (New Haven: Yale, 1992), 9.

7. P. David Searles, *The Peace Corps Experience: Challenge and Change: 1969–1976* (Lexington: University of Kentucky, 1997), 39.

8. This book does not make use of any oral history interviews. The temptation was tremendous to include interviews—after all, almost every one of the actors in this book is still alive. There were two main reasons I decided to avoid oral history. First, the tremendous wealth of written sources obviated the need for more primary material. Second, and most importantly, I believe oral history did not serve the purposes of this study. This study examines the attitudes, rather than the events, of the past. Its central argument relates to how attitudes and culture have changed since the 1960s. I believe it would be very difficult for interviewer and interviewee to separate current attitudes and cultural understandings from those held in the past.

9. Michael H. Hunt, *Ideology and U.S. Foreign Policy* (New Haven: Yale, 1987), 160.

10. Ibid., 12.

11. For important discussions of the role of culture in diplomatic history, see William O. Walker III, "Bernath Lecture: Drug Control and the Issue of Culture in American Foreign Relations," *Diplomatic History* 12, no. 4 (fall 1988): 365–82; and Michael H. Hunt, "The Long Crisis in Diplomatic History," *Diplomatic History* 16, no. 1 (winter 1992): 115–40. For examples of how scholars have used these ideas in books on international relations, see Hunt, *Ideology;* William O. Walker, *Drug Control in the Americas* (Albuquerque: University of New Mexico, 1989); and Cobbs, *Rich Neighbor Policy.*

12. Hunt, *Ideology,* 159.

13. Catherine Lutz and Jane Collins, *Reading National Geographic* (Chicago: University of Chicago, 1993), 108, 110.

14. Lutz and Collins, *Reading National Geographic,* 13.

15. Thomas Paterson, J. Gary Clifford, and Kenneth Hagan, *American Foreign Policy* (Lexington, Mass.: D. C. Heath, 1988), 537.

CHAPTER 1

1. Gary May, "Passing the Torch and Lighting Fires: The Peace Corps," in *Kennedy's Quest for Victory,* ed. Thomas G. Paterson (Lexington, Mass.: D.C. Heath, 1988), 285.

2. Gerard T. Rice, *The Bold Experiment: JFK's Peace Corps* (Notre Dame, Ind.: Notre Dame, 1985), 21.

3. Ibid., 26.

4. Walt Whitman Rostow, *Eisenhower, Kennedy and Foreign Aid* (Austin: University of Texas, 1985), 44.

5. Educational Policy Commission, *Point Four and Education* (Washington, D.C.: National Education Association, 1950), 2.

6. See Robert Packenham, *Liberal America and the Third World: Political Development Ideas in Foreign Aid and Social Science* (Princeton: Princeton University Press, 1973).

7. Rostow, *Eisenhower,* 158.

8. Dennis Merrill, *Bread and the Ballot* (Chapel Hill: University of North Carolina, 1990), 154.

9. Ibid., 85.

10. Douglas Brinkley, *Dean Acheson: The Cold War Years, 1953–1971* (New Haven: Yale, 1992), 304.

11. John F. Kennedy, "Speech on the Independence of Algeria," July 2, 1957, in *Strategy of Peace* (New York: Harper and Row, 1960), 66.

12. William Burdick and Eugene Lederer, *The Ugly American* (New York: W. W. Norton, 1958), 236–39.

13. Packenham, *Liberal America,* 62–63.

14. May, "Passing the Torch," 286.

15. Theodore Sorenson, "The Election of 1960," in *The History of American Presidential Elections,* vol. 4, ed. Arthur Schlesinger Jr., Fred Israel, and William Hansen (New York: McGraw Hill, 1971), 3464.

16. Rice, *Bold Experiment,* 34.

17. Harris Wofford, *Of Kennedys and Kings: Making Sense of the Sixties* (New York: Farrar, Straus & Giroux, 1980), 360.

18. John F. Kennedy, "Special Message to the Congress on Foreign Aid," March 22, 1961, *Public Papers of the President, John F. Kennedy,* vol. 1 (Washington, D.C.: U.S. Government Printing Office, 1962), 207–8.

19. Rice, *Bold Experiment,* 60.

20. Coates Redmon, *Come As You Are: The Peace Corps Story* (San Diego: Harcourt, Brace, Jovanovich, 1986), 40.

21. Rice, *Bold Experiment*, 79.

22. Ibid., 140.

23. Wofford, *Of Kennedys and Kings*, 266.

24. May, "Passing the Torch," 287.

25. Wofford, *Of Kennedys and Kings*, 40.

26. Ibid., 45.

27. Brent Ashabrannar, *A Moment in History: The First Ten Years of the Peace Corps* (Garden City, N.Y.: Doubleday, 1971), 21.

28. William Peters, *Passport to Friendship: The Story of the Experiment in International Living* (Philadelphia: J. B. Lippincott, 1957), 94.

29. Ibid., 120, 128.

30. Rice, *Bold Experiment*, 51.

31. Mark Harris, *Twentyone Twice: A Journal* (Boston: Little, Brown, 1966), 166.

32. Redmon, *Come As You Are*, 153; Harris, *Twentyone Twice*, 41.

33. Redmon, *Come As You Are*, 164.

34. Julius A. Amin, *The Peace Corps in Cameroon* (Kent, Ohio: Kent State University, 1992), 32.

35. Rice, *Bold Experiment*, 91.

36. Ibid., 93.

37. Thomas Scott, "The Peace Corps and the Private Sector: The Failure of a Partnership," *Annals of the American Academy of Political and Social Science* 365 (May 1966): 94.

38. Packenham, *Liberal America*, 67.

39. Address, Sargent Shriver, November 19, 1961, in "Speeches of Sargent Shriver 1961–1962," Peace Corps Library, Washington, D.C. (hereafter referred to as PCL).

40. Robert G. Athearn, *The Mythic West in Twentieth Century America* (Lawrence: University of Kansas, 1986), 234.

41. Thomas Kenneally, *Schindler's List* (New York: Simon and Schuster, 1982), 232.

42. David B. Davis, "Ten-Gallon Hero," *American Quarterly* 6 (summer 1954): 120.

43. Hal Borland, *America Is Americans* (New York: Harper and Brothers, 1941), 101.

44. John Hellman, *The American Myth and the Legacy of Vietnam* (New York: Columbia University, 1986), 20.

45. Ibid., 43.

46. Robert H. Shaffer, "Peace Corps: Antidote for Provincialism," in *School and Society* 95 (April 15, 1967): 262.

47. Address, Sargent Shriver, Worthington, Minnesota, October 1961, in binder, "Speeches of Sargent Shriver, 1961–1962," PCL.

48. Richard Slotkin, *Gunfighter Nation: The Myth of the Frontier in Twentieth Century America* (New York: Atheneum, 1992), 503.

49. Address, Sargent Shriver, Kansas State University, June 3, 1963, in binder, "Speeches of Sargent Shriver, 1963–64," PCL.

50. William James, *Memories and Studies* (New York: Longmans, Green, 1911), 287, 290.

51. Ashabrannar, *Moment in History*, 78.

52. Wofford, *Of Kennedys and Kings*, 113.

53. Paul Cowan, *The Making of an Un-American* (New York: Viking, 1967), 81.

54. Harris Wofford, *Road to World Republic: Policy and Strategy for Federalists* (Chicago: Federalist Press, 1948), 5.

55. Wofford, *Of Kennedys and Kings*, 33.

56. Ibid., 256.

57. Harris Wofford, *It's Up to Us: Federal World Government in Our Time* (New York: Harcourt, Brace, 1946), 102.

58. Wofford, *It's Up to Us,* 111.

59. May, "Passing the Torch," 292.

60. Ibid.

61. Wofford, *It's Up to Us,* 52.

62. Clare Wofford and Harris Wofford, *India Afire* (New York: John Day, 1951), 332.

63. May, "Passing the Torch," 292.

64. Hellman, *American Myth,* 25.

65. Rice, *Bold Experiment,* 40.

66. Redmon, *Come As You Are,* 286–87.

67. Ibid., 293.

68. Ibid., 146, 245.

69. Jack Valenti, *A Very Human President* (New York: Norton, 1975), 71.

70. Tom Wicker, "Bill Moyers: Johnson's Good Angel," *Harper's,* October 1965, 42–45.

71. Redmon, *Come As You Are,* 50, 61, 82.

72. Wicker, "Bill Moyers," 283.

73. Redmon, *Come As You Are,* 118.

74. Wofford, *Of Kennedys and Kings,* 5.

75. Redmon, *Come As You Are,* 115.

76. *Peace Corps Volunteer Magazine,* February 1964, 3, and November 1962, 7.

77. Memo, Walter K. Davis to Shriver, June 30, 1966, "Orientation of Volunteers," in folder, "Peace Corps Training, 1966–67," PCL.

78. Arnold Zeitlin, *To the Peace Corps with Love* (Garden City, N.Y.: Doubleday, 1965), 83.

79. Roy Hoopes, *The Complete Peace Corps Guide* (New York: Dial, 1968), 13.

80. John Coyne, "A View from the Rear of the Room," *Peace Corps Volunteer Magazine,* August 1966, 5.

81. Harris Wofford, "Training: Ideas Wanted," *Peace Corps Volunteer Magazine,* February 1966, 13.

82. Andrew Kopkind, "The Peace Corps' Daring New Look," *New Republic* 6 (February 1966): 16.

83. Jack Vaughn, "The Peace Corps," in *The Peace Corps Reader,* ed. Peace Corps Office of Public Information (Washington, D.C.: Peace Corps, 1968), 8.

84. Ashabrannar, *Moment in History,* 229.

85. "Diplomacy: A Field Trip," *Time,* September 3, 1965, 41.

86. Redmon, *Come As You Are,* 56.

87. Ashabrannar, *Moment in History,* 215, 216; "Diplomacy," 41.

88. Ashabrannar, *Moment in History,* 216.

89. Redmon, *Come As You Are,* 130.

90. Kopkind, "Peace Corps' Daring New Look," 17.

91. Jack Vaughn, "Report to the President," September 10, 1965, in *Annals of the Department of State* (Washington, D.C.: U.S. Department of State, 1965), 548.

CHAPTER 2

1. Rice, *Bold Experiment,* 142.

2. Redmon, *Come As You Are,* 34.

3. Alan Weiss, *High Risk/High Gain: A Free-Wheeling Account of Peace Corps Training* (New York: St. Martin's, 1968), 11.

4. Rice, *Bold Experiment,* 144.

5. Sargent Shriver, *Point of the Lance* (New York: Harper and Row, 1964), 18.

6. Weiss, *High Risk,* 11.

7. Paul Bell, Evaluation Report, Guatemala, Agricultural Extension Project, October 10, 1964, Peace Corps Records Group, National Archives, Washington, D.C. (hereafter referred to as PCRG/NA).

8. Maurice L. Albertson, Andrew E. Rice, and Pauline E. Birky, *New Frontiers for American Youth: Perspectives on the Peace Corps* (Washington, D.C.: Public Affairs, 1961), 156.

9. Eugene Burdick and William Lederer, Evaluation Report, Philippines, January 1963, 36, PCRG/NA.

10. Roy Hoopes, in *The Peace Corps Reader,* ed. Peace Corps Office of Public Information (Washington, D.C.: Peace Corps, 1968), 13.

11. Ibid.

12. George Carter, "The Beginnings of Peace Corps Programming," *Annals of the American Association of Political and Social Science* 365 (May 1966): 50.

13. George Guthrie, "Cultural Preparation for the Philippines," in *Cultural Frontiers of the Peace Corps,* ed. Robert Textor (Cambridge: MIT, 1966), 20.

14. Hoopes, *Complete Peace Corps Guide,* 139.

15. Albertson et al., *New Frontiers,* 155.

16. For a more detailed examination of the training schedule, including timetables of daily regimens and hourly breakdowns of classes, see Amin, *Peace Corps in Cameroon,* chapter 4, 68–99.

17. Hoopes, *Complete Peace Corps Guide,* 144.

18. James Cross, "Letter from Dakar," *Modern Language Journal,* November 1963, 328.

19. Amin, *Peace Corps in Cameroon,* 88.

20. Paul L. Doughty, "Pitfalls and Progress in the Peruvian Sierra," in *Cultural Frontiers of the Peace Corps,* ed. Robert Textor (Cambridge: MIT, 1966), 231–32.

21. Slotkin, *Gunfighter Nation,* 499.

22. Rice, *Bold Experiment,* 158.

23. Policy Research Institute, Report on Philippines, December 12, 1962, 4, in folder, "Country Program Evaluation 1962," PCRG/NA.

24. Paul Jacobs, Training Evaluation 1962, 8, in folder, "Country Program Evaluation, Philippines VIII, 1962," PCRG/NA.

25. Amin, *Peace Corps in Cameroon,* 77.

26. Cowan, *Making of an Un-American,* 99.

27. Memo, Walter K. Davis to Sargent Shriver, "Social Behavior Responsibilities Overseas," June 30, 1966, 8, in folder, "Peace Corps: Training 1966–67," PCL.

28. Santha Rama Rau, "It's a Long, Long Way from Old Camp Shawnee," in *The Peace Corps Reader,* ed. Peace Corps Office of Public Information (Washington, D.C.: Peace Corps, 1968), 110.

29. Training Document, in folder, "Philippines Training Files: Philippines V, VI, VII," July 1962, 2, PCRG/NA.

30. Edna McGuire, *The Peace Corps: Kindlers of the Spark* (New York: MacMillan, 1966), 19, 21.

31. "Training for Pacific Assignment," *Peace Corps Volunteer Magazine,* November 1966, 19.

32. John Snyder, "From Judgment Ridge to India," *Peace Corps Volunteer Magazine,* August 1966, 9, 8.

33. Cowan, *Making of an Un-American,* 99.

34. Snyder, "From Judgment Ridge," 9.

35. Robert Textor, "Conclusions, Problems and Prospects," in *Cultural Frontiers of the Peace Corps,* ed. Robert Textor (Cambridge: MIT, 1966), 312.

36. Rice, *Bold Experiment,* 153.

37. Richard McManus, "I Shall Never Forget: The Story of a Peace Corps Volunteer," ca. 1968, 14, Philippine section, PCL.

38. Iris Luce, ed., *Letters from the Peace Corps* (Washington: Robert B. Luce, 1964), 15.

39. Albertson et al., *New Frontiers,* 108.

40. Ibid., 38.

41. Cowan, *Making of an Un-American,* 104.

42. Robert. L. Gaudino, *The Uncomfortable Learning: Some Americans in India* (Bombay: Popular Prakashan, 1964), 184.

43. Albertson et al., *New Frontiers,* 109.

44. Redmon, *Come As You Are,* 115.

45. Gerald Caplan, *Addendum to Manual for Psychiatrists Participating in the Peace Corps Program* (Washington, D.C.: Peace Corps Medical Division, 1969), 6, PCL.

46. Hellman, *American Myth,* 44, 73.

47. Esther M. Warber diary, box 173R, Record Group Aa 2, p. 1, Bentley Historical Library, University of Michigan, Ann Arbor, Michigan (hereafter referred to as UM).

48. George M. Guthrie, "Cultural Preparation for the Philippines," in *Cultural Frontiers of the Peace Corps,* ed. Robert Textor (Cambridge: MIT, 1966), 29.

49. Mary Williams, "No Sacrifice Here," *Peace Corps Volunteer Magazine,* June 1966, 22.

50. Richard K. Lazarus, *Letters from Colombia* (Cincinnati: Ralph Lazarus Foundation, 1984), 85.

51. Ibid., 47.

52. "Peace Corps: Fact Book," April 1, 1961, 7, in folder, "Peace Corps: History. (beginnings) 1960–61," PCL.

53. Eugene Burdick and William Lederer, Evaluation Report, Philippines, January 1963, 15, PCRG/NA.

54. *Time,* September 8, 1961, 22.

55. William J. Fuller, "A View of the Peace Corps," *Educational Forum* 30 (November 1965): 95.

56. Anne Wilson, "An Experience to Declare," *Social Action* 30, no. 5 (January 1964): 30.

57. Mrs. James Liser, letter to the editor, *Peace Corps Volunteer Magazine,* July 1967, 23.

58. Morris I. Stein, *Volunteers for Peace* (New York: John Wiley and Sons, 1966), 1.

59. Lawrence H. Fuchs, *Those Peculiar Americans: The Peace Corps and the American National Character* (New York: Merideth, 1967), 3.

60. Maureen Carroll, Completion of Service Conference Report (hereafter referred to as COSCR), Dominican Republic XVI (66-02-03), 1, PCRG/NA.

61. Thorburn Reid, Evaluation Report, El Salvador, September 28, 1963, 2, PCRG/NA.

62. Fred McCluskey to Pat Kennedy, July 25, 1962, 3, collection 4486, UM.

63. Myron Gildesgame journal, 60, in folder, "70. Myron Gildesgame, Ecuador, 1968–70," Smithsonian Museum of Natural History, Anthropology Archives (hereafter referred to as AA).

64. Richard Poston, COSCR, Dominican Republic XII (65-1-01), May 30, 1966, 9, PCRG/NA.

65. Michael Parrish, "Peace Corps Revisited," *Life,* March 1985, 84.

66. Chad Bardone (to family?), December 29, 1964, 3, in file, "30. Chad Bardone. Bolivia. 1964–1966," AA.

67. Raymond Stock journal, 4, in file, "48. Raymond Stock. Ethiopia. 1965–66," AA.

68. McManus, "I Shall Never Forget," 38.

69. William Buss, "Mato Grasso: In Some Cases Like Bonanza," *Peace Corps Volunteer Magazine,* September 1965, 18.

70. McManus, "I Shall Never Forget," 2.

71. Jerald Posman, "Making Rules Work in the Peace Corps," *Peace Corps Volunteer Magazine,* April 1968, 2.

72. Philip Cook, Evaluation Report, Ivory Coast, December 15, 1965, 38, PCRG/NA.

73. Chad Bardone journal, December 29, 1964, 4, in folder, "30. Chad Bardone. Bolivia. 1964–66," AA.

74. *Peace Corps Volunteer Magazine,* December 1962, 3.

75. Ibid., December 1963, 22–23.

76. Ibid., January 1966, 3.

77. Ibid., June 1963, 1.

78. Ibid., January 1966, August 1963, December 1963.

79. Ibid., June 1964, 13.

80. Ibid., June 1964, 13.

81. Ibid., March 1963.

82. Ibid., July 1963.

83. Ibid., November 1963.

84. Ibid., May 1963.

85. Earle and Rhoda Brooks, "Ecuador," *National Geographic Magazine*, September 1964, 340–45.

86. Parrish, "Peace Corps Revisited," 88.

87. Roy Furomizo, "By Raft and Jeep to Malaria," *Peace Corps Volunteer Magazine*, December 1962, 13.

88. Olcott Gates, "Ghana Receives 12 Peace Corps Geologists to Assist Survey Work in Backcountry," *Peace Corps Volunteer Magazine*, August 1963, 4.

89. Frances Cunha diary, January 14, 1963, in file, "55. Brazil. Mrs. Frances Cunha. 1962–64," AA.

90. Lillian Carter and Gloria Carter Spann, *Away from Home: Letters to My Family* (New York: Simon and Schuster, 1977), 1.

91. Fuchs, *Those Peculiar Americans*, 80.

92. Albertson et al., *New Frontiers*, 18.

93. John Groebli, COSCR, Peru VIII, June 8, 1965, 4, PCRG/NA.

94. Leveo Sanchez, Evaluation Report, Dominican Republic, December 17, 1962, 13, PCRG/NA.

95. Gaudino, *Uncomfortable Learning*, 200.

96. Robert Drew, "Snake Charming for Fun and Profit," *Peace Corps Volunteer Magazine*, July 1966, 20.

97. Phil Barrow, "Volunteer Shifts from T-square to Teaching," *Peace Corps Volunteer Magazine*, August 1966, 20.

98. Robert Bates, "Nepal," *Peace Corps Volunteer Magazine*, May 1963, 10.

99. Jim Grant, "Lahijan Gets a Grant," *Peace Corps Volunteer Magazine*, November 1964, 10.

100. Cynthia Erskine, "Evolution in the Lab," *Peace Corps Volunteer Magazine*, April 1963, 18.

101. Herb Wegner, Evaluation Report, Peru, 1963, 64, PCRG/NA.

102. Carol Schnebel, "Jamaica: 'No Place Like Home,'" *Peace Corps Volunteer Magazine*, November 1963, 10.

103. Leonard Levitt, *An African Season* (New York: Simon and Schuster, 1966), 153.

104. Richard Richter, Evaluation Report, Ghana, January 6, 1965, PCRG/NA.

105. John Halloran to family, May 8, 1962, in folder, "27. John Halloran. Philippines. 1962–1963," AA.

106. Kathryn Saltonstall, *Small Bridges to One World: A Peace Corps Perspective, Nigeria, 1963–65* (Portsmouth, N.H.: Peter E. Randall, 1986), 195–96.

107. Eric Broudy, "Paradise at River Cess," *Peace Corps Volunteer Magazine*, July 1964, 15.

108. Polly Kirkpatrick diary, January 30, 1969, 81, in folder, "68. Polly Kirkpatrick. Togo. 1968–1970," AA.

109. Lula Muller, "The Yellow Balcony," 54, in folder, "3. Lula Muller. Nepal. 1962–1964," AA.

110. Fuchs, *Those Peculiar Americans*, 144.

111. Anna Zentella, "Who's Lonesome? I Never Left Home," *Peace Corps Volunteer Magazine*, July 1963, 4.

112. McManus, "I Shall Never Forget," 108.

113. *Peace Corps Volunteer Magazine*, summer 1971, 58.

114. Gaudino, *Uncomfortable Learning*, 133.

115. Cowan, *Making of an Un-American,* 163.

116. David Nelson to family, January 25, 1963, collection 4417, UM.

117. Charlene Duline, "Dreams of Powdered Milk," *Peace Corps Volunteer Magazine,* July 1963, 19.

118. Angene Nelson, February 1965, in folder, "Peace Corps: Volunteer Experiences," PCL.

119. Sargent Shriver, "The Moral Force of Sport," *Sports Illustrated,* June 3, 1963, 18.

120. Velma Adams, *The Peace Corps in Action* (Chicago: Follett, 1964), 139.

121. Dee Jacobs, Evaluation Report, Guatemala, August 7, 1963, 17–18, PCRG/NA.

122. Richard Richter, Evaluation Report, Ghana, January 6, 1965, 64, PCRG/NA.

123. McManus, "I Shall Never Forget," 75.

124. Thorburn Reid, Evaluation Report, El Salvador, September 28, 1963, 5, PCRG/NA.

125. Cowan, *Making of an Un-American,* 277.

126. Peace Corps Office of Volunteer Service, "Cases and Material on Problems of Social Behavior among Peace Corps Volunteers," 15, in folder, "Peace Corps: Office of Volunteer Support," PCL.

127. Eduard Santomayor, "'Hola, Pedro . . . Hola, Pedrito,'" *Peace Corps Volunteer Magazine,* August 1964, 14–15.

CHAPTER 3

1. Bill Cull, "Some Days, I Just Talk," *Peace Corps Volunteer Magazine,* February 1965, 6.

2. Lutz and Collins, *Reading National Geographic,* 89–90.

3. Ibid., 13.

4. May, "Passing the Torch," 294.

5. Karen Schwarz, *What You Can Do for Your Country: An Oral History of the Peace Corps* (New York: William Morrow, 1991), 36.

6. A. W. Lewis, "I Was in the Chorus that Answered Him," *Peace Corps Volunteer Magazine,* December 1963, 2.

7. Francis Henzel, "Peace Corps or Missionary: Does It Really Make Any Difference?" *Catholic World* 208 (February 1969): 206.

8. Saltonstall, *Small Bridges,* 146.

9. Luce, *Letters from the Peace Corps,* 41.

10. Linda Muller diary, November 1, 1968, in folder, "3. Linda Muller. Nigeria. 1970–1971," AA.

11. David Riesman, "A Mixture of Motives," in *The Peace Corps Reader,* ed. Peace Corps Office of Public Information (Washington, D.C.: Peace Corps, 1966), 16.

12. Tom deVries, "The Activist: A Definition," *Peace Corps Volunteer Magazine,* December 1965, 10.

13. Fuchs, *Those Peculiar Americans,* 37.

14. James McDonough, "Notes of a Peace Corps Reject," *Esquire* 65 (January 1966): 90.

15. Amin, *Peace Corps in Cameroon,* 70.

16. Carter and Spann, *Away from Home,* 19.

17. Moritz Thomsen, *Living Poor: A Peace Corps Chronicle* (Seattle: University of Washington, 1969), 4.

18. Jaclyn Hyland diary, November 8, 1966, in folder, "44. Jaclyn Hyland. Liberia. 1966–1968," AA.

19. Luce, *Letters from the Peace Corps,* 14.

20. Cowan, *Making of an Un-American,* 110.

21. Luce, *Letters from the Peace Corps,* 13.

22. John Groebli, COSCR, Peru VIII, June 8, 1965, 4, PCRG/NA.

23. Mark Simpson (to family?), May 24, 1967, in folder, "28. Mark Simpson. Niger. 1967–1969," AA.

24. Richard Richter, Evaluation Report, Ghana, January 6, 1965, 73, PCRG/NA.

25. Mark Simpson (to family?), May 24, 1967, in folder, "28. Mark Simpson. Niger. 1967–1969," AA.

26. Frederick McCluskey diary, August 24, 1961, collection 4486, UM.

27. Ashabrannar, *Moment in History,* 99.

28. George Sullivan, *The Story of the Peace Corps* (New York: Fleet, 1964), 69.

29. Weiss, *High Risk,* 19.

30. Amin, *Peace Corps in Cameroon,* 77.

31. Cowan, *Making of an Un-American,* 99.

32. Eugene Burdick and William Lederer, Evaluation Report, Philippines, January 1963, 41, PCRG/NA.

33. COSCR, El Salvador, Education I (64-01-02), January 3, 1966, 2, PCRG/NA.

34. Lazarus, *Letters from Colombia,* 35–40.

35. Ann Anderson, ed., *The Evaluation Reader* (Washington, D.C.: Peace Corps Office of Evaluation and Research, 1967), 194, PCL.

36. Paul Bell, COSCR, Guatemala I, October 10, 1964, 2, PCRG/NA.

37. Tim Adams and Robert McGuire, Evaluation Report, Nigeria, December 4, 1963, 26, PCRG/NA.

38. Thomsen, *Living Poor,* 6.

39. Zeitlin, *To the Peace Corps with Love,* 34.

40. Thomsen, *Living Poor,* 5.

41. Luce, *Letters from the Peace Corps,* 20.

42. *Peace Corps Volunteer Magazine,* April 1968, 10.

43. Carter and Spann, *Away from Home,* 26.

44. Roz Paris, *Peace Corps Volunteer Magazine,* November 1966, 22.

45. "Training: Shaping of Volunteers Is an Ever-Changing Process," *Peace Corps Volunteer Magazine,* February 1964, 12.

46. Bill Steife, "One Man's Junket," *Peace Corps Volunteer Magazine,* February 1964, 18.

47. Allan Bérubé, *Coming out under Fire: The History of Gay Men and Women in World War Two* (New York: Free Press, 1990), 10.

48. Helen Swick Perry, *Psychiatrist of America: The Life of Harry Stack Sullivan* (Cambridge: Belknap, 1992), 404.

49. Christopher Lasch, *Haven in a Heartless World: The Family Besieged* (New York: Basic, 1977), 98, 100.

50. Sullivan, *Story of the Peace Corps,* 88.

51. Caplan, *Addendum to Manual for Psychiatrists,* 67.

52. Scott, "Peace Corps and the Private Sector," 99.

53. Amin, *Peace Corps in Cameroon,* 87.

54. "COSC History," internal Peace Corps memo, 1969, p. 1, in folder, "Peace Corps: COSC/MSC," PCL.

55. Caplan, *Addendum to Manual for Psychiatrists,* 28.

56. Fuchs, *Those Peculiar Americans,* 201.

57. Weiss, *High Risk,* 43.

58. El Salvador Country File, Appendix 5, in folder, "El Salvador, 1963, Country File, Screened," PCRG/NA.

59. Jesse G. Harris Jr., "A Science of the South Pacific: Analysis of the Character Structure of the Peace Corps Volunteer," *American Psychologist* 28, no. 3 (March 1973): 241.

60. Stein, *Volunteers for Peace,* 19–20.

61. Weiss, *High Risk,* 30.

62. Schwarz, *What You Can Do,* 37.

63. Weiss, *High Risk,* 161.

64. Caplan, *Addendum to Manual for Psychiatrists,* 236.

65. "Lesson Plan for Social Behavior," in folder, "Peace Corps: Training, 1961–65," PCL.

66. "Cases and Material on Problems of Social Behavior Encountered by Peace Corps Volunteers," 1–2, in folder, "Peace Corps, Office of Volunteer Support," PCL.

67. El Salvador Country File, Appendix 3, in folder, "El Salvador, Country File, Screened, 1963," PCRG/NA.

68. Harris, "Science of the South Pacific," 236.

69. Donald Shea, "The Preparation of Peace Corps Volunteers for Overseas Service," *Annals of the American Society of Political and Social Science* 365 (May 1966): 41.

70. Internal memo, Department of Volunteer Services, 1969, in folder, "Peace Corps, COSC/MSC," PCL.

71. Thomsen, *Living Poor,* 6.

72. Don Chamberlain, Memo on Training, May 2, 1962, 3–4, in folder, "1962: Philippines III and IV; Penn St. Training Files," PCRG/NA.

73. Weiss, *High Risk,* 137.

74. Al Carp, "A Response," *Peace Corps Volunteer Magazine,* October 1965, 28.

75. Katie Mayer journal, in folder, "47. Katie Mayer. Ceylon. 1962–1964," AA.

76. Cowan, *Making of an Un-American,* 101.

77. Paul Jacobs, Training Evaluation, August 6, 1962, 2, in folder, "Philippines, Training files, July 1962, Philippines V, VI, VII," PCRG/NA.

78. Frederick McCluskey diary, August 24, 1961, collection 4486, UM.

79. Weiss, *High Risk,* 185.

80. McDonough, "Notes of a Peace Corps Reject," 26.

81. Redmon, *Come As You Are,* 372.

82. McDonough, "Notes of a Peace Corps Reject," 122.

83. Weiss, *High Risk,* 110.

84. Henry Gilgoff, "Assessment or Assistance?" *Peace Corps Volunteer Magazine,* April 1968, 10.

85. McDonough, "Notes of a Peace Corps Reject," 122.

86. Zygmunt Nagorski, "The Peace Corps and the Rebel," 8, in folder, "Peace Corps: Volunteer Personality," PCL.

87. *Peace Corps Volunteer Magazine,* April 1966, 14.

88. John Freivalds manuscript, 9, in folder, "22. Mr. and Mrs. John Freivalds. Panama/Colombia. 1969–1970," AA.

89. Richard Hopkins, "Thoughts from the Rain Forest: On Alley Cats, Tame Tabbies and Peace Corps Training," 1966, 2, in folder, "Peace Corps: Training, 1966–1969," PCL.

90. "OID file 1962–1963," in folder, "Office of the Director, Country File, Philippines 1962–1963," PCRG/NA.

91. Bonnie Jo Dopp, letter to the editor, *Peace Corps Volunteer Magazine,* February 1965, 2.

92. Thomsen, *Living Poor,* 8.

CHAPTER 4

1. Gaudino, *Uncomfortable Learning,* 184.

2. Lewis Butler, "The Overseas Staff," *Annals of the American Academy of Political and Social Science* 365 (May 1966): 86.

3. Adams, *Peace Corps in Action,* 224.

4. Cowan, *Making of an Un-American,* 176.

5. Ruth McKenzie and Frank Mankiewicz, COSCR, Peru XII, June 7, 1966, 10, PCRG/NA.

6. COSCR, Philippines I, May 27, 1963, 18, PCRG/NA.

7. Memo, Walter K. Davis to Jack Vaughn, "Peace Corps Orientation of Trainees," June 30, 1966, 4, in folder, "Peace Corps: Training, 1966–1967," PCL.

8. COSCR, Guatemala V (65-01-02), May 13, 1967, 10, PCRG/NA.

9. Saltonstall, *Small Bridges,* 81.

10. William Mangin, COSCR, Ghana IV (64-01-06), May 30, 1966, 5, PCRG/NA.

11. Dee Jacobs, Evaluation Report, Guatemala, August 7, 1963, 9, PCRG/NA.

12. "Jamaican Bullsheet," vol. 2, 2, Kenneth Gibbs papers, collection 4538, UM.

13. Hoopes, *Complete Peace Corps Guide,* 159.

14. "Photograph Causes Flap," *Peace Corps Volunteer Magazine,* January 1968, 24.

15. Roger Hagler, Arthur Herzog, and Jack MacDonald, Evaluation Report, Malaysia, April 19, 1968, in folder, "Peace Corps: Volunteer Performance," PCL.

16. Richard Hopkins, "Thoughts from the Rainforest," 1966, in folder, "Peace Corps: Training, 1966–1969," PCL.

17. Adams, *Peace Corps in Action,* 270.

18. Zeitlin, *To the Peace Corps with Love,* 80.

19. Philip S. Cook, Evaluation Report, Ivory Coast, December 15, 1965, 24, PCRG/NA.

20. Gerald Anderson, "Peace Corps Intrigue in the Philippines," *Christian Century,* January 7, 1970, 4–6.

21. O. M. Scruggs, COSCR, Peru XIII (64-01-06), June 7, 1966, 5, PCRG/NA.

22. "Volunteer Life Called Unsentimental Education," *Peace Corps Volunteer Magazine,* September 1963, 2.

23. Ashabrannar, *Moment in History,* 96.

24. Fuchs, *Those Peculiar Americans,* 32.

25. Letter, June 28, 1963, in folder, "OIG [Office of the Inspector General] Country File, Guatemala, 1963–1964," PCRG/NA.

26. Redmon, *Come As You Are,* 169.

27. Efrem Siegal, "A Peace Corpsman Looks Back," in *The Peace Corps Reader,* ed. Peace Corps Office of Public Information (Washington, D.C.: Peace Corps, 1968), 50.

28. Parrish, "Peace Corps Revisited," 84.

29. Schwarz, *What You Can Do,* 119.

30. Gaudino, *Uncomfortable Learning,* 169.

31. Cowan, *Making of an Un-American,* 290–302.

32. Harris Wofford, Ernest Fox, and George Nicolau, *Citizen in a Time of Change* (Washington, D.C.: Peace Corps, 1965), 19.

33. Fuller, "View of the Peace Corps," 97.

34. Jane Campbell and Thomas Scott, COSCR, Philippines IV, April 14, 1964, addendum 2, PCRG/NA.

35. Scott, "Peace Corps and the Private Sector," 95.

36. Zeitlin, *To the Peace Corps with Love,* 152.

37. Ken Bredeson, COSCR, Philippines XIX (66-03-06), June 25, 1968, 21, PCRG/NA.

38. Richard Posten, COSCR, Dominican Republic XII (65-1-01), May 30, 1966, 10, PCRG/NA.

39. Posman, "Making Rules Work," 2.

40. Lazarus, *Letters from Colombia,* 50.

41. Lee Leardini, "Off the Soapbox," *Peace Corps Volunteer Magazine,* January 1968, 20.

42. John Freivalds manuscript, 55 and 99, in folder, "22. Mr. and Mrs. John Freivalds. Panama/Colombia. 1969–1970," AA.

43. Howard Tolley Jr., "Political Issue," *Peace Corps Volunteer Magazine,* January 1968, 20.

44. "Volunteers Play Neutral Role in Dominican Republic Strife," *Peace Corps Volunteer Magazine,* May 1965, 3.

45. Schwarz, *What You Can Do,* 82.

46. Zeitlin, *To the Peace Corps with Love,* 228–32.

47. Cowan, *Making of an Un-American,* 356.

48. Robert F. Arnove and Jonathan F. Seeley, "Teaching English in Venezuela," *Overseas,* December 1963, 8.

49. John Freivalds manuscript, 68, in folder, "22. Mr. and Mrs. John Freivalds. Panama/Colombia. 1969–1970," AA.

50. Alicia Teichman to Joseph Smaldone, November 21, 1967, in folder, "67. Joseph Smaldone. Tanzania. 1966–1968," AA.

51. John Freivalds manuscript, 15, in folder, "22. Mr. and Mrs. John Freivalds. Panama/Colombia. 1969–1970," AA.

52. Ed Smith, *Where to, Black Man?* (Chicago: Quadrangle, 1967), 60.

53. Lazarus, *Letters from Colombia,* 64.

54. Brian Walsh and David Livingston, excerpts from article in *Worldview Magazine,* summer 1989, in folder, "Peace Corps: Draft," PCL.

55. Cowan, *Making of an Un-American,* 160.

56. COSCR, Guatemala V (65-01-07), May 3, 1967, 15, PCRG/NA.

57. Alicia Teichman to Joseph Smaldone, March 3, 1968, in folder, "67. Joseph Smaldone. Tanzania. 1966–1968," AA.

58. Schwarz, *What You Can Do,* 103–8.

59. COSCR, Guatemala V (65-01-07), May 3, 1967, 12, PCRG/NA.

60. Ashabrannar, *Moment in History,* 280.

61. For a more detailed discussion of the Murray case, see "The Bruce Murray Case," *Peace Corps Volunteer Magazine,* March–April 1970, 11–12; and Schwarz, *What You Can Do,* 97–108.

62. Schwarz, *What You Can Do,* 117.

63. Cowan, *Making of an Un-American,* 113.

64. Robert Thomson, "On Compulsory Service," *Peace Corps Volunteer Magazine,* August 1967, 9.

65. William Mangin , COSCR, Ghana IV (64-01-06), May 30, 1966, 6, PCRG/NA.

66. Richard Richter, Evaluation Report, Ghana, January 6, 1965, 33–36, PCRG/NA.

67. Mary McGrory, "Seminarians to the Peace Corps?" *America* 114 (January 29, 1969): 167.

68. Evaluation Report, Cameroon, December 20, 1962, 12, PCRG/NA.

69. Adams, *Peace Corps in Action,* 215.

70. Evaluation Report, Cameroon, December 20, 1962, 8, PCRG/NA.

71. George W. Shepherd Jr., "Christian Hope for the Peace Corps: Peace, Freedom and Service," *Social Action* 30 (January 1964): 7, 12.

72. Henzel, "Peace Corps Volunteer or Missionary," 206.

73. Myron Gildesgame journal, 71, in folder, "70. Myron Gildesgame. Ecuador. 1968–1970," AA.

74. Anne Wilson, "An Experience to Declare," *Social Action* 30, no. 5 (January 1964): 31.

75. McManus, "I Shall Never Forget," 11, 51.

76. Julien Phillips, COSCR, Peru XIX (65-01-01), May 10, 1967, 4, PCRG/NA.

77. Frederick McCluskey journal, September 7, 1962, collection 4486, UM.

78. Carl Pope, *Sahib: An American Misadventure in India* (New York: Liveright, 1972), 163.

79. COSCR, El Salvador CAU III (66-03-08), August 18, 1968, 1, PCRG/NA.

80. Judy Bowsman and Janet Wallbeck, *Mister, Where You Go?* (Washington, D.C.: Peace Corps), 23, Afghanistan Section, PCL.

81. Vincent D'Andrea, COSCR, Thailand VII (63-04-09), August 17, 1965, 2, PCRG/NA.

82. Athearn, *Mythic West,* 170.

83. Martin Green, *The Great American Adventure* (Boston: Beacon Press), 6.

84. Peace Corps Office of Public Information, "You Can't Send a Girl There!" (Washington, D.C.: Peace Corps, 1966), 2.

85. Richard Starkey, Evaluation Report, Turkey, December 23, 1966, 18, 23, PCRG/NA.

86. "Soft Hearted City Girls Learn to Kill Chickens for Dinner," *National Geographic*, September 1964, 306–8.

87. Charles E. Wingenbach, *The Peace Corps: Who, How and Where* (New York: John Day, 1961), 116.

88. *Peace Corps Volunteer Magazine*, October 1968, 12.

89. Philip S. Cook, Evaluation Report, Ivory Coast, December 15, 1965, 6, PCRG/NA.

90. Betty Friedan, *The Feminine Mystique* (New York: W. W. Norton, 1963), 34–36.

91. Richard Hancock, "Volunteers a New Presence in El Salvador," *Peace Corps Volunteer Magazine*, December 1962, 7.

92. Richard Starkey, Evaluation Report, Turkey, December 23, 1966, 20, PCRG/NA.

93. Albertson et al., *New Frontiers*, 62.

94. Hoopes, *Complete Peace Corps Guide*, 126.

95. George M. Coleman Jr., "Progress on the Farm," *Peace Corps Volunteer Magazine*, February 1963, 13.

96. "Jane," "From the Distaff Side," *Peace Corps Volunteer Magazine*, April 1968, 29.

97. Kevin Delaney, exit interview, August 6, 1963, in folder, "Office of the Inspector General, Country File, Philippines, 1963–1964," PCRG/NA.

98. Thorburn Reid, Evaluation Report, El Salvador, September 28, 1963, 10, PCRG/NA.

99. Peace Corps Office of Public Information, "You Can't Send a Girl There!" 12.

100. Ibid., 5–6.

101. George Summerson Jr., "Femininity as Fact," *Peace Corps Volunteer Magazine*, September 1968, 20.

102. Peace Corps Office of Volunteer Support, "Cases and Material on Problems of Social Behavior Encountered by Peace Corps Volunteers," 1966, 4–5, in folder, "Peace Corps: Office of Volunteer Support," PCL.

103. Memo, Walter K. Davis to Jack Vaughn, "Peace Corps Orientation of Trainees," June 30, 1966, in folder, "Peace Corps: Training, 1966–1967," PCL.

104. Alicia Teichman to Joseph Smaldone, May 23, 1967, in folder, "67. Joseph Smaldone. Tanzania. 1966–1968," AA.

105. Neil Boyer, "Volunteers in the Field: Great Expectations," *Annals of the American Society of Political and Social Scientists* 365 (May 1966): 61.

106. Eeta B. Freeman diary, September 11, 1963, box 236P, UM.

107. "Sex Makes an Impact," *Peace Corps Volunteer Magazine*, January 1966, 17.

108. Richard Starkey, Evaluation Report, Turkey, December 23, 1966, 24, PCRG/NA.

109. Walter K. Davis to Jack Vaughn, "Peace Corps Orientation of Trainees in Social Behavior Responsibilities Overseas," June 30, 1966, 1, in folder, "Peace Corps: Training, 1966–1967," PCL.

110. Luce, *Letters from the Peace Corps*, 114.

111. "Cases and Material on Problems of Social Behavior Encountered by Peace Corps Volunteers," 35, in folder, "Peace Corps: Office of Volunteer Support, 1966," PCL.

112. Zeitlin, *To the Peace Corps with Love*, 30.

113. Walter K. Davis, COSCR, Nigeria X (64-01-02), January 16, 1966, 8, PCRG/NA.

114. Memo, Sargent Shriver to Peace Corps representatives, August 3, 1963, 2, in folder, "Peace Corps: Training, 1966–1967," PCL.

115. John Griffin, exit interview, July 13, 1963, in folder, "Office of the Inspector General, Country File, Philippines, 1963–1964," PCRG/NA.

116. Fuchs, *Those Peculiar Americans*, 120.

117. Redmon, *Come As You Are*, 96–97.

118. Michael T. Field, "A Modest Proposal," *Peace Corps Volunteer Magazine*, February 1965, 23.

119. COSCR, Philippines I, May 27, 1963, 13, PCRG/NA.

120. Memo, Dan Chamberlain, May 2, 1962, in folder, "1962, Philippines III and IV; Penn St. Training Files," 8, PCRG/NA.

121. Redmon, *Come As You Are,* 98.

122. Shriver, *Point of the Lance,* 73.

123. C. Payne Lucas, *Black Pride, Black Action* (Washington, D.C.: Peace Corps, 1968), 10.

124. Shriver, *Point of the Lance,* 140.

125. Eeta B. Freeman diary, May 20, 1964, box 236P, UM.

126. Rice, *Bold Experiment,* 220.

127. Ashabrannar, *Moment in History,* 259.

128. *Attitudes towards the Peace Corps among Black Americans* (New York: Pinkett-Brown-Black, 1968), iv.

129. Ibid., 12.

130. "A Costly Interlude," *Peace Corps Volunteer Magazine,* July–August 1968, 4.

131. Athearn, *Mythic West,* 235.

132. *Attitudes,* 4, 8, 9.

133. Ibid., 11.

134. Peace Corps news release, "Project Peace Pipe," 1969, in folder, "Peace Corps: American Indian," PCL.

135. Ashabrannar, *Moment in History,* 270.

136. Jack Anderson, "Project Peace Pipe," *Washington Post,* November 4, 1970.

137. Summary of COSCRs, March 1964, p. 3, PCL.

138. Nicholas Hobbs, COSCR, Nigeria/Nsukka, May 29, 1963, 3, PCRG/NA.

139. COSCR, Philippines I, May 27, 1963, 23, PCRG/NA.

140. John Groebli, COSCR, Peru IX (63-05-06), June 11, 1965, 8, PCRG/NA.

141. For other examples, see COSCRs, Peru VII; Thailand I, PCRG/NA; and Compilation, 1964, PCL.

142. Nicholas Hobbs and Jane Campbell, COSCR, Nigeria/Nsukka, May 27, 1963, 3, PCRG/NA.

143. Ashabrannar, *Moment in History,* 1.

144. John Groebli, COSCR, Peru VIII, June 8, 1965, 3, PCRG/NA.

145. Wofford et al., *Citizen in a Time of Change,* 15.

146. "What Direction Change?" *Peace Corps Volunteer Magazine,* July–August 1968, 13.

147. Adams, *Peace Corps in Action,* 266.

148. Gaudino, *Uncomfortable Learning,* 37.

149. Zeitlin, *To the Peace Corps with Love,* 21.

150. Fuchs, *Those Peculiar Americans,* 66.

151. John Coyne, "A View from the Rear of the Room," *Peace Corps Volunteer Magazine,* August 1966, 5.

152. Fuchs, *Those Peculiar Americans,* 169.

153. Ibid., xvii.

154. Ibid., 40.

CHAPTER 5

1. Robert Coughlan, "Black Africa Surges to Independence," *Life,* January 26, 1959, 100–110, and February 2, 1959, 85–94.

2. Lutz and Collins, *Reading National Geographic,* 109.

3. Herbert Feis, *Foreign Aid and Foreign Policy* (New York: St. Martin's, 1964), 74.

4. Margaret Balfe, "Wet Foot Harvest," *Peace Corps Volunteer Magazine,* April 1963, 18.

5. Thomsen, *Living Poor,* 24.

6. Jaclyn Hyland journal, 19, in folder, "44. Jaclyn Hyland. Liberia. 1966–68," AA.

7. Zeitlin, *To the Peace Corps with Love,* 142.

8. "Sabah and Sarawak," *Peace Corps Volunteer Magazine,* December 1963, 10.

9. Barbara Lorimer, "North Borneo," *Peace Corps Volunteer Magazine,* July 1963, 8.

10. McManus, "I Shall Never Forget," 18.

11. Jim Fisher, "Letter from 'Land of Yak and Yeti,'" *Peace Corps Volunteer Magazine,* May 1963, 11.

12. Coleman, "Progress on the Farm," 13.

13. Saltonstall, *Small Bridges,* 163.

14. Bob Siegal, "Trip's Treat: Nkungoburger," *Peace Corps Volunteer Magazine,* November 1963, 20.

15. "Books and Buzkashi," *Peace Corps Volunteer Magazine,* January 1964, 20.

16. Jaclyn Hyland journal, 6, in folder, "44. Jaclyn Hyland. Liberia. 1966–1968," AA.

17. See, for example, Rosalind Person (to family?), May 17, 1963, UM.

18. Gena Reissner, "My African Father," *Peace Corps Volunteer Magazine,* October 1965, 10.

19. See, for example, Esther Pierce, "A Top Story from Kenlanton," *Peace Corps Volunteer Magazine,* January 1965, 6; or Hollis Burke, "Festive Turks Aid Volunteer Wedding Rites," *Peace Corps Volunteer Magazine,* August 1966.

20. Adams, *Peace Corps in Action,* 78.

21. William Mangin, COSCR, Ghana IV (64-01-06), May 30, 1966, 6, PCRG/NA.

22. Fuchs, *Those Peculiar Americans,* 129.

23. John Freivalds manuscript, 65, in folder, "22. Mr. and Mrs. John Freivalds. Panama/Colombia. 1969–1970," AA.

24. Jaclyn Hyland to family, 1, in folder, "44. Jaclyn Hyland. Liberia. 1966–1968," AA.

25. Peace Corps, "Discussion Materials on the Peace Corps Experience: 1967," vol. 2, 6, in file, "Discussion Materials," PCL.

26. Nelson Stahlman diary, January 25, 1965, in folder, "36. Nelson Stahlman. Ethiopia. 1965–66," AA.

27. David Wallendar to brother Peter, January 22, 1970, in folder, "62. David Wallendar. Upper Volta. 1969–1971," AA.

28. Chad Bardone (to family?), August 9, 1964, in folder, "30. Chad Bardone. Bolivia. 1964–1966," AA.

29. Lazarus, *Letters from Colombia,* 77.

30. Robert Major, "Cyprus: Its Problems Are Different," *Peace Corps Volunteer Magazine,* February 1963, 20.

31. Levitt, *African Season,* 33.

32. Pope, *Sahib,* 2.

33. Levitt, *African Season,* 209.

34. Stein, *Volunteers for Peace,* 62.

35. Adams, *Peace Corps in Action,* 258.

36. Philip Cook, Evaluation, Ivory Coast, December 15, 1965, 1, PCRG/NA.

37. Chris Beemer, "Fighting Apathy in a Rio Suburb," *Peace Corps Volunteer Magazine,* September 1966, 10.

38. Judith Nordblom, "The Real Job of the Volunteer Can Best Be Achieved in the City," *Peace Corps Volunteer Magazine,* September 1966, 14.

39. Judy Thelen, "Almost Like Home," *Peace Corps Volunteer Magazine,* September 1966, 6.

40. Cowan, *Making of an Un-American,* 192.

41. David Palmer, "Peru," *Peace Corps Volunteer Magazine,* July 1963, 10.

42. Sidney Werkman, COSCR, Afghanistan III (63-02-10), 2, PCRG/NA.

43. Gary Engelberg, "Urban and Rural Environments Produce Two Different Kinds of Volunteers," *Peace Corps Volunteer Magazine,* September 1966, 32.

44. Susan and Robert Calhoun, "A Case of Readjusted Expectations," *Peace Corps Volunteer Magazine,* September 1966, 8.

45. "Bolivia Volunteers Make a Go at Urban Jobs," *Peace Corps Volunteer Magazine,* May 1963, 2.

46. "The Peace Corps in the City," *Peace Corps Volunteer Magazine,* September 1966, 5.

47. Ann Friesan, "Urban Setting Complicated Entry Problems of New Volunteers," *Peace Corps Volunteer Magazine,* September 1966, 36.

48. Lazarus, *Letters from Colombia,* 19.

49. Fuchs, *Those Peculiar Americans,* 52.

50. Thomsen, *Living Poor,* 20.

51. Lazarus, *Letters from Colombia,* 2.

52. Jaclyn Hyland journal, 1, in folder, "44. Jaclyn Hyland. Liberia, 1966–1968," AA.

53. Margot Morrow, "A Glimpse at Teaching in the Peace Corps," *Chicago Schools Journal* 45 (October 1963): 2.

54. Kevin Haverty, "A Cliff-Hanging Tale of a Sunday Ascent to La Paz," *Peace Corps Volunteer Magazine,* August 1966, 12.

55. Frank Brechin to family, September 16, 1962, collection 4388, UM.

56. Anderson, *Evaluation Reader,* 15.

57. Mark Simpson to family, September 23, 1967, in folder, "28. Mark Simpson. Niger. 1967–1969," AA.

58. Zeitlin, *To the Peace Corps with Love,* 170, 195.

59. Levitt, *African Season,* 209.

60. Fuchs, *Those Peculiar Americans,* 110.

61. Schwarz, *What You Can Do,* 66.

62. Peace Corps Office of the Inspector General, letter, June 28, 1963, in file, "OIG Country File, 1963–1964, Guatemala," PCRG/NA.

63. *Peace Corps Volunteer Magazine,* summer 1971.

64. Cowan, *Making of an Un-American,* 216.

65. Seth Tillman, *Diary of a Trip to Asia,* 36–37.

66. Thomsen, *Living Poor,* 84.

67. Pope, *Sahib,* 64.

68. Parrish, "Peace Corps Revisited," 86.

69. Herb Wegner, Evaluation Report, Peru, 1963, 78, PCRG/NA.

70. Linda Muller journal, February 25, 1970, in folder, "3. Linda Muller. Nigeria. 1970–1971," AA.

71. Frederick McCluskey journal, November 24, 1961, collection 4486, UM.

72. Adams, *Peace Corps in Action,* 44.

73. Carter and Spann, *Away from Home,* 42.

74. Zeitlin, *To the Peace Corps with Love,* 11.

75. Lula Muller, "The Yellow Balcony," 1, in folder, "3. Lula Muller. Nepal. 1962–1964," AA.

76. Hilary Whittaker to family, November 9, 1967, collection 5166, UM.

77. Greg Maronek, "One's Status Is Unclearly Defined," *Peace Corps Volunteer Magazine,* September 1966, 17.

78. Cowan, *Making of an Un-American,* 220.

79. Frank Brechin journal, April 12, 1963, collection 4388, UM.

80. H. David Grunwald, "As the Months Fly By," *Peace Corps Volunteer Magazine,* March 1965, 12.

81. Luce, *Letters from the Peace Corps,* 42.

82. Ibid., 29.

83. Ann Friesan, "Urban Setting Complicated Entry Problems of New Volunteers," *Peace Corps Volunteer Magazine,* September 1966, 35.

84. Richard Richter, Evaluation Report, Ghana, January 6, 1965, 49, PCRG/NA.

85. Christopher Wiles, "The Curious Marriage of Basketball and Urban Community Development," *Peace Corps Volunteer Magazine,* September 1966, 26.

86. Leon Weintraub, "A Dance Leads to Bush," *Peace Corps Volunteer Magazine,* July 1964, 19.

87. Alonzo Smith, "Ivory Coast," *Peace Corps Volunteer Magazine,* August 1965, 10.

88. Smith, *Where to, Black Man?* 154.

89. McCarthy, Evaluation, Cameroons, December 20, 1962, 3, PCRG/NA.

90. Schwarz, *What You Can Do,* 41–42.

91. Luce, *Letters from the Peace Corps,* 44.

92. Levitt, *African Season.*

93. Luce, *Letters from the Peace Corps,* 39.

94. Pope, *Sahib,* 23.

95. Cowan, *Making of an Un-American,* 229.

96. Adams, *Peace Corps in Action,* 93.

97. Zeitlin, *To the Peace Corps with Love,* 12.

98. Adams, *Peace Corps in Action,* 115.

99. Levitt, *African Season,* 123.

100. Eugene Burdick and William Lederer, Evaluation, Philippines, January 1963, 24, PCRG/NA.

101. Lazarus, *Letters from Colombia,* 18.

102. Peter Deekle (to family?), January 1, 1969, in folder, "10. Peter Deekle. Iran. 1969–1970," AA.

103. See, for example, COSCRs, Ghana, I, IV and IX, PCRG/NA.

104. William Mangin, COSCR, Ghana IV, May 30, 1966, PCRG/NA.

105. Sidney Werkman, COSCR, Afghanistan III (63-02-10), September 4, 1965, 3, PCRG/NA.

106. Luce, *Letters from the Peace Corps,* 101, 102.

107. Philip Delfeld, "Hammer, Wrench Were Not Enough," *Peace Corps Volunteer Magazine,* May 1964, 15.

108. David Schickele, "When the Right Hand Washes the Left," in *The Peace Corps Reader,* ed. Peace Corps Office of Public Information (Washington, D.C.: Peace Corps, 1968), 35.

109. "Volunteers Rank Problems," *Peace Corps Volunteer Magazine,* August 1966, 3.

110. John Freivalds manuscript, 220, in folder, "22. Mr. and Mrs. John Freivalds. Panama/Colombia. 1969–1970," AA.

111. "Congress Told of Volunteer Problems, Too," *Peace Corps Volunteer Magazine,* June 1963, 4.

112. Adams, *Peace Corps in Action,* 251.

113. COSCR, Philippines I, May 27, 1963, 11, PCRG/NA.

114. COSCR, Ghana (67-02-06), June 2, 1969, 10, PCRG/NA.

115. Paul Bell, COSCR, Guatemala I, October 10, 1964, PCRG/NA.

116. Frederick McCluskey (to family?), November 1, 1961, collection 4486, UM.

117. Wanda Montgomery, "The Peace Corps Volunteer and His Medical Kit," *Peace Corps Volunteer Magazine,* December 1962, 18.

118. May, "Passing the Torch," 298.

119. Fuchs, *Those Peculiar Americans,* 93.

120. Frank Brechin to family, November 4, 1962, collection 4388, UM.

121. Esther Warber to family, August 4, 1963, box 173R, UM.

122. "Bullsheet," 4, in Kenneth Gibbs papers, Peace Corps Collection 4538, UM.

123. Adams, *Peace Corps in Action,* 127.

124. O. M. Scruggs, COSCR, Peru XII (64-01-06), 4, PCRG/NA.

125. May, "Passing the Torch," 159.

127. Siegal, "Peace Corpsman Looks Back," 50.

128. Neil Boyer, "Volunteers in the Field: Great Expectations," *Annals of the American Academy of Political and Social Science* 365 (May 1966): 59.

129. Luce, *Letters from the Peace Corps,* 125.

130. Smith, *Where to, Black Man?* 40.

131. Mark Simpson diary, January 15, 1968, in folder, "28. Mark Simpson. Niger. 1967–1969," AA.

132. Peace Corps, Compilation of Evaluation Reports, 1964, 6, PCL.

133. David Barnet, "Researcher Tells Findings," *Peace Corps Volunteer Magazine,* July 1963, 24.

134. Frank J. Mahony, "Success in Somalia," in *Cultural Frontiers of the Peace Corps,* ed. Robert Textor (Cambridge: MIT, 1966), 131.

135. Myron Gildesgame diary, October 19, 1968, 78, in folder, "70. Myron Gildesgame. Ecuador 1968–1970," AA.

136. See, for example, Gaudino, *Uncomfortable Learning,* 93.

137. Thomsen, *Living Poor,* 139.

138. Raymond Stock diary, September 30, 1966, in folder, "48. Raymond Stock. Ethiopia. 1965–66," AA.

139. Chad Bardone (to family?), December 29, 1964, 4, in folder, "30. Chad Bardone. Bolivia, 1964–1966," AA.

140. Smith, *Where to, Black Man?* 81.

141. Thomsen, *Living Poor,* 96.

142. Carter and Spann, *Away from Home,* 51.

143. Smith, *Where to, Black Man?* 72.

CHAPTER 6

1. "The Volunteer Image," *Peace Corps Volunteer Magazine,* February 1963, 4.

2. Gaudino, *Uncomfortable Learning,* 4.

3. Ibid., 206.

4. Ibid., 24.

5. Seymour Greben, COSCR, Peru, Rural Community Development (66-06-08), November 5, 1968, 6, PCRG/NA.

6. Bates, "Nepal," 10.

7. Richard Richter, Evaluation Report, Ghana, January 6, 1965, 21, PCRG/NA.

8. Gene Shreiber, "E. Africa Volunteers Finish Up: Sure of Value of U.S. Aid," *Peace Corps Volunteer Magazine,* June 1963, 6.

9. Luce, *Letters from the Peace Corps,* 88.

10. Victor Joos, "Growing a Green Thumb," *Peace Corps Volunteer Magazine,* June 1963.

11. Scott Evans, "A Glimpse of Forestry in the Peace Corps," *Journal of Forestry* 65 (August 1967): 572–73.

12. Frank Brechin to family, May 21, 1963, collection 4388, UM.

13. Will Weiss, "Progress: At 70 m.p.h.," *Peace Corps Volunteer Magazine,* April 1963, 21.

14. Terry Carpenter, "Professional Duties Come before Image," *Peace Corps Volunteer Magazine,* September 1966, 12.

15. Adams, *Peace Corps in Action,* 70.

16. Christopher Wiles, "The Curious Marriage of Basketball and Urban CD," *Peace Corps Volunteer Magazine,* September 1966, 26.

17. William Friedland, "Nurses in Tanganyika," in *Cultural Frontiers of the Peace Corps,* ed. Robert Textor (Cambridge: MIT, 1966), 147.

18. Jane Campbell, COSCR, Nigeria/Kaduna, June 19, 1963, 14, PCRG/NA.

19. Gaudino, *Uncomfortable Learning,* 13.

20. Mary Williams, "No Sacrifice Here," *Peace Corps Volunteer Magazine,* June 1966, 22.

21. Lazarus, *Letters from Colombia,* 51.

22. Jane Campbell, COSCR, Philippines V, April 14, 1964, 1, PCRG/NA.

23. Gaudino, *Uncomfortable Learning,* 121.

24. Larry Godfrey, "Graduate Students in India Got Out and Dug," *Peace Corps Volunteer Magazine,* May 1963, 21.

25. George Carter, "The Beginning of Peace Corps Programming," *Annals of the American Political and Social Science Association* 365 (May 1966): 52.

26. Stein, *Volunteers for Peace,* 55, 158.

27. Frank Mankiewicz, "A Revolutionary Force," in *The Peace Corps Reader,* ed. Peace Corps Office of Public Information (Washington, D.C.: Peace Corps, 1968), 87.

28. Cowan, *Making of an Un-American,* 91–92.

29. Stein, *Volunteers for Peace,* 101.

30. Kirby Jones, "The Peace Corps Volunteer in the Field: Community Development," *Annals of the American Political and Social Science Association* 365 (May 1966): 70.

31. Cowan, *Making of an Un-American,* 218.

32. Frederick McCluskey to Pat Kennedy, July 25, 1962, 2, collection 4486, UM.

33. Ibid., 5.

34. David Pearson, COSCR, Peru I, February 18, 1964, 1, PCRG/NA.

35. O. M. Scruggs, COSCR, Peru XIII (64-02-06), June 7, 1966, 1, PCRG/NA.

36. Lazarus, *Letters from Colombia,* 70.

37. David Nelson to parents, April 11, 1963, 1, box 3J, collection 4417, UM.

38. Louis Rapoport, "On Unidentified Project, an Unidentified Person," *Peace Corps Volunteer Magazine,* March 1965, 18.

39. COSCR, Ghana IX (66-02-10), April 18, 1968, 5, PCRG/NA.

40. Ashabrannar, *Moment in History,* 162.

41. Fred McCluskey to family, April 5, 1962, and to parents, September 7, 1962, collection 4486, UM.

42. Richard Posten, COSCR, Dominican Republic XII (65-1-01), May 30, 1966, PCRG/NA.

43. Frederick McCluskey to family, November 1, 1961, collection 4486, UM.

44. Chad Bardone to family, March 1, 1966, in folder, "30. Chad Bardone. Bolivia. 1964–1966," AA.

45. Memorandum, Peace Corps Office of Evaluation and Research, 1965, in folder, "Peace Corps: Community Development, Volunteer Experiences," PCL.

46. COSCR, Guatemala V (65-01-07), May 3, 1967, 5, PCRG/NA.

47. Bernard Isaacson, "Fruitless Labor," *Peace Corps Volunteer Magazine,* September 1963, 21.

48. Thomsen, *Living Poor,* 82.

49. Ibid., 103.

50. "New Focus on Urban CD," *Peace Corps Volunteer Magazine,* July 1966, 3.

51. Alex Zipperer, "An Operational Criticism," *Peace Corps Volunteer Magazine,* September 1966, 24–25.

52. Thomsen, *Living Poor,* 200.

53. James Dean, "Specialists—with a Flourish," *Peace Corps Volunteer Magazine,* August 1964, 13.

54. Thomsen, *Living Poor,* 184.

55. Stanley Frankel, "View of a One-Eyed King," *Peace Corps Volunteer Magazine,* March 1966, 9.

56. Cowan, *Making of an Un-American,* 24.

57. Ibid., 52.

58. John Freivalds manuscript, 104, in folder, "22. Mr. and Mrs. John Freivalds. Panama/Colombia, 1969–1970," AA.

59. COSCR, Guatemala V (65-01-07), May 3, 1967, PCRG/NA.

60. Stein, *Volunteers for Peace,* 235.

61. Peace Corps Office of Evaluation, *Bi-Monthly Compilation of Evaluation Reports* 6 (1969): 46.

62. COSCR, Guatemala V (65-01-07), May 3, 1967, PCRG/NA.

63. Fred McCluskey to Pat Kennedy, July 25, 1962, 6, UM.

64. Schwarz, *What You Can Do,* 75.

65. Ibid., 56.

66. Tom Newman, letter to the editor, *Peace Corps Volunteer Magazine,* November 1965, 13.

67. Robert Sebring, letter to the editor, *Peace Corps Volunteer Magazine,* June 1966, 10.

68. COSCR, Ghana (67-02-06), June 2, 1969, 5, PCRG/NA.

69. Paul Cromwell, COSCR, Nigeria VII (63-01-06), April 17, 1965, 3, PCRG/NA.

70. COSCR, El Salvador (64-01-02), January 3, 1966, 4, PCRG/NA.

71. Arnold Deutchman, "Volunteers in the Field: Teaching," *Annals of the American Academy of Political and Social Science* 365 (May 1966): 73.

72. Philip Cook, Evaluation Report, Ivory Coast, December 15, 1965, 1, PCRG/NA.

73. Bennett Oberstein, "Drama? Send Me a Nutritionist!" *Peace Corps Volunteer Magazine,* September 1965, 10.

74. COSCR, Ghana I, June 2, 1963, 11, PCRG/NA.

75. Seth Tillman, *The Peace Corps: From Enthusiasm to Disciplined Idealism* (Washington, D.C.: U.S. Government Printing Office, 1969), 11.

76. COSCR, Ghana IX (66-02-10), April 18, 1968, 4–5, PCRG/NA.

77. William Mangin, COSCR, Ghana IV (64-01-06), May 30, 1966, 8, PCRG/NA.

78. Dr. William Gaymon, COSCR, Nigeria, Groups XVII–XXI, December 21, 1967, PCRG/NA.

79. William Mangin, COSCR, Ghana IV (64-01-06), May 30, 1966, 2, PCRG/NA.

80. Peter Deekle diary, February 18, 1969, in folder, "10. Peter Deekle. Iran. 1969–1970," AA.

81. Deutchman, "Volunteers in the Field," 81.

82. Peace Corps Office of Evaluation, "Bimonthly Bulletin of Evaluation Reports," 3–5, PCL.

83. William Haddad, Evaluation Report, Ghana, April 4, 1962, 3, PCRG/NA.

84. Robert Lystad, Evaluation Report, Ghana, December 20, 1962, 16, PCRG/NA.

85. Anderson, *Evaluation Reader,* 106.

86. COSCR, Ghana I, June 12, 1963, 5, PCRG/NA.

87. Richard Nishihara and David Sears, "Farming on the Stumps," *Peace Corps Volunteer Magazine,* May 1963, 18.

88. Saltonstall, *Small Bridges,* 152–53.

89. Samuel Abbott, "On the Making of a Peace Corps Volunteer," *Peace Corps Volunteer Magazine,* November 1966, 10.

90. Saltonstall, *Small Bridges,* 140.

91. Alonzo Smith, "Ivory Coast," *Peace Corps Volunteer Magazine,* August 1963, 10.

92. Deutchman, "Volunteers in the Field," 76.

93. Paul Gilbert, History of Somalia, in folder, "16. Paul Gilbert. Somalia. 1964–1966," AA.

94. McManus, "I Shall Never Forget," 50.

95. Alan and Judith Guskin, "University Teachers: They Also Serve," *Peace Corps Volunteer Magazine,* December 1962, 16.

96. L. Cowan, Evaluation Report, Nigeria, April 12, 1964, 14, PCRG/NA.

97. Judy Thelen, "Almost Like Home," *Peace Corps Volunteer Magazine,* September 1966, 6.

98. Levitt, *African Season.*

99. Timothy Adams and Robert McGuire, Evaluation Report, Nigeria, December 4, 1963, 5, PCRG/NA.

100. Halsey Beemer, COSCR, Ethiopia III (64-01-06), April 7, 1966, 3, PCRG/NA.

101. Zeitlin, *To the Peace Corps with Love,* 252.

102. Gwynne Douglass, "That Girl in the Fourth Row," *Peace Corps Volunteer Magazine,* March 1965, 20.

103. See, for example, Jaclyn Hyland diary, April 5 or 19, 1967, in folder, "44. Jaclyn Hyland. Liberia. 1966–1968," AA.

104. COSCR, Ghana VII (65-01-06), April 24, 1968, 8, PCRG/NA.

105. Bowsman and Walbeck, *Mister, Where You Go?* 13.

106. Gardiner Jones and Maureen Carroll, Evaluation Report, Philippines, March 19, 1965, PCRG/NA.

107. Seth Tillman, *Diary of a Trip to Asia,* 23.

108. John Lunstrum, "The Mystique of the Peace Corps: A Dilemma," *Phi Delta Kappan* 48 (November 1966): 99.

109. Thorburn Reid, Evaluation Report, Senegal, July 2, 1963, 43, PCRG/NA.

110. William F. Marquardt, "The Training of Teachers of English as a Second Language in the Peace Corps," *Language Learning* 12, no. 2 (1962): 108.

111. Scott, "Peace Corps and the Private Sector," 99.

112. Harris,"Science of the South Pacific," 237.

113. James Robinson, "Why Remain a Slave to an Idea?" *Peace Corps Volunteer Magazine,* March 1966, 22.

114. Chester Bowles, "Wanted: Professional Technicians as Amateur Volunteers," *Peace Corps Volunteer Magazine,* March 1966, 13.

115. Frances Hopkins, "A Capital: The Toughest Place to Excel," *Peace Corps Volunteer Magazine,* September 1966, 12.

116. Gardiner Jones and Maureen Carroll, Evaluation Report, Philippines, March 19, 1965, 51, PCRG/NA.

117. Anderson, *Evaluation Reader,* 98–99.

118. Jaclyn Hyland diary, 9, in folder, "44. Jaclyn Hyland. Liberia. 1966–1968," AA.

119. Saltonstall, *Small Bridges,* 60.

120. Luce, *Letters from the Peace Corps,* 59.

121. Zeitlin, *To the Peace Corps with Love,* 87.

122. Schwarz, *What You Can Do,* 61.

123. Levitt, *African Season,* 133.

124. J. Norman Parmer, Evaluation Report, Korea, June 1967, 13, PCRG/NA.

125. Polly Kirkpatrick diary, November 5, 1968, in folder, "68. Polly Kirkpatrick. Togo. 1968–1970," AA.

126. May, "Passing the Torch," 304–5.

127. Jim Bain and Randy Clare, "Old to New: A Slow Pace," *Peace Corps Volunteer Magazine,* November 1963, 14.

128. David Nelson to family, March 3, 1963, collection 4417, box 3J, UM.

129. Letter from John Halloran, June 8, 1962, in folder, "27. John Halloran. Philippines. 1962–1963," AA.

130. L. Gray Cowan, "The Nigerian Experience and Career Reorientation," in *Cultural Frontiers of the Peace Corps,* ed. Robert Textor (Cambridge: MIT, 1966), 159.

131. Dennis Shaw, "A Puppeteer Gives Teaching Tips," *Peace Corps Volunteer Magazine,* November 1966, 20.

132. John Halloran to family, October 18, 1962, in folder, "27. John Halloran. Philippines. 1962–1963," AA.

133. Peace Corps Office of Evaluation, "Bimonthly Bulletin of Evaluation Reports," 1968–69, 22, PCL.

134. Jaclyn Hyland journal, 8, in folder, "44. Jaclyn Hyland. Liberia. 1966–1968," AA.

135. Bowsman and Walbeck, *Mister, Where You Go?* 4.

136. Fannie R. Shaftel, "Peace Corps Teachers in Malaya," *Educational Leadership* 21 (March 1964): 349.

137. Zeitlin, *To the Peace Corps with Love,* 103.

138. Lewis Butler, "Malaya: Syllabuses and Ghosts," *Peace Corps Volunteer Magazine,* April 1963, 12.

139. Deutchman, "Volunteers in the Field," 75.

140. Adams, *Peace Corps in Action,* 167.

141. Alicia Teichman to Joseph Smaldone, February 2, 1967, in folder, "67. Joseph. Smaldone. Tanzania. 1966–1968," AA.

142. Levitt, *African Season,* 61, 63.

143. Schickele, "When the Right Hand Washes the Left," 18.

144. *Peace Corps Volunteer Magazine,* summer 1971, 60.

145. Angene Wilson journal, February 1965, in folder, "Peace Corps: Volunteer Experiences," PCL.

146. Zeitlin, *To the Peace Corps with Love,* 95.

147. McGuire, *Peace Corps: Kindlers of the Spark,* 70.

148. John Freivalds manuscript, 159, in folder, "22. Mr. and Mrs. John Freivalds. Panama/Colombia. 1969–1970," AA.

149. Julien Phillips, COSCR, Peru XIX (65-01-01), May 10, 1967, 7, PCRG/NA.

150. Samuel Abbot, "On the Making of a Peace Corps Volunteer," *Peace Corps Volunteer Magazine,* November 1966, 9.

CHAPTER 7

1. Thomsen, *Living Poor,* 74.

2. Letter from John Halloran, October 18, 1962, 2, in folder, "27. John Halloran. Philippines. 1962–1963," AA.

3. Levitt, *African Season,* 16.

4. William Martin, "In Brazil, Beware of the 'Faz Mals,'" *Peace Corps Volunteer Magazine,* September 1965, 8.

5. John Halloran (to family?), May 10, 1962, in folder, "27. John Halloran. Philippines. 1962–1963," AA.

6. COSCR, El Salvador VII (66-02-08-4H), September 25, 1968, 46, PCRG/NA.

7. John Halloran (to family?), July 14, 1963, in folder, "27. John Halloran. Philippines. 1962–63," AA.

8. Levitt, *African Season,* 90.

9. David Nelson manuscript, chapter 2, 5, box 3J, collection 4417, UM.

10. Richard Richter, Evaluation Report, Ghana, January 6, 1965, 44, PCRG/NA.

11. COSCR, Philippines IX, November 16, 1964, PCRG/NA.

12. COSCR, El Salvador VII (66-02-08-4H), September 25, 1968, 2, PCRG/NA.

13. Richard Ottinger, "Hey, Peace Corps! Take the Lead," *Peace Corps Volunteer,* March 1966, 17.

14. "Discussion Materials on the Peace Corps Experience," 1967, section 2, 8, PCL.

15. William Burdick and Eugene Lederer, Evaluation Report, Philippines, January 1963, 17, PCRG/NA.

16. John Freivalds manuscript, 30, in folder, "22. Mr. and Mrs. John Freivalds. Panama/Colombia. 1969–1970," AA.

17. B. P. R. Vithal, "Old Fences and New Frontiers," in *The Peace Corps Reader,* ed. Peace Corps Office of Public Information (Washington, D.C.: Peace Corps, 1968), 97.

18. John Hurley, COSCR, Thailand XI (65-03-06), April 25, 1967, 7, PCRG/NA.

19. Zeitlin, *To the Peace Corps with Love,* 187.

20. Gaudino, *Uncomfortable Learning,* 51.

21. Sam Adams, "Why, Indeed?" *Peace Corps Volunteer Magazine,* January 1965, 24.

22. Raymond Stock journal, 28, in folder, "48. Raymond Stock. Ethiopia. 1965–1966," AA.

23. Luce, *Letters from the Peace Corps,* 108.

24. Thomsen, *Living Poor,* 128.

25. Pope, *Sahib,* 73, 175.

26. Thomsen, *Living Poor,* 67.

27. Zeitlin, *To the Peace Corps with Love,* 115.

28. Levitt, *African Season,* 130.

29. Gaudino, *Uncomfortable Learning,* 72.

30. Myron Gildesgame journal, July 21, 1969, in folder, "70. Myron Gildesgame. Ecuador. 1968–1970," AA.

31. Lazarus, *Letters from Colombia,* 45.

32. Letter from Mrs. Frances Cunha, March 22, 1963, in folder, "55. Mrs. Frances Cunha. Brazil. 1962–1964," AA.

33. Hilary Whitaker journal, November 22, 1967, collection 5166, UM.

34. Luce, *Letters from the Peace Corps,* 126.

35. Mark Simpson to family, March 7, 1968, in folder, "28. Mark Simpson. Niger. 1967–1969," AA.

36. May, "Passing the Torch," 311.

37. Myron Gildesgame manuscript, 2, in folder, "70. Myron Gildesgame. Ecuador. 1968–1970," AA.

38. Schwarz, *What You Can Do,* 61.

39. David Pearson, COSCR, Peru I, February 18, 1964, 2, PCRG/NA.

40. Frederick McCluskey diary, June 1962, collection 4486, UM.

41. Jones, "Peace Corps Volunteer in the Field," 64.

42. John Freivalds manuscript, 133, in folder, "22. Mr. and Mrs. John Freivalds. Panama/Colombia. 1969–1970," AA.

43. Cowan, *Making of an Un-American,* 231, 180.

44. Timothy Adams and Robert McGuire, Evaluation Report, Nigeria, December 4, 1963, 38, PCRG/NA.

45. Dr. William Gaymon, COSCR, Nigeria XVII–XXI, 4, PCRG/NA.

46. COSCR, Ghana, June 2, 1963, 7, PCRG/NA.

47. Timothy Adams and Robert McGuire, Evaluation Report, Nigeria, December 4, 1963, 26, PCRG/NA.

48. Esther Warber to family, April 6, 1963, box 173R, UM.

49. Leveo Sanchez, Evaluation Report, Dominican Republic, December 17, 1962, 24, PCRG/NA.

50. COSC Ghana (67-02-06), June 2, 1969, 8, PCRG/NA.

51. Richard Richter, Evaluation Report, Ghana, January 6, 1965, 2, PCRG/NA.

52. David Nelson to parents, June 29, 1963, 1, box 3J, collection 4417, UM.

53. J. Norman Parmer, Evaluation Report, Korea, June 1967, 64, PCRG/NA.

54. David Nelson manuscript, chapter 4, 3, box 3J, collection 4417, UM.

55. The Group, *Tidbits: Nkwantabisa,* 5, PCL.

56. John Freivalds manuscript, 186, in folder, "22. Mr. and Mrs. John Freivalds. Colombia/Panama. 1969–1970," AA.

57. Frederick McCluskey to parents, October 5, 1962, collection 4486, UM.

58. Pope, *Sahib,* 6.

59. Leslie Hanscom, "The Magic of Caring," in *The Peace Corps Reader,* ed. Peace Corps Office of Public Information (Washington, D.C.: Peace Corps, 1968), 111.

60. Carl Moore, "Two Volunteers Treat Indians on Bolivia's Sky-High Plateau," *Peace Corps Volunteer Magazine,* July 1963, 6.

61. Lila Schoenfeld, "Volunteer Nurse Finds Her Work in Chardigarh," *Peace Corps Volunteer Magazine,* April 1964, 12.

62. Sally Yudelman, "Finding Jobs for Women," *Peace Corps Volunteer Magazine,* October 1968, 12.

63. Fuchs, *Those Peculiar Americans,* 113.

64. J. Norman Parmer, Evaluation Report, Korea, June 1967, 36–37, PCRG/NA.

65. Joan Marasciulo, "A Third Kind of Single Woman," *Peace Corps Volunteer Magazine,* September 1965, 15.

66. Gaile Nobel, "Limits Same for Both Sexes," *Peace Corps Volunteer Magazine,* February 1969, 22.

67. Nancy Galvin Petty, "Teacher Wore Funny Shoes," *Peace Corps Volunteer Magazine,* January 1965, 14.

68. Nancy Scott, "Maman Goes to School," *Peace Corps Volunteer Magazine,* August 1963, 14.

69. Leslie Hanscom, Evaluation, Afghanistan, 1966, in *The Evaluation Reader,* ed. Ann Anderson (Washington, D.C.: Peace Corps Office of Evaluation and Research, 1967), 22, PCL.

70. Gaudino, *Uncomfortable Learning,* 137.

71. Sullivan, *Story of the Peace Corps,* 135.

72. Fuchs, *Those Peculiar Americans,* 118.

73. Adams, *Peace Corps in Action,* 291.

74. Schwarz, *What You Can Do,* 76–77.

75. Lucas, *Black Pride,* 9.

76. Zimmerman, "Beyond Double Consciousness," 1000.

77. Ibid., 1001.

78. Ed Smith, *Where to, Black Man?* 22.

79. Ibid., 19, 20.

80. Ibid., 41.

81. Ibid., 119, 200.

82. Letter, Calvin Sparks, *Pokok: The Newsletter of Peace Corps/Malaysia,* April–May 1969, 6, in folder, "Peace Corps, Minorities," PCL.

83. Willie Hankins, "On Being a Negro in India," *Peace Corps Volunteer Magazine,* April 1964, 6.

84. Fuchs, *Those Peculiar Americans,* 123.

85. Jane Campbell and Thomas Scott, COSCR, Philippines V, April 14, 1964, 6, PCRG/NA.

86. Ann Covington, "Negro Volunteer in Ethiopia Finds Color an Advantage," *Peace Corps Volunteer Magazine,* May 1964, 4.

87. Zimmerman, "Beyond Double Consciousness," 1016.

88. *Ibid.,* 1017.

89. *Ibid.,* 1018.

90. Smith, *Where to, Black Man?* 105.

91. Zeitlin, *To the Peace Corps with Love,* 249.

92. Mankiewicz, "Revolutionary Force," 91.

93. Herb Wegner, Evaluation Report, Peru 1963, 71, PCRG/NA.

94. Dave Buentello, "The Minority Volunteer," *Peace Corps Volunteer Magazine,* October 1968, 18.

95. Ashabrannar, *Moment in History,* 262.

96. Dolores Trevino, "The Minority Volunteer," *Peace Corps Volunteer Magazine,* October 1968, 16.

97. Robert Ishikawa, "Very Poor Americans," *Peace Corps Volunteer Magazine,* April 1964, 11.

98. Toshi Watanabe, "The Non-American Volunteer," *Peace Corps Volunteer Magazine,* January 1965, 5.

99. Glenn Tamanaha, "The Minority Volunteer," *Peace Corps Volunteer Magazine,* October 1968, 19.

100. Dave Matsushita, "The Minority Volunteer," *Peace Corps Volunteer Magazine,* October 1968, 18.

101. William Mercer, "On 'Minority Volunteers,'" *Peace Corps Volunteer Magazine,* February 1969, 23.

102. Cowan, *Making of an Un-American,* 130.

103. Stein, *Volunteers for Peace,* 212.

104. John Briscoe, "The Peace Corps Helps with Plans of Ag-Extension," *Peace Corps Volunteer Magazine,* April 1964, 21.

105. Coleman, "Progress on the Farm," 12.

106. Robert McAndrews, "Liberian Village Trial and 'American Justice,'" *Practical Anthropology* 14 (May 1967): 103–9.

107. Stein, *Volunteers for Peace,* 161.

108. Thomsen, *Living Poor,* vi.

109. Alan Guskin, "Tradition and Change in a Thai University," in *Cultural Frontiers of the Peace Corps,* ed. Robert Textor (Cambridge: MIT, 1966), 101.

110. Lunstrum, "Mystique of the Peace Corps," 101.

111. McGuire, *Peace Corps: Kindlers of the Spark,* 105.

112. Pope, *Sahib.*

113. John Freivalds manuscript, 127, 134, in folder, "22. Mr. and Mrs. John Freivalds. Panama/Colombia. 1969–1970," AA.

114. David Szanton, "Cultural Confrontation in the Peace Corps," in *Cultural Frontiers of the Peace Corps,* ed. Robert Textor (Cambridge: MIT, 1966), 36.

115. Mark Harris, *Twentyone Twice,* 205.

116. Peter Deekle diary, April 7, 1969, in folder, "10. Peter Deekle. Iran. 1969–1970," AA.

117. Bowsman and Wallbeck, *Mister, Where You Go?* 32.

118. Tom Carter, "If You Think It Will Be Picturesque, Forget It!" in *The Peace Corps Reader,* ed. Peace Corps Office of Public Information (Washington, D.C.: Peace Corps, 1968), 78, 79.

119. Fuchs, *Those Peculiar Americans,* 83.

120. Robert Doerr, "The Peace Corps Experience: A Phenomenological Analysis of the In-Country Event," August 9, 1980, PCL.

121. David Nelson to family, March 11, 1963, box 3J, collection 4417, UM.

122. Carter and Spann, *Away from Home,* 21.

123. Cowan, *Making of an Un-American,* 253–55.

124. John Freivalds manuscript, 4, in folder, "22. Mr. and Mrs. John Freivalds. Panama/Colombia. 1969–1970," AA.

125. Dan Boucher, "Conference Notes," *Peace Corps Volunteer Magazine,* April 1965, 13.

126. Carter and Spann, *Away from Home,* 103.

127. Rice, *Bold Experiment,* 220.

128. Polly Kirkpatrick to family, September 30, 1968, in folder, "68. Polly Kirkpatrick. Togo. 1968–1970," AA.

129. Schickele, "When the Right Hand Washes the Left," 42.

130. Zeitlin, *To the Peace Corps with Love,* 250.

131. Saltonstall, *Small Bridges,* 159.

132. Luce, *Letters from the Peace Corps,* 105.

133. May, "Passing the Torch," 297.

134. David Pearson, "The Peace Corps Volunteer Returns," *Saturday Review,* October 17, 1964, 75.

135. COSCR, Ghana I, June 2, 1963, 13, PCRG/NA.

136. Hoopes, *Complete Peace Corps Guide,* 183.

137. James Michener, "An Interview with James A. Michener," in *The Peace Corps Reader,* ed. Peace Corps Office of Public Information (Washington, D.C.: Peace Corps, 1968), 74.

138. Riesman, "Mixture of Motives,"18.

139. Mary Ellen Craig, "Person to Person," *Social Action* 30, no. 5 (January 1964): 27.

140. Myron Gildesgame journal, 70, October 12, 1968, in folder, "70. Myron Gildesgame. Ecuador. 1968–1970," AA.

141. Zeitlin, *To the Peace Corps with Love,* 346.

142. Richard Poston, COSCR, Dominican Republic XII (65-1-01), May 30, 1966, 14, PCRG/NA.

143. *Attitudes,* 5.

144. COSCR, Guatemala V (65-01-07), May 3, 1967, 5, PCRG/NA.

145. Donald Sharfe, "One Worldly Civil Servants Belong in Geneva, Not Washington," *Peace Corps Volunteer Magazine,* March 1966, 26.

146. Ross Pritchard and Warren Wiggins, COSCR, Thailand VIII (64-01-02), January 8, 1966, 8, PCRG/NA.

147. COSCR, Guatemala V (65-01-07), May 3, 1967, 11, 12, PCRG/NA.

148. Jane Campbell and Thomas Scott, COSCR, Philippines V, April 14, 1964, 7, PCRG/NA.

149. Cowan, *Making of an Un-American,* 119.

150. Gaudino, *Uncomfortable Learning,* 147.

151. Mrs. Frances Cunha diary, September 11, 1963, in folder, "55. Mrs. Frances Cunha. Brazil. 1962–1964," AA.

152. Zentella, "Who's Lonesome?" 4.

153. Adams, *Peace Corps in Action,* 56.

154. Bee Hegelson, "Interview with an Ex-Intern," *Parks and Recreation* 7, no. 12 (December 1972): 21.

155. James Oliver and Will Prior, "A Lesson in Respect," *Peace Corps Volunteer Magazine,* June 1964, 13.

156. Ann Weir, "Babysitting in the 'Wild West,'" *Peace Corps Volunteer Magazine,* September 1965, 12.

157. Sharon Omohundro, "Happiness Can Be a Beanbag," *Peace Corps Volunteer Magazine,* November 1964, 2.

158. May, "Passing the Torch," 307.

159. Seymour Greben, COSCR, Peru, Rural CD (66-06-08), November 5, 1968, 14, PCRG/NA.

160. Lazarus, *Letters from Colombia,* 64.

161. deVries, "Activist," 10.

162. Wofford et al., *Citizen in a Time of Change,* 12.

163. David Nelson to family, file 4417, box 3J, UM.

164. Robert Attaway, "Love Taken to Task," *Peace Corps Volunteer Magazine,* April 1968, 29.

165. Gaudino, *Uncomfortable Learning,* 119.

166. Policy Research Institute, Report on Philippine Volunteers, December 12, 1962, 4, in folder, "Philippines 1962, Country Program Evaluation file," PCRG/NA.

167. Linda Muller journal, July 29, 1970, in folder, "3. Linda Muller. Nigeria. 1970–1971," AA.

168. Alicia Teichman to Joseph Smaldone, November 1968, in folder, "67. Joseph Smaldone. Tanzania. 1966–1968," AA.

169. The Group, *Tidbits: Nkwantabisa,* November 1969, 2, PCL.

170. Ibid., May 1970, 4.

171. Francis Pollack, "The New World They See," *Nation,* July 3, 1967, 17.

172. "The Peace Corps on Campus," *Peace Corps Volunteer Magazine,* June 1968, 4.

173. Stein, *Volunteers for Peace,* 215.

174. John Groebli and Larry Horne, COSCR, Peru IX (63-05-06), June 11, 1965, 3, PCRG/NA.

175. Jane Campbell and Thomas Scott, COSCR, Philippines V, April 14, 1964, 4, PCRG/NA.

176. Walter Davis, COSCR, Nigeria X (64-01-02), January 16, 1966, 4, PCRG/NA.

177. COSCR, Philippines II (61-02-08), June 14, 1963, 4, PCRG/NA.

178. Mrs. Frances Cunha to family, March 8, 1963, and February 2, 1963, in folder, "55. Mrs. Frances Cunha. Brazil. 1962–1964," AA.

179. Myron Gildesgame journal, March 6, 1970, 263, in folder, "70. Myron Gildesgame. Ecuador. 1968–1970," AA.

180. Lazarus, *Letters from Colombia,* 63.

CONCLUSION

1. James Clifford, *The Predicament of Culture: Twentieth Century Ethnography, Literature and Art* (Cambridge: Harvard, 1988), 8.

2. Ibid., 5–6.

3. Ibid., 14.

4. Ibid., 8.

5. Ibid., 284, 344.

6. Ibid., 273.

7. Searles, *Peace Corps Experience,* 206.

8. Searles joins the ranks of those who want historians of American foreign affairs to concentrate more on the effects of American policies on other countries and the resultant cultural changes. For a coherent and eloquent discussion of this argument, see Hunt, "The Long Crisis in Diplomatic History," 128–32. I agree wholeheartedly with the need for such studies while at the same time defending the critical importance of studies such as this one, which examine the domestic cultural roots of American foreign policy.

9. David Halberstam, *The Best and the Brightest* (New York: Random House, 1969), 215.

10. Robert S. McNamara, *In Retrospect: The Tragedy and Lessons of Vietnam* (New York: Random House, 1995), 6.

11. Robert S. McNamara, *One Hundred Countries, Two Billion People: The Dimensions of Development* (New York: Praeger, 1973), 18.

12. Ibid., 17.

13. Ibid., 20.

14. Ibid., 8.

15. Schwarz, *What You Can Do,* 179.

16. Martha L. Cottam, *Images and Intervention: US Policies in Latin America* (Pittsburgh: University of Pittsburgh, 1994), 19, 35, 39, 179.

17. Jimmy Carter, *Keeping Faith: Memoirs of a President* (Toronto: Bantam, 1982), 143, 151, 155.

18. Cottam, *Images and Intervention,* 120–21.

19. Ibid., 118.

20. Bruce Watson, "The New Peace Corps Steppes Out—in Kazakhstan," *Smithsonian* 25, no. 5 (August 1994): 27.

21. Howard Witt, "Russia Saps Esprit from Peace Corps," *Chicago Tribune,* December 4, 1994, 1, 12.

22. Zimmerman, "Beyond Double Consciousness," 1027.

23. Cobbs, *Rich Neighbor Policy,* 4.

24. Jack G. Sheehan, "Arab Images in American Comic Books," *Journal of Popular Culture* 28 (summer 1994): 123–33.

25. Paul Theroux, "When the Peace Corps Was Young," *New York Times,* February 25, 1986.

26. Jonathan Alter, "Jumping to Conclusions," *Newsweek,* May 1, 1995, 55. See also "Rushing to Bash Outsiders," *Time,* May 1, 1995, 70.

27. "'Far East' Erased from Peace Corps Maps," *Peace Corps Volunteer Magazine,* November 1966, 4.

Index

Page numbers in italics indicate photographs